The sea in Russian strategy

Edited by Andrew Monaghan
and
Richard Connolly

Manchester University Press

Published by Manchester University Press
Oxford Road, Manchester M13 9PL
www.manchesteruniversitypress.co.uk

British Library Cataloguing-in-Publication Data
A catalogue record for this book is available from the British Library

ISBN 978 1 5261 6878 8 paperback
ISBN 978 1 5261 6880 1 hardback

First published 2023

Typeset
by Cheshire Typesetting Ltd, Cuddington, Cheshire
Printed in Great Britain
by Bell and Bain Ltd, Glasgow

Contents

Contents

Part III: The challenge: the Russian Navy
in practice

Figures

Tables

Tables

Contributors

Richard Connolly is Director of Eastern Advisory Group and an Associate Fellow at the Royal United Services Institute in London.

Dmitry Gorenburg is a Senior Research Scientist in the Strategic Studies division at CNA, a not-for-profit research and analysis organisation.

Clive Johnstone is Head of Strategy at BMT and a former Commander of NATO Allied Maritime Command (MARCOM).

Michael Kofman is the Director of the Russia Studies Program at CNA and a Fellow of the Center for a New American Security.

Andrew Lambert is Laughton Professor of Naval History at King's College London.

Andrew Monaghan is Director of the Russia Research Network and a Senior Associate Fellow at the Royal United Services Institute in London.

Michael B. Petersen is Director of the Russia Maritime Studies Institute and an Associate Professor at the US Naval War College. He writes in a personal capacity.

Contributors

Eleanor Stack is a former Commanding Officer of HMS *Duncan*.

Geoffrey Till is Emeritus Professor of Maritime Studies of King's College London and Chairman of the Corbett Centre for Maritime Policy Studies.

Foreword

Commander (rtd) Eleanor Stack (RN)

Steaming round the corner of Kola Bay to see the entire Northern Fleet at anchor, glistening in the Arctic sun, was a sight to behold for a twenty-four-year-old sub lieutenant on the Bridge of a Royal Navy minehunter. As the first Royal Navy ship to sail down the Kola Inlet since the Arctic convoys, HMS *Ramsey* was there, in the summer of 2002, to act as the flagship for the UK's Commander-in-Chief Fleet to review the Northern Fleet in company with the Russian Fleet Commander. As a young officer undertaking navigation training, my time alongside in Severomorsk was a memorable experience. Cooperation, understanding, and mutual respect were the central tenets of the time we spent with our Russian counterparts, underpinned by sincere and convivial interaction. The most poignant episode of our time together was a visit to the Northern Fleet Museum in Murmansk, where we were shown an exhibition dedicated to the testimony of the courage and resolve demonstrated by those in the Arctic convoys. Included in the museum was a harrowing exhibit for those in Severomorsk to those who had lost their lives in the sinking of the *Kursk* two years previously. These exhibitions served as a reminder that the histories and fortunes of seafaring nations are often complex and entwined, and, yet, there is a common thread that binds us: the might, volatility, and magnificence of the maritime environment in which we operate.

Fast forward fourteen years, and I had assumed command of HMS *Duncan*, which will be the first Type 45 destroyer to act as the flagship to a NATO Task Group, Standing NATO Maritime Group 2 (SNMG2), covering the Mediterranean and Black Sea. In those intervening years, relations with Russia had changed considerably, and the changing dynamic with Russia was at the forefront of our planning and training for this mission. The perception that Russia had seized the initiative in the Black Sea and Eastern Mediterranean set the tone for this NATO deployment: an uncompromising focus on readiness for combat operations. From the perspective of the UK, HMS *Duncan*'s contribution was to be a clear statement of intent in showcasing the UK's leadership role in the alliance and emphasising NATO's position at the heart of UK defence.

HMS *Duncan*'s world-class combat and contingency capabilities made her a platform of choice for allies and partners in pursuing operational and training opportunities. We were asked to "operationalise" the SNMG2 Joint Operating Area by acting as the hub for a reinvigorated Allied network-centred approach. Building trust in HMS *Duncan*'s capabilities with our Allies and partners could enable us to provide them with a counter anti-access/area denial (commonly known as A2/AD) umbrella in the Black Sea and Eastern Mediterranean under which less-capable warships could exercise and operate with confidence: a rarity given the ever-increasing attempts at Russian coercion fielded against them. What was less clear throughout the planning and initial operating stages, though, was how Russia would react to the presence of such a potent warship operating as the flagship of a NATO Task Group operating in waters that Russia considered its own.

HMS *Duncan*'s tenure as SNMG2 flagship spanned three months in 2017 and six months in 2018. During that time, the Task Group conducted three patrols in the Black Sea, and each was characterised by differing responses from the Russian forces that can be linked to changes in military priorities on both sides. Despite the build-up in expectations of a reaction to the sustained presence of a Type 45 in the Black Sea, the patrol of the summer of 2017 drew a routine response in the presence of Black Sea "gatekeepers" and shadowing units. This appeared surprising given the Task Group's scheduled visit to Odessa – the first visit of a Royal Navy warship since 2003. The visit to Odessa brought home to us all the reality of the Russian invasion of Crimea in 2014, articulated in the many stories of members of the Ukrainian Navy. Forced to leave their homes and families at short notice, they faced a difficult balance of maintaining relations with those left behind and establishing trust with those in their new places of work. Working with the Ukrainians and other Black Sea partners, the first patrol was vital in building relationships and understanding the regional maritime environment. The Task Group operated in accordance with the well-publicised schedule during this exploratory phase, so, in retrospect, it was perhaps less surprising that the Russian response was routine.

Sailing again from the UK in early 2018, the Task Group was directed to conduct another patrol in the Black Sea, undertaking operations in support of NATO allies in the region. So, we were reunited with old friends from Bulgaria, Romania, and Turkey who joined the Task Group for that patrol. The Commander of SNMG2, in line with NATO Maritime Command's intent, was determined to use the opportunity to support NATO's objective to conduct overt freedom of navigation patrols. The Commander and I knew of the A2/AD capability that Russia deploys in the Black Sea, in the form of coastal defence cruise missile systems combined with maritime air power. But the NATO perspective is that this should not deter the Alliance from exercising its right to freedom of navigation in the region, while also supporting its regional partners in their right to do so.

And the execution of NATO's intent led to a unique event that took place on 14 February 2018 in waters and airspace to the south of Crimea. Throughout our careers in the Royal Navy, we train and train and train again for different scenarios. "Train hard, fight easy" is a common mantra in militaries, and it's one we espouse in the Royal Navy. When a particular situation that you have trained for materialises and the adrenaline starts coursing through your veins, your kneejerk reaction is to fall back on your training. And this is what happened on that day off Crimea when we witnessed what the Russians refer to as a "vnezapnaya proverka", or what we call a snap exercise. The timing of the event was clearly in reaction to our presence in the area off Crimea (well outside territorial waters and airspace). The power and accuracy of a Type 45's radars and sensors enabled us to witness the launching from Sevastopol of seventeen Russian combat aircraft and their approach to the Task Group. I had the chance to stand back and analyse what we were witnessing and respond appropriately: we knew from experience that Russia wanted to test our resolve and reactions, so it was vital that our assessment of the threat, in terms of capability and intent, was accurate. To overreact could have severe geopolitical implications, but to underestimate the threat could result in immediate damage or loss within the Task Group.

This might be an appropriate juncture to mention that the latest addition to HMS *Duncan* was a Channel 5 documentary team. Their mandate was to capture unprecedented footage of a Type 45 on operations. What the documentary team did not expect was to be filming Russian Flankers and Fencers flying close to the Task Group, with Operations Room screens adorned with red radar contacts, whistles being blown endlessly by our electronic warfare operators on detecting threat emitters, and a NATO Battle Staff and Ship's Command Team locked in action and reaction to the evolving situation. This was high-end drama.

As we analysed what was unfolding in the skies around us, it was clear that Russian aviation was conducting a demonstration of its air defence plan for Crimea. At no point did any of the aircraft act in a way that met NATO's criteria of hostile intent or hostile action. It was therefore vital that our response remained commensurate with what we were witnessing. That said, it was significant enough that Russia had reacted in this way to the presence of the Task Group. The Commander summed it up in his debrief to my Operations Team when he stated that we were 'probably the only maritime asset that has seen a raid of that magnitude in the last twenty-five years'. During this period of interaction, HMS *Duncan* enabled the Commander and the staff of SNMG2 by offering unparalleled situational awareness to him and his staff by working hand-in-hand with the NATO Control and Reporting Centres and airborne early warning aircraft over southern Europe.

The intervening period on the 2018 deployment was characterised by two events: the poisonings in Salisbury and the Douma chemical attack. The combined effect of these events reinforced NATO's commitment to supporting regional partners by enforcing freedom of navigation in the Black Sea and Eastern Mediterranean. The build-up of Russian forces in the Eastern Mediterranean had been noticeable, and our final patrol of the Black Sea in May 2018 was comparable to the 2017 patrol in terms of low levels of Russian interaction due to many Russian units being re-deployed from the Black Sea to the Eastern Mediterranean. What this re-deployment did result in, though, was a greater level of NATO focus on Russian activity in the Eastern Mediterranean. Following the chemical weapons attack in April, HMS *Duncan* was ordered to reposition from the Adriatic to the Eastern Mediterranean at best speed to provide NATO options in terms of a military response. It was a fascinating time for my Ship's Company to witness the counterbalance of live media reporting and military orders: from President Trump's tweets to Russian verbal retaliation, and where the good ship *Duncan* would end up as a result.

The news reporting at the time of the chemical weapons attack made clear Russia's position and involvement in Syria. This was given tangible effect in the waters of the Eastern Mediterranean by the numbers of Russian units present across the operating environments. Russia had been forthright in its support of its Syrian ally and had made overt threats in the media to respond to any military strikes conducted against the Syrian regime. As our tasking to support the coalition strikes was promulgated, the unpredictability of the Russian response became ever clearer, with Russian units clearly marking warships that could be involved in a strike package. And so, it came to the night of Friday, 13 April when the timing of H Hour was communicated to me. This required me to ensure that *Duncan* was ready at the appointed time to react to whatever might occur, bearing in mind the proximity of highly capable Russian warships. Yet again, the Russians tried to test the resolve of the NATO and coalition units in the vicinity: venturing to provoke a reaction yet being very careful not to put themselves in a position where there was justifiable evidence of Russian hostile intent. A wrong move from *Duncan*, or one of the coalition warships, would have reinforced the Russian narrative in support of the Syrian regime.

What supports and sustains you in command during times of such challenging operational situations is the extraordinary commitment and calibre of the men and women of your Ship's Company. The Channel 5 documentary offered the public an indication of Russia's renewed capability at sea and the connection between the Russian Navy and its international policy. It also gave an understanding of the unique disposition of the sailors of the Royal Navy: sailors in navies of any nation have a shared maritime core that comes from years of operating in a maritime environment that can be as challenging an adversary as a hostile nation. To understand this relationship, one needs look no further than the bond that unites submariners in response to submarine disasters, including the sinking of the *Kursk* and the loss in April 2021 of the KRI *Nanggala*.

That said, we spend years studying each other's histories, evaluating each other's capabilities and limitations, and analysing each other's doctrines and tactics to gain operational advantage over our adversaries. Books like this one contribute to that understanding in adding academic analysis and perspective to the information presented by nations in publicising their maritime power. Nowhere is this more relevant than in the case of Russia, recently described by the UK's Secretary of State as 'our number one threat' as he noted that the UK had observed a Russian submarine in the Irish Sea. The reality behind the rhetoric of current and future Russian maritime power is what fascinates military practitioners and academics alike. The intrigue surrounds not just the proven capabilities and sustainability of Russian maritime power from space to subsea but also future maritime doctrine encompassing the vision of how Russian maritime power will be used to cement Russia's self-belief in its status as a global power.

Rewinding to 2002, the hope was that those moments of shared training could coalesce with the common bonds of the maritime into a relationship that would enable a greater depth of understanding on both parts. Almost twenty years later, the 180-degree shift in relations with Russia poses a challenge for the interpretation of Russian maritime power in the future. The assessment of the interactions off Crimea and in the Eastern Mediterranean led to a hypothesis that Russian maritime power was kept in check: despite the overt posturing and rhetoric, the political will did not exist to exacerbate the situation on either axis. This book, as a comprehensive analysis of Russian maritime power, will help revise earlier assessments and, most importantly, provide an intellectual anchor with which to inform UK military strategy.

Acknowledgements

This volume emerged from a workshop entitled "The Sea in Russian Strategy" held at the Oxford Changing Character of War Centre at Pembroke College, Oxford University, in September 2019. We are grateful both to the University of Birmingham and Pembroke College for financing the workshop, and for the contributions made by all the participants at the event, which have helped inform the contents of this volume. And to the authors who have contributed to the volume: thank you! It has been a pleasure to work together.

We would also like to thank Manchester University Press for their support for the project and help in seeing it through to publication, and to two anonymous reviewers for their useful comments.

Introduction: the fall and rise of Russia's power at sea

Andrew Monaghan

A sense that the Russian Navy poses a challenge for the North Atlantic Treaty Organization (NATO) in the Atlantic and Arctic Oceans and the Baltic, Black, and Mediterranean Seas began to brew through the second half of the 2010s. Senior officials and observers pointed to Russian submarine activity throughout the North Atlantic, asserting the emergence of a "Fourth Battle of the Atlantic". They also voiced concerns about how Russian surface ships undertook forceful and dangerous manoeuvres in the Eastern Mediterranean, as well as Moscow hindering freedom of navigation in the Arctic and access to the Sea of Azov in 2018.[1]

This challenge took very real form in February 2022 when Moscow launched its "Special Military Operation" and invaded Ukraine. Through its navy, Russia has dominated the Black Sea since the war began. The navy has played an active role in the assault, bombarding Ukraine from ships in the Black and Caspian Seas in support of ground operations. It also seized Snake Island on the first day of the invasion as part of the imposition of a blockade on Ukraine's Black Sea Coast, cutting its maritime trade. The navy has suffered losses, including the Black Sea Fleet's flagship, the missile cruiser *Moskva*, and there was prolonged fighting over Snake Island before Russia abandoned it on 30 June 2022. But so far, the blockade is having a major impact on Ukraine's economy, which relies heavily on grain and industrial exports by sea. Indeed, some see the blockade of Ukrainian grain to be contributing to the wider, even global, food crisis emerging and thus have argued for the Euro-Atlantic community to intervene to break the blockade – either through the supply of sophisticated anti-ship weapons to Ukraine or by asserting freedom of navigation and convoying Ukrainian vessels.[2] Suddenly, the prospect of Euro-Atlantic navies coming into direct contact with the Russian Navy in a dynamic wartime context has become very real.

This represents a complete reversal in our understanding of Russian maritime and naval power over a generation. For the great majority of the post-Cold War era, Russian maritime power hardly featured in the Euro-Atlantic community's thinking. When it did, it was a question of Russian crisis and tragedy, dysfunction and accident; it was a question of Western assistance to mitigate Russian problems, whether in decommissioning aging nuclear submarines in the 1990s or helping to raise the stricken deep sub-mergence rescue vehicle AS-28 in 2005.

From the *Kursk* to the "Fourth Battle of the Atlantic"

Through the 1990s, the Russian Navy faced a complex crisis char-acterised by the risk of nuclear disaster, underfunding, and under-staffing. By the middle of the decade, in terms of ships, the navy had shrunk by nearly 50 per cent: it may have received fifteen new ships annually from 1992 to 1995, but it simultaneously lost an average of 174. Likewise, the strength of naval aviation was reduced by some 60 per cent, and manning of the combat and support forces was at approximately two thirds. Some of this could be attributed to the active and deliberate decommissioning of old and unnecessary ships. But Felix Gromov, the then Commander in Chief of the Fleet, acknowledged that the navy was receiving half of the funding that it needed, and that many of those ships that remained in service were past the time of their mid-term repair.

Indeed, while it claimed to remain combat ready, the Northern Fleet, Russia's primary naval force, was deep in economic and social crisis. If the state's non-payment of the defence budget led to the knock-on effects of the navy not paying either wages or its bills to the city budget such that production and social services were badly affected, there were further consequences for the training and morale of personnel. Russian reports pointed to the moral degradation of officers, drunkenness, and crime, and hospitalisation with psychological disorders. As Rear Admiral Valery Aleksin, then Russia's Chief Navigator, put it: without an urgent state programme to reconstruct Russia's naval forces, by the year 2000 Russia 'may lose its status as the world's second strongest naval power'. In the Baltic, Russia would become inferior to Germany and Sweden, in the Black Sea region, it would be inferior to Turkey.[3]

Instead, in 2000 the Oscar-II class nuclear submarine *Kursk* sank with the loss of all 118 of its crew in the first major naval exercises of the post-Soviet era, shedding tragic light on the ongoing nature of the situation. The serious mismanagement of the events at the time both by the Russian Navy and Moscow was widely criticised in the Russian and international media. The Admiralty misled Russian officials and media alike about the nature of the tragedy and who was to blame. And with limited and largely decrepit rescue resources available, the Russian Navy initially handled the rescue attempt poorly, rejecting British and Norwegian assistance while itself failing to attach submersibles to the *Kursk*'s escape hatch.

Launched in 1994, the *Kursk* had been one of Russia's newest vessels. But it had had limited time at sea due to lack of funds for fuel, and though the crew was considered the best in the fleet, it was inexperienced, and subsequent reviews pointed to poor training, maintenance, and oversight. An official explanation for the sinking emerged only two years later, stating that a High-Test Peroxide leak (due to a faulty weld) caused a torpedo to explode, setting off a chain reaction causing other torpedoes to explode and destroying the submarine.[4]

The tragedy symbolised the poor condition of the Russian Navy. For many in the Euro-Atlantic community, it confirmed the poor state of the Russian armed forces more broadly at the time, encouraging a view that Russia could safely be ignored as a military or international power.[5] The tragedy of the *Kursk* remained the most obvious point of attention in the Euro-Atlantic community to Russia's navy and maritime power long after the event, even being the subject of a film in 2018.[6]

Even twenty years later, there are high-profile illustrations of Russia's naval and maritime troubles. The *Admiral Kuznetsov*, a heavy aircraft-carrying cruiser, has long been plagued by mechanical problems and has suffered repeated misfortunes. When it took part in the Syrian campaign in 2016, it was accompanied by an ocean-going tug because of concerns about the reliability of its propulsion. Subsequently, it was damaged during a refit in 2018 when Russia's largest floating dry dock, PD-50, suffered a power failure and sank, killing one sailor and injuring four more and nearly taking the *Kuznetsov* with it. One of the dry dock's cranes crashed into the flight deck, tearing a hole in it. And again in 2019 as the refit continued, a fire broke out on board *Kuznetsov*, killing two and injuring fourteen.[7]

A degree of dysfunctionality remains in the Russian Navy, too: in 2016, some fifty officers in the Baltic Sea Fleet command were fired for what the Ministry of Defence called 'serious lapses in service'. The official explanation is that Rear Admiral Kravchuk and other senior officers were fired for 'serious omissions in the organisation of combat preparation, of the daily activity of the forces, a lack of measures to improve the life of personnel, the neglect of subordinates, and the distortion of the real state of affairs' when reporting to the Minister of Defence. Igor Kasatonov, a former commander of the Baltic Fleet and Deputy Commander of the navy, suggested that similar high-profile firings are likely to arise in future because of the low levels of preparation of personnel – 'we do not have the Soviet school of preparing officers for the fleet'.[8]

The Russian Navy suffered a number of other accidents, including fatal fires on ships and submarines in 2008, 2011, and 2012. Perhaps most notable, though, was the fire on the Russian deep-diving nuclear-powered submarine *Losharik* in July 2019 in which fourteen of its crew, including many senior officers, died. Observers also point to ongoing problems modernising older platforms, integrating components with old and new platforms, and delivering vessels on time and on budget, as well as wider constraints on the navy, not least its place as the junior service in the Russian armed forces.

But since the mid-2010s, a complete change has taken place both in the international situation and in terms of Russia's maritime and naval presence. The Euro-Atlantic community has become increasingly focused on a new era of Great Power Competition as Russia and China are understood to be vying for influence and challenge the international order. In this competition, most attention has focused on the way these states use measures short of war to achieve their ends: propaganda and disinformation, cyber-attacks, and the use of special forces and proxies. These questions have driven much discussion of conflict in the "grey zone" or "hybrid warfare".

Nevertheless, both China and Russia also pose significant maritime and naval challenges. Much attention is being devoted, for example, to the growth of the Chinese navy such that it has become the largest naval force in the world, as well as Chinese attempts both to control the South China Sea and to acquire access to ports across the world. China's emerging naval presence is felt on a global scale through its connection to the maritime silk road and building of a string of ports in the Indian Ocean and beyond, and its interest in the Northern Sea Route (NSR).[9]

There is also official recognition that Moscow's sustained effort to modernise its capabilities at sea in the 2010s is showing results, and much discussion about how, through the significant increase in the quantity and quality of its naval presence in the Baltic, North Atlantic, and Arctic, Russia is changing the security environment of NATO and its member states.[10] In 2021, the UK's Secretary of State for Defence stated that since 2013 there had been more than 150 instances of Russian naval assets being detected by the UK (there was just one detection in 2010). This was a level of activity not displayed since the end of the Cold War, according to the (then) UK Chief of Defence Staff.[11]

This increase in activity led some to assert the emergence of a "Fourth Battle of the Atlantic". As Admiral James Foggo, then Commander of the US 6th Fleet and Commander of NATO's Striking and Support Forces, put it, Russia now appears as a 'significant and aggressive maritime power', claiming a maritime battlespace across Europe and closing the technological gap with Western navies. Russia's reappearance in the North Atlantic changes the "strategic reality" for NATO, since it is seen to threaten the Euro-Atlantic community's Sea Lines of Communication (SLOCs).[12] This concern about lines of communication is twofold. First, it relates to the alliance's more traditional ability to deploy forces and supplies across the Atlantic. Second, it relates to the communications and internet cables that run under the sea. According to one senior official, Russia's modernisation challenges both forms of communication – that in addition to new ships and submarines, Russia 'continues to perfect both unconventional capabilities and information warfare'.[13]

But the challenge of Russian power at sea goes beyond NATO's SLOCs in the North Atlantic. It is felt in the Mediterranean, where the Russian Navy has established a substantial presence,[14] and in the High North, where Russia has both built up substantial military capabilities including coastal defence and anti-access weapons systems and sought to establish command over the NSR. Concern about Russia's so-called anti-access/area denial (A2/AD) capabilities has shaped much of the debate about its military modernisation and challenge,[15] but the question of freedom of navigation, including in the NSR, is likely to become only more important.

It is also felt in the Black Sea, not only in terms of Russia's annexation of Crimea and the embellishment of capabilities on the peninsula to create another "A2/AD bubble", but also in the way it has asserted control over the Sea of Azov. Through its control of the Kerch Strait, for instance, Russia has been able to control Ukrainian access to two of Ukraine's own ports, Mariupol and Berdiansk. A crisis emerged in 2018 when vessels of the Russian Federal Security Service (FSB) stopped and then confiscated three Ukrainian navy vessels, accusing them of illegally entering Russian waters.

This change in debate and understanding of the situation has already driven a change in policy: in May 2018, the United States announced the re-establishment of the 2nd Fleet, and the launch of a new naval command (Joint Forces Command (JFC), Norfolk), which became active in 2019 and fully operational in 2021. As a Pentagon spokesman stated, the 'return to great power competition and a resurgent Russia demands that NATO refocus on the Atlantic to ensure dedicated reinforcement of the continent and demonstrate a capable and credible deterrence effect'. JFC Norfolk is to be the 'linchpin of trans-Atlantic security'.[16]

This fresh discussion about Russia's new prominence at sea is important. But it both misses a number of significant themes in Russian maritime thinking and is characterised by old problems of mirror-imaging and imposing Western concepts on Russian thinking that do not correlate to Russian concepts, and refighting the last war. One example is the debate about Russia's so-called "A2/AD" bubbles, which refers to a series of long-range anti-air and anti-ship capabilities that create exclusion zones or bubbles that reach well beyond Russia's coastline. While this fits logically with Western, and especially US military concepts, it does not relate to Russian military thinking and so is misleading in the way it frames Russian capability and activity.

The discussion of the "Fourth Battle of the Atlantic" is another example, and it echoes a debate that took place during the Cold War about Soviet intentions.[17] As analysts pointed out at the time, the Soviet Navy was neither equipped for nor intended to fight in a similar way to the German Kriegsmarine in the First and Second World Wars (by attacking NATO's SLOCs). Soviet intentions were misread with regard to SLOCs and also anti-submarine warfare – indeed, the scenario bore no similarity to what the Soviet Navy intended to do in case of war. Thus, the West was preparing to fight a battle that its adversary was not intending to wage; the 2nd Fleet was 'aimed at a shadow' and was 'essentially pointless except for use in dealing with Soviet spoilers sent into the Atlantic on a one-way mission to tie up larger US forces in defence'. Veterans of this Cold War-era discussion see a similar disconnect between US expectations and actual Russian naval behaviour taking shape today, with the newly re-established 2nd Fleet preparing to fight a war that the Russian Navy is unlikely to come out to fight.[18]

Russia as one of the world's leading seafaring nations?

One way to mitigate mirror-imaging is to examine the Russian discussion about maritime and naval power. What are Russian priorities, concepts, and problems? What are the main headlines and themes under debate? There are some important similarities, most notably about the increase in activity: perhaps the most obvious feature of the discussion in Russia is the emphasis on the Russian Navy being equipped and more active globally, not just in the North Atlantic and Arctic Oceans, and Baltic, Black, and Mediterranean Seas, but also in the Red Sea and South Atlantic, Indian, and Pacific Oceans. The rising importance of maritime matters is accepted by officials and observers alike and has become the focus of some debate.

Thus, Russian observers noted in 2015 that the activities of the Russian Navy had increased sharply, and the number of exercises was growing to levels unheard of 'even in the Soviet heyday', with a constant expansion of voyages.[19] Officials too have emphasised this trend. Valeriy Gerasimov, the Russian Chief of General Staff, stated in 2017 that the navy had in recent years increased the intensity of its missions in the key areas of the global ocean and conducted 672 missions, including thirty-one in the Arctic and twenty-two in dangerous pirate areas, and 650 port visits.[20] Nikolai Yevmenov, Commander in Chief of the Russian Navy since 2019, pointed to Russia's major exercises in the Bering Sea in September 2020 and in the Arctic in 2021 as 'unprecedented' as the navy seeks to 'ensure the economic development of the region'.[21] The Russian Navy joined the search to help the Argentinian navy when one of its submarines sank in 2017 and has conducted numerous long-distance voyages: in 2019, a small flotilla led by the frigate *Admiral Gorshkov* conducted Russia's first circumnavigation since the nineteenth century. Russia participated in exercises with Iran and China, including in the North Indian Ocean, and with South Africa in the South Indian Ocean.[22] It also contributes to the international counter-piracy effort off Africa's east coast.

Russian naval exercises grow in size and complexity – indeed, "the largest since the Cold War" is an often-repeated description of exercises, as are comparisons to those held by the Soviet Navy at its peak. Exercise Ocean Shield in 2018, for instance, was a large-scale inter-fleet exercise bringing together the Northern and Black Sea Fleets off Syria, and two corvettes from the Caspian Flotilla. The major VOSTOK exercises also practised linking different distant regions and fleets, connecting the North Atlantic with the Pacific Oceans. Exercise Ocean Shield 2020 saw activity in all four fleets, with coordination between surface, sub-surface, and coastal complexes and amphibious landings. Groupings of ships and aircraft operated in Eastern, Arctic, and Western strategic directions.

In 2021, the Ministry of Defence held a large-scale oceanic exercise in the far sea zone bringing together the Northern and Pacific Fleets in different regions under a single leadership. The exercise was intended to test automated command and control, and to examine both inter-fleet and inter-service cooperation, particularly with aerospace forces. This is all intended to mark Russia's return to the "ocean zone" after a long break.[23] This activity is symptomatic of Moscow's maritime ambitions, but it also shows that there are some important distinctions in the Russian discussion that frame the question differently from how it is discussed in the West.

The most obvious distinction is in the emphasis on Russia's maritime power. President Putin has repeatedly emphasised Russia's status as a great maritime and naval power. He points to Russia having the world's longest maritime boundary with access to three oceans, and the major effort the Russian government has made to modernise and strengthen the navy. He has stated that the navy 'remains an important, if not key component ensuring national defence and security in the 21st century and we must also preserve and enhance our country's status as one of the world's leading seafaring nations'. Putin has emphasised his intent that the navy should be modernised to include high-precision, state-of-the-art weapons, in other words, to create a fleet of 'unique capabilities', and the fleet of a 'strong and sovereign nation'.[24]

Yet it is significant, though, that Putin points not just to the *military* role the navy has played, but the much wider range of Russia's experience and capabilities at sea. Alongside the military elements – both victories and defeats, achievements and accidents – he emphasises Russia's other accomplishments at sea. He thus points to Russia's 'legendary research voyages' and discovery of Antarctica, and its contributions to science with its geographic, biological, and geological discoveries through the use of the latest equipment and 'unparalleled design solutions'. Following the March 2021 "Umka" exercise, he emphasised not only the combat training, but also the research measures – the integrated nature of the expedition, which included study and exploration of the Far North.[25] Likewise, Russian experts point to the combination of Russia's maritime resources, maritime instruments, and maritime activities and place Russia within the top three "great sea powers" of the current era. For them, though Russia lags well behind the United States and China in the *overall* index (because of much less activity), its maritime resources and instruments are among the most substantial in the world, and Russia possesses significantly more overall maritime might than the next three states, Japan, South Korea, and the United Kingdom.[26]

This shift to a maritime focus reflects the wider attention that needs to be given to how Moscow understands sea power, even how the Russian leadership thinks about international affairs. For much of the period between the late 2000s and early 2020s, senior officials and experts have emphasised what they see as an emergent and intensifying geo-economic competition over access to resources, transit routes, and markets – and for Russia, much of this is a maritime question given its export-based economy.[27]

Much of this is laid out in Russia's official strategic planning documentation, such as the Strategy for the Development of the Shipbuilding Industry, the Maritime Doctrine, and the Fundamentals of Naval Policy. It also features in strategies for regional development (particularly the Arctic) and the strategic planning documents of major Russian companies such as Rosatom and Rosneft. The most recent versions of these documents (published since the mid-2010s) are broadly coordinated with other major documents including the National Security Strategy, Military Doctrine, and Foreign Policy Concept to suggest a deliberate and considered expression of Russian strategic thinking.

The documents also set out the importance of securing Russia's place as the second most powerful maritime power in the world, protecting and promoting Russia's global interests, and the deliberate recoupling of the military to Russia's geostrategic interests at sea.

Six regional priorities are set out: the Atlantic, Pacific, Indian Oceans, the Caspian Sea, and the Arctic. Concerns about the impact of regional conflicts in the Middle East, South Asia, and Africa are stated, including piracy in the Gulf of Guinea, Indian, and Pacific Oceans. It is noteworthy, though, that the documents point to threats in the North and West, particularly in the shape of NATO moving closer to Russia's adjacent seas, while suggesting a more cooperative approach in the East and South.[28]

The documents offer sober analysis of ends and means and realistic missions for the navy as well as a broader maritime agenda. The navy is intended both to respond to Russian security concerns – from implementing strategic deterrence and dealing with military threats to anti-piracy operations – and to be a tool for cooperation. To this end, the documents include a range of state tools, including the role of the FSB as border guards, and set out the intention for the long-term modernisation of the navy, particularly the improvement of command and control and the "kalibrisation" of a range of ships.[29]

This is the context in which officials and analysts point to the large-scale renovation of the navy. In the spring of 2021, Vladimir Pospelov, a member of the government's marine collegium, announced the major modernisation of the Udaloy-class (anti-submarine) destroyer *Marshal Shaposhnikov*, which was handed over to the Pacific Fleet in April 2021; the modernisation of the *Admiral Nakhimov* heavy cruiser, which will be in service for at least another twenty years; and that a further ten Borei-A-class submarines will be commissioned by 2030.[30] Others point to the introduction of new and upgraded naval aviation, and the looming introduction of an automated command system to improve the navy's ability to create 'continuous zones of destruction with an area of hundreds, even thousands of kilometres'.[31] The Russian population appears to agree with the positive assessment of Russia's power at sea: one poll suggested, for instance, that two thirds of the population think that the Russian Navy is the strongest in the world, and 89 per cent think that it is able to defend the coast in case of a real threat.[32]

There are critics, though. Some suggest that Russian ports are 'dead places' where there are only customs and FSB officers, 'poverty and desolation'.[33] Others, acknowledging the growing importance of maritime matters in international affairs, point to a range of broader issues, including the 'acute problems', even 'crisis' in Russia's maritime transport, fishing, and research fleets, which face significant 'depreciation' as they simultaneously shrink and age. Some estimate that large percentages of the vessels in these fleets are past their standard service lives and note that there is a lack of 'new-generation' technical facilities.[34]

There is also substantial debate about the extent of modernisation and state of the navy, the priorities in development, and even its value as a force. Some point to the incomplete modernisation process, asserting, for instance, the 'complete absence' of modern anti-torpedo protection, and the ongoing obsolescence of important equipment such as the Tu-142 anti-submarine warfare aircraft's search and sighting systems and hydroacoustic buoys.[35] Others point to the real costs and effectiveness of the modernisation process as a whole and the priorities within it. Such observers argue that the modernisation of the *Admiral Nakhimov*, for instance, is a 'very controversial decision, a rather expensive pleasure'. Not only is the real cost unknown (perhaps 90 to 100 billion roubles), but the actual usefulness of such a large ship is questionable, since such a 'mastodon' will prove an easy target. Instead, they suggest, international trends are moving towards stealth and miniaturisation, and even allowing for increasing prices, embezzlement, and Russia's 'other realities', the money spent on modernising the *Admiral Nakhimov* would have paid for eight smaller rocket ships that are both harder to hit and can still deliver substantial firepower.[36] The sinking of the *Moskva* on 14 April 2022 will likely ensure that this debate continues. Moreover, some suggest that

Russia's ability to have a strong fleet is scuppered by the 'harsh fact' that funds must be divided into five parts (to serve Russia's four fleets and flotilla). Having 4.5 fleets means that despite spending three times as much on the navy as Turkey does, for example, the Russian Navy locally is significantly weaker than the Turkish Navy.[37]

Even officially, there appears to be some debate about the priority directions of the navy's development, for instance over whether aircraft carriers are appropriate for the Russian Navy. If some former senior naval figures have pointed to plans for a multi-purpose aircraft carrier, Project 23000E (Shtorm), others have emphasised the ongoing delays and asked whether such a ship is necessary for Russia. As Pospelov has stated, 'in theory, the navy needs three carriers', but at the moment there is no construction plant capable of producing them, and the financing would absorb all other naval funding, so it would need a separate state programme. Consequently, it would take at least a decade, even given the (currently lacking) scientific and technical groundwork for the aircraft and the readiness of the shipyard.[38]

The sea in Russian strategy in the twenty-first century

This book examines Russia's strategic approach to the sea in depth, looking at the longer historical trajectory, and how the Russian leadership conceptualises maritime affairs and attempts to assert Russia's position, before drawing this together to reflect on why it is a key question for the Euro-Atlantic community. It is increasingly important to have a nuanced grasp of the sea in contemporary Russian strategy for three main reasons, all intimately connected. First, there is a wider "maritime turn" in international affairs – and Russia is part of this. Second, the sea is more significant in the Russian leadership's thinking and activity than is widely recognised in the Euro-Atlantic community. And third, there are a number of differences in how Russia views power at sea. Let us briefly look at these in turn.

First, the wider "maritime turn" in global affairs reveals the significance of these issues in their own right. It emphasises questions of national security, marine environment, economic development, and human security at the forefront of thinking. The seas serve as a connective fibre of global power, with growth in global trade by sea: analysts suggest that some 80–90 per cent of global trade by volume is seaborne. This has led to a dramatic increase in spending on navies, especially in East Asia. As noted above, Chinese spending on the navy is such that it has become, in terms of numbers of ships, the largest navy. But Japan, India, and Australia have likewise increased spending. This turn drives the emergence of a new agenda and questions about the role (and sanctity) of the global commons and freedom of navigation, concerns about transit routes and choke points, and what constitutes "sea power" in the twenty-first century.[39]

Some, therefore, emphasise that though shipping is the 'great ignored subject at the centre of the global economy', it is '90% of everything', and that the shipping industry is bigger 'and more consequential than ever'. The sea is the 'physical equivalent of the internet', the other 'instrument which makes globalisation possible'. But if shipping has become so cheap as to change the shape of the world economy, it still faces important questions: the outsized influence of maritime choke points was illustrated when the Suez Canal was blocked in March 2021 (at a cost of some $9.6 billion each day) and vessels had to re-route, and the way the shipping industry has worked hard to hide itself behind 'impenetrably secure, razor wired ports' that are no longer coastal "ports" but purely transport hubs.[40] Others point to a "paradigm shift" in naval matters, with the development of carrier-killer missiles and new submarine detection methods, such that they ask whether the age of warships, submarines, and aircraft carriers is over, since they are 'even vulnerable while bobbing at their moorings in home ports, never mind at sea'.[41]

Russia is part of a much wider trend, therefore: and all of these questions matter to, and feature in, the Russian discussion about the sea. The "maritime turn" is recognised in Russia,[42] and there is discussion among Russian experts and officials alike about competition for the global commons, for instance, and concern about maritime choke points. We have already seen how Russian ports are described as secure hubs, rather than ports. Some suggest that advances in technology have implications for the navy such that they question the need for a strong navy at all: the long ranges of missiles mean that fleets, their bases, and airfields are under constant targeting and so have a 'very ambiguous survival rate', and there is a real chance that the Black Sea Fleet, for instance, could be destroyed within minutes with up to two thirds of its ships shot at the pier. Aviation, some argue, therefore, plays a 'disproportionately large role' in naval affairs, and without it, the fleet does not 'seem functional'. The concept of the sea battle 'ceases to exist as something independent'.[43] Again, these debates are likely to continue given developments in the Black Sea, not only in terms of how the navy can be used to strike targets at distance, but also including the vulnerability of large ships, such as the *Moskva*.

This links to the second point: the importance of the sea to the Russian leadership, especially from an economic perspective. While Russian imports from Asia have grown since 2014, largely by sea, the Russian economy depends on the ability to exploit and export hydrocarbons and agricultural products by sea. Logistical and transport infrastructure is being built to support this. The former is exemplified by Russia's development of hydrocarbons in the High North and facilities for the NSR,[44] the latter by the development of Black Sea infrastructure to facilitate the export of grain to the Middle East and North Africa. The linking of railway and port infrastructure to create a cross-continental connection between seas and oceans is a prominent feature in speeches by senior officials, as is the concern about geo-economic competition posing potential threats to Russia and its interests.[45] Of course, when the Suez Canal was blocked, Moscow seized the opportunity to emphasise the advantages that the NSR would bring to global trade.[46]

Finally, third, geography and history mean there are a number of noteworthy specificities in the way Russia looks at the sea. Geography imposes significant challenges on the way Moscow makes strategy at sea, creating specific ambiguities at the heart of thinking about power at sea. While Russia is usually thought of as a continental power, it also has the longest seaboard in the world. Though it is true that the two main "Fatherland Wars" that form the core pillars of Russian military history were fought largely on land, it is also the case that a number of Russia's most significant military defeats have been brought about from the sea, for instance in the Crimean War (1854–56) and in the Russo-Japanese War (1904–5). Moreover, Russia's primary contenders in the nineteenth and twentieth centuries – Great Britain and the United States – were both major maritime powers, able to project significant power across the sea. This question of potentially hostile power being delivered from the sea remains relevant into the twenty-first century. Russia is challenged by power projected from the sea, therefore, but it prioritises its ground forces – the navy is a junior service and has long been allocated resources accordingly.

Moreover, despite its long seaboard, Russia has few outlets for its own naval deployment: its bases are separated by thousands of miles, and access to the seas and oceans is only possible through narrow exits and choke points. This is what drives the Russian Navy's division into four fleets and a flotilla and automatically puts it at serious disadvantage compared to other major powers since it generates logistical problems and difficulties in reinforcement. The starting point for the Russian Navy is fragmentation and the need to operate from isolated theatres.

These points are the foundation of a number of category and conceptual differences in the way Moscow thinks of power at sea, and how the Russian leadership uses naval forces to achieve it.

In contrast to Euro-Atlantic thinking, for instance, there is no specific or uniquely "naval strategy" in Russian thinking. The navy is a tool wrapped into the successful fulfilment of other political or military tasks; it does not act independently. This is perhaps suitably illustrated by the point that in thinking of Russian power at sea, we must consider not only the Russian Navy and how it links in to unified strategic commands and military districts, but also the Ministry of Defence's Main Directorate for Undersea Research, which has special submarines, of which *Losharik* is one, and the FSB border service, so active during the crisis in the Sea of Azov in 2018.

Moreover, the idea of "command of the sea", so central to Euro-Atlantic thinking, has long been understood very differently in Russia, and not considered a priority task for the navy. Indeed, for the Soviets, the command of the sea was not considered to be the proper objective of navies in war, since not only is it unrealisable except through all arms combat, but it distracts the navy from its proper tasks. Instead, the Soviets dedicated much thought to the possibility of conducting naval operations without having command of the sea, and usually in the face of an adversary's superior force. This resulted in the development of concepts for combat stability (*boevaya ustoichivost*) and area defence concepts to achieve command by exclusion, by denial, or through temporary local superiority of force. In the main, the intent was to avoid fleet engagement and rely on successive combined attacks with aircraft, submarines, torpedo craft, and mines.[47]

Finally, the Soviet and now Russian Navy was not intended to be a "balanced" fleet in the way Western navies are conceived; nor do Russian ships reflect Western designs. Russian ships, intended for specific purposes (often to counter Western maritime superiority), are designed on different lines, either as unique weapons systems or as adapted versions, as ship killers with substantial armament (and little comfort for the crews). Thus, as some note, much is lost in translation between ship classes: when the Russians class a ship as a corvette, this means the firepower of a Western frigate, and when they class a ship as a frigate, this means the firepower of a Western destroyer. Similarly, Russian aircraft carriers, for example, are intended to fulfil different functions from Western aircraft carriers, in effect to extend the combat capability of anti-submarine operations further from Russian shores.

Indifferent performances in war at sea should not obscure the original and inventive approaches the Russian Navy adopts to mitigate the geographical and historical contexts. Russian ship designers have often proved very innovative, being among the first to experiment with explosive shells, torpedoes, mines, and naval aircraft, and in producing warships that are orthodox and tailored to their own specific needs.[48] Platforms may be spread thinly across 4.5 fleets, but the introduction of long-range missiles – the "kalibri-sation" process noted above – allows them to strike targets at sea and land at considerable distance. Problems remain, but this acts as a significant force multiplier that gives the navy central roles in Russian thinking about military strategy. Soviet and Russian designers have also shown particular innovation in submarines and submersibles: in May 2020, the autonomous unmanned deep-sea submersible Vityaz-D reached the world's deepest ocean point in the Mariana Trench, the first unmanned submersible to achieve this.[49]

All told, therefore, Russia's strategy at sea illuminates a key feature of contemporary national power and long-term trajectory of growth, and, within this, Moscow's priorities and choices as well as the concepts that underpin its activities. Importantly, it shines a light on the significant complexities that the Russian leadership faces – not only the setbacks and limitations but also ongoing indecision and problems within the chain of command. This is the substance of strategy. Finally, it shows where Russian thinking is similar to, if hardly in accord with, Western thinking about maritime affairs, but also the differences in Russian views, and distinct cultural aspects.

Understanding the sea's importance to Moscow, the role it plays in Russian thinking, and the specificities of Russian concepts is crucial to shaping good Russia-related policy – whether it be deterrence, defence, or even dialogue. To be sure, at the time of writing in late 2022, questions of deterrence and defence are at the forefront of thinking. But it is worth remembering that the sea has in the past offered the context for dialogue (in terms of port visits), or even more cooperative relations: the UK-led NATO expedition to raise the stricken AS-28 in 2005 led to a visit to the UK by Putin and the signing of a number of agreements.

For the time being, though, in the context of a Great Power Competition, it is worth recalling that in the past, Moscow has pursued its policy objectives behind advanced naval screens. Russian naval activity has often formed just the initial stage of a complex programme aimed at expanding Moscow's influence in a region. Indeed, naval activity facilitated the application of military power without initiating hostilities and thus remaining below the threshold of war and not provoking a Western response.[50] Both of these features of Russian international activity are visible today, and we should understand them better – as the Euro-Atlantic community adopts a more explicitly global focus in its security thinking, it is likely to rub up against Russia more often, including at sea. Consequently, without a nuanced understanding of purpose, strengths, and weaknesses, the ambiguities of Moscow's power at sea are more likely to confuse and cause a misdiagnosis of Russian activity. In the pithy words of Michael Kofman, one of the contributors to this volume, those who wish to test the notion that the Russian Navy is weak or disappearing should 'pack a life raft'.[51]

This book sets an introductory platform for better understanding Moscow's strategy at sea and Russian maritime power. The chapters flesh out these themes. The book is in three parts. The two chapters in Part I provide broad context by offering views of Russian sea power informed by history and concepts of maritime and sea power. The chapters in Part II focus more specifically on contemporary questions of concepts and capabilities, examining Russian views of the oceans and seas, and maritime state planning and the ability to achieve these plans, including shipbuilding and infrastructure capacity. Part III offers a change in perspective with a comparative view of what this means for the Euro-Atlantic community.

Russia's strategy at sea is a vast subject that raises many interesting questions that could be addressed from different angles. The intent here is to open up these questions, reflecting on key themes of continuity and change from the Tsarist and Soviet eras through to today and into the 2020s. Our core interest is in strategy and how Moscow understands the value of the sea: hence "the sea in Russian strategy". There is, of course, much debate about what "strategy" actually means. In this volume, it is understood to be an executive process – the formulation of plans and their implementation. It is the art of using the resources of the state to create power in pursuit of political ends and securing the state against enemies real and perceived. It is a complex, dynamic, and difficult process that involves coordinating resources and people – conducting the orchestra of the state.[52]

The chapters adopt a broad thematic approach to examine Russia's maritime power, with a particular emphasis on naval power. This highlights Moscow's efforts to rebuild its naval power and what this consists of, but also the difficulties the Russian leadership has in implementing these plans, and the ongoing debates in Russia about maritime power at sea and more specifically the role of the navy. Indeed, the lack of consensus over some key questions in Russia is echoed in a certain lack of consensus among the contributors to this volume.

Moreover, though the contributors touch on them, in some cases quite substantially, there is much more to be said about the history of Russian maritime power, wider aspects of contemporary Russia's non-naval maritime power, such as fishing, commerce, research, and constabulary, and regional priorities, whether in the Baltic or Black Sea regions, the Arctic and Pacific. Both this and the current need to focus on the navy and to understand its capabilities are highlighted by the Russian invasion of Ukraine and the substantial role the navy has played in it, and there will be much more to examine in terms of the broader strengths and shortcomings of the Russian Navy, and Moscow's attempt to turn Russia into one of the world's leading sea-faring nations, and the implications of this for Western thinking about Russian maritime power.

Indeed, as this volume was being written and prepared, Moscow launched its invasion of Ukraine, and the war is ongoing as the book goes to press. Though specific episodes from the first few months of the war feature in the chapters, the book does not seek to offer a sustained examination of the war or to detail the role of the Russian Navy. To date, the Russian Navy has certainly played an active role, operating a blockade first close to Ukraine and then at distance, and conducting both coastal defence and stand-off land-attack operations, and seeking to offer maritime support for troops ashore. Results have been mixed, but not only has the navy has shown itself to be a significant feature of the Russian military, but the war has made the sea ever more important to Russia. These wartime activities all deserve detailed examination in future, both as more evidence emerges and the longer-term consequences of the war and of Western measures against Russia, such as sanctions, take shape over time. The latter, in particular, have the potential to further stymie the modernisation of Russia's maritime capabilities and to constrain Moscow's efforts to use the sea to advance its geo-economic ambitions. In the meantime, this book sets out a broader context for thinking about the challenge Russia poses at sea – a reflection on the longer-term trajectory and "how and why we got here, and where might we be going" – framing Moscow's intent to establish Russia as a leading seafaring nation with significant interests at sea.

Notes

1 'Exclusive: Russia Is "Our Number 1 Threat" as Its Submarines Circle Britain', *Telegraph*, 22 May 2021; 'NATO Flotilla Goes North to Put Russia in Its Place', Bloomberg, 8 May 2020, www.bloomberg.com/opinion/articles/2020-05-08/nato-flotilla-goes-north-to-put-russia-in-its-place (accessed 13 November 2022); J. Foggo and A. Fritz, 'The Fourth Battle of the Atlantic', *Proceedings*, Vol. 142, No. 6 (2016), www.usni.org/magazines/proceedings/2016/june/fourth-battle-atlantic (accessed 13 November 2022); R. Hilton, 'Moscow's Strategic Miscalculation in Blockading the Sea of Azov', European Leadership Network, 27 November 2018, www.europeanleadershipnetwork.org/commentary/russias-strategic-miscalculation-in-blockading-the-sea-of-azov (accessed 7 October 2022).

2 Indeed, Kyiv accused Moscow of imposing a blockade even in the weeks prior to the invasion. 'The Black Sea Blockade: Mapping the Impact of War in Ukraine on the World's Food Supply; Interactive', *Guardian*, 9 June 2022, www.theguardian.com/global-development/ng-interactive/2022/jun/09/the-black-sea-blockade-mapping-the-impact-of-war-in-ukraine-on-the-worlds-food-supply-interactive (accessed 13 November 2022). Also see: 'Russian Warships in Caspian Sea Join in Bombardment of Ukraine', *Telegraph*, 20 March 2022; L. Freedman, 'Russia's Black Sea Blockade Causes Food Shortages for the Whole World', *New Statesman*, 19 May 2022, www.newstatesman.com/world/europe/ukraine/2022/05/black-sea-blockade-crimea (accessed 7 October 2022); 'Russia's Black Sea Blockade Will Turbocharge Global Food Crisis', *Foreign Policy*, 24 May 2022, https://foreignpolicy.com/2022/05/24/russia-ukraine-blockade-food-crisis-black-sea (accessed 7 October 2022).

3 For discussion and quotes, see S. G. Simonson, 'Russia's Northern Fleet in Heavy Seas', *Journal of Slavic Military Studies*, Vol. 9, No. 4 (1996), pp. 713–31.

4 Retired Russian naval officers were among those who criticised the navy's performance. Vice Admiral Valery Ryazantsev, for instance, subsequently wrote a particularly scathing report, accusing the navy's commanders of 'illiteracy and incompetence', and an inability to manage the fleet even in peacetime. 'Vospominaniya: Chapter 9. Spasatelnaya operatsiya', http://www.avtonomka.org/vospominaniya/vitse-admiral-ryazantsev-valeriy-dmitrievich/45-glava-ix-spasatelnaya-operatsiya.html (no longer active). Though it did not officially apportion blame to individuals, the government report also pointed to poor equipment, negligence, and poor management and breaches of discipline. See discussion in Z. Barany, *Democratic Breakdown and the Decline of the Russian Military*. Princeton: Princeton University Press, 2007, p. 32.

5 Russia's armed forces had suffered a number of humiliating military reverses in the first Chechen war (1994–96), and at the time were facing the early stages of a renewal of that war. There was also widespread reportage of poor equipment, hazing, and low morale in the ground and air forces. The problems the *Kursk* disaster revealed in the chain of command had important consequences for how the new President, Vladimir Putin, began to shape Russian politics more broadly, including attempting to implement a "vertical of power" by appointing reliable and loyal people. A. Goltz, 'Russia's Power Vertical Stretches Back to Kursk', *Moscow Times*, 17 August 2010. For a wider discussion of this, see A. Monaghan, *Power in Modern Russia: Strategy and Mobilisation*. Manchester: Manchester University Press, 2017.

6 The *Kursk* has been the subject of many articles and several books including R. Flynn, *Cry from the Deep: The Sinking of the Kursk, the Submarine Disaster that Riveted the World and Put the New Russia to the Ultimate Test*. London: HarperCollins, 2011; P. Truscott, *Kursk: Russia's Lost Pride*. London: Simon & Schuster, 2002; R. Moore, *A Time to Die: The Untold Story of the Kursk Tragedy*. London: Crown, 2003. The latter book was made into a film, *Kursk: The Last Mission*, which premiered at the Toronto Film Festival in 2018. Soviet or Russian submarines and their tragedies are the subject of other well-known films, including *K-19: The Widowmaker* (2002).

7 See, for instance, 'Russia's Unlucky Aircraft Carrier Is Getting Ready for Its Return to Action', Business Insider, 19 April 2021, www.businessinsider.com/russian-aircraft-carrier-kuznetsov-getting-ready-for-return-to-action-2021-4?r=US&IR=T (accessed 13 November 2022); 'Belching Smoke through the Channel, Russian Aircraft Carrier So Unreliable It Sails with Its Own Tugboat', *Telegraph*, 22 October 2016.

8 'SMI soobshchili ob uvolnenii 50 rukovoditelei Baltflota', Lenta.ru, 30 June 2016, https://lenta.ru/news/2016/06/30/new37th (accessed 13 November 2022); 'Komanduyushchevo i nachshtaba Baltflota snyali za priukrashivanie deistvitelnost', Lenta.ru, 29 June 2016, https://lenta.ru/news/2016/06/29/za_upuschenia (accessed 13 November 2022); 'Commanders of Russia's Baltic Fleet Fired', Russia Beyond the Headlines, 30 June 2016, https://www.rbth.com/defence/2016/06/30/commanders-of-russias-baltic-fleet-fired_607579 (accessed 13 November 2022).

9 T. Yoshihara and J. Holmes, *Red Star over the Pacific*. 2nd edn. Annapolis: US Naval Institute Press, 2018; 'Yes, China Has the Largest Navy in the World: That Matters Less Than You Might Think', The Diplomat, 7 April 2021, https://thediplomat.com/2021/04/yes-china-has-the-worlds-largest-navy-that-matters-less-than-you-might-think (accessed 13 November 2022).

10 N. Soames (rapporteur), 'Evolving Security in the North Atlantic', NATO Parliamentary Assembly's Defence and Security Committee Report, 138 DSCTC 19E, 13 October 2019.

11 'Exclusive: "Russia Is Our Number One Threat" as Its Submarines Circle Britain', *Telegraph*, 22 May 2021; 'Russia Is "Flexing Muscles in Britain's Back Yard" after 10 Warships Arrive Off UK Coast', *Telegraph*, 17 December 2020; 'Royal Navy Warships Monitor Significant Russian Presence Close to UK Waters', Website of the Royal Navy, 4 December 2020, www.royalnavy.mod.uk/news-and-latest-activity/news/2020/december/04/200412-russian-monitoring (accessed 13 November 2022); 'RUSI Sea Power Conference Speech', Website of the UK Government, 24 May 2018, www.gov.uk/government/speeches/rusi-sea-power-con ference-speech (accessed 13 November 2022).

12 Foggo and Fritz, 'The Fourth Battle of the Atlantic'; J. Olsen (ed.), 'NATO and the North Atlantic: Revitalising Collective Defence', RUSI Whitehall Paper, 2016.

13 'Annual Chief of Defence Staff Lecture', Royal United Services Institute, London, 17 December 2017.

14 For some of the implications of this presence, see 'Why Is a Russian Naval Fleet Gathering Near Syria?', *National Interest*, 4 September 2018. Though the Russian Navy established its presence in the Eastern Mediterranean, including at a port facility in Tartus, there is also a strong sense of Russia moving to develop a presence in the Central Mediterranean, especially through its involvement in the Libyan Civil War.

15 Soames, 'Security in the North Atlantic'.

16 Cited in '"Great Power Competition": NATO Announces Atlantic Command to Counter Russia', *Guardian*, 5 May 2018.

17 A. Monaghan, *Dealing with the Russians*. Cambridge: Polity, 2019; D. Adamsky, 'Moscow's Aerospace Theory of Victory: What the West Is Getting Wrong', *Russian Analytical Digest*, No. 259, 30 November 2020, https://css.ethz.ch/content/dam/ethz/special-interest/gess/cis/center-for-securities-studies/pdfs/RAD259.pdf (accessed 13 November 2022).

18 B. Dismukes, 'The Return of Great Power Competition: Cold War Lessons about Strategic Anti-Submarine Warfare and the Defence of Sea Lines of Communication', *Naval War College Review*, Vol. 73, No. 3 (2020), https://digital-commons.usnwc.edu/nwc-review/vol73/iss3/6 (accessed 13 November 2022); S. Wills, '"These Aren't the SLOCs You're Looking For": Mirror Imaging Battles of the Atlantic Won't Solve Current Atlantic Security Needs', *Defense and Security Analysis*, Vol. 36, No. 1 (2020), pp. 30–41.

19 R. Pukhov, 'Russia's Naval Doctrine: New Priorities and Benchmarks', Valdai, 17 August 2015, https://valdaiclub.com/a/highlights/russia_

s_naval_doctrine_new_priorities_and_benchmarks/ (accessed 13 November 2022).

20 V. Gerasimov, 'Vystuplenue nachalnika Generalnovo shtaba Vooruzhonnykh Sil Rossiiskoi Federatsii – pervovo zamestitelya Ministra oborony Rossiiskoi Federatsii generala armii Valeriya Gerasimova na otkrytom zasedanii Kollegii Minoborony Rossii 7 noyabrya 2017', Website of the Ministry of Defence, 7 November 2017, https://function. mil.ru/news_page/country/more.htm?id=12149743@egNews (accessed 13 November 2022).

21 'Prezident zaslushal doklad glavkoma VMF Nikolaya Evmenova o khode kompleksnoi arkticheskoi ekspeditsii', Website of the Presidential Administration, 26 March 2021, http://kremlin.ru/events/presid ent/news/65229 (accessed 13 November 2022); 'Russia's Pacific Fleet Conducts Drills near Alaska', Asia Times, 1 September 2020, https:// asiatimes.com/2020/09/russias-pacific-fleet-conducts-drills-near-alaska/ (accessed 13 November 2022).

22 For some, this indicates how Russo-Chinese cooperation is shifting from the continental to the maritime. 'China–Russian Strategic Partnership: From Continental to Marine', Russian International Affairs Council, 9 August 2021, https://russiancouncil.ru/en/analytics-and-comments/ analytics/china-russian-strategic-partnership-from-continental-to-marine (accessed 13 November 2022).

23 A. Lavrov and A. Ramm, 'Floty vroz: v 2021 godu VMF provedyot krupneishie okeanskie ucheniya', *Izvestiia*, 2 March 2021, https:// iz.ru/1131152/anton-lavrov-aleksei-ramm/floty-vroz-v-2021-godu-vmf- provedet-krupneishie-okeanskie-ucheniia (accessed 7 October 2022).

24 'Glavniy voenno-morskoi parad', Website of the Presidential Administration, 26 July 2020, http://kremlin.ru/events/president/ news/63753 (accessed 13 November 2022); 'Priyom po sluchayu Dnya Voenno-Morskovo Flota', Website of the Presidential Administration, 28 June 2019, http://kremlin.ru/events/president/news/61179 (accessed 7 October 2022).

25 'Prezident zaslushal doklad'; 'Glavniy voenno-morskoi parad'; 'Priyom po Sluchayu'. For a detailed examination of Russia's prioritisation and development of the Arctic and the NSR, see N. Mehdiyeva, 'Polar Power: Russia's Twenty-First-Century Power Base', in A. Monaghan (ed.), *Russian Grand Strategy in the Era of Global Power Competition*. Manchester: Manchester University Press, 2022, pp. 128–54.

26 A. P. Polivach and P. A. Gudev, *Morskie derzhavy 2021: Indeks IMEMO RAN*. Moscow: IMEMO, 2021, pp. 13–19, www.imemo.ru/files/File/ru/ publ/2021/SPR-21.pdf (accessed 7 October 2022).

27 For detailed discussion, see Monaghan, *Russian Grand Strategy*.

28 See reviews by Richard Connolly of the 'Strategy for the Development of Marine Activities to 2030, the Maritime Doctrine, and Foundations of State Policy in the Field of Activities in the Period to 2030', and by Nazrin Mehdiyeva of Russia's Arctic strategies and the 'Development Strategy of the State Corporation Rosatom to 2030' published by the NATO Defense College in the Russian Studies series, available at www.ndc.nato.int/research/research.php?icode=0 (accessed 7 October 2022).

29 "Kalibrisation" refers to the introduction of a family of long-range missiles that can be used to attack targets on land or at sea.

30 'Vladimir Pospelov: desyati "Borei" sdadut do 2030 goda', RIA Novosti, 17 May 2021, https://ria.ru/20210517/pospelov-1732338234.html (no longer active). Its new designation is "Fregat".

31 'S dalnym pritselom: korabli protivnika zametyat za sotni kilometrov', *Izvestiia*, 3 March 2021, https://iz.ru/1131632/anton-lavrov-aleksei-ramm/s-dalnim-pritcelom-korabli-protivnika-zametiat-za-sotni-kilometrov (accessed 7 October 2022).

32 'Bolshinstvo Rossiyan – 67% – schitayut, shto Voenno-Morskoi Flot v Rossii samyi silniyi v mire', Echo Moskvy, 31 July 2019, https://echo.msk.ru/news/2474093_echo.html (accessed 7 October 2022).

33 'Vechno myortvaya zona: pochemu nyet zhizni v rossiiskikh portakh', *Novie izvestiia*, 29 April 2021, https://newizv.ru/news/society/29-04-2021/vechno-mertvaya-zona-pochemu-net-zhizni-v-rossiyskih-portah (accessed 13 November 2022). Under the "pretext" of state security, the authorities restrict access to the coast, including of small vessels.

34 'Kakie korabli nuzhni na more', *Nezavisimoe voennoye obozrenie*, 2 December 2021, https://nvo.ng.ru/realty/2021-12-02/1_1168_ship.html (accessed 13 November 2022).

35 'Protivotorpednaya katastrofa Rossisskovo flota', Topwar, 8 March 2021, https://topwar.ru/180576-protivotorpednaja-katastrofa-rossijskogo-flota.html?yrwinfo=1615460355883848-1479323153271533580100110-production-app-host-vla-web-yp-183 (accessed 7 October 2022).

36 'Shto poleznee: Admiral Nakhimov ili desyat "Buyanov"', Topwar, 15 March 2021. https://topwar.ru/180862-chto-poleznee-admiral-nahimov-ili-desjat-bujanov.html (accessed 7 October 2022).

37 'Nuzhen li Rossii silnii flot?', Topwar, 9 March 2021, https://topwar.ru/178933-chernovik-1.html (accessed 7 October 2022).

38 'Vladimir Pospelov: novy avianosets mozhet stoit 500 milliardov rublei', RIA Novosti, 18 May 2021, https://ria.ru/20210518/pospelov-1732345158.html (accessed 13 November 2022).

39 See, for instance, discussion in G. Till, *Seapower: A Guide for the Twenty-First Century*. Revised and updated 4th edn. London: Routledge, 2018.

For discussion of Russian views of intensifying geo-economic competition, especially over the global commons, see Monaghan, *Russian Grand Strategy*.

40   J. Lanchester, 'Gargantuanisation', *London Review of Books*, 22 April 2021.

41   C. Bueger, T. Edmunds, and B. Ryan, 'Maritime Security: The Uncharted Politics of the Global Sea', *International Affairs*, Vol. 95, No. 5 (2019), pp. 971–8; R. Kaplan, *The Return of Marco Polo's World: War, Strategy and American Interests in the Twenty First-Century*. London: Random House, 2018; J. Holmes, 'Are Navies Dying?', *National Interest*, 7 September 2019.

42   'Kakie korabli nuzhni na more'.

43   'Nuzhen li Rossii silnii flot?'

44   The connection between the sea and Russia's energy interests is wide ranging. Not only does Moscow lay claim to extensive offshore resources, but it has invested heavily in developing transit capabilities, whether by port and ship or by pipelines, many of which – including Nord Stream 1 and 2 – pass along the seabed.

45   'Zasedaniye diskussionovo kluba "Valdai"', Website of the Presidential Administration, 3 October 2019, http://kremlin.ru/events/presi dent/news/61719 (accessed 7 October 2022); 'V period do 2030 goda uroven potentsialnoi voennoi opasnosti znachitelno povysetsya – Valerii Gerasimov', *Voenno-promyshlenniy kurier*, 18 February 2013, https://vpk. name/news/84463_v_period_do_2030_goda_uroven_potencialnoi_voe nnoi_opasnosti_znachitelno_povysitsya_valerii_gerasimov.html (accessed 7 October 2022).

46   'As Suez Canal Remains Blocked, Russia Promotes Northern Sea Route', The Maritime Executive, 26 March 2021, https://maritime-executive. com/article/as-suez-canal-remains-blocked-russia-promotes-northern-sea-route (accessed 13 November 2022). For discussion of the NSR, see Mehdiyeva, 'Polar Power'.

47   M. MccGwire, 'Command of the Sea in Soviet Naval Strategy', in M. MccGwire, K. Booth, and J. McDonnell (eds), *Soviet Naval Policy: Objectives and Constraints*. London: Praeger, 1975, pp. 623–36.

48   E. Morris, *The Russian Navy: Myth and Reality*. London: Hamish Hamilton, 1977, p. 59; M. Kofman and J. Edmonds, 'Why the Russian Navy Is a More Capable Adversary than It Appears', *National Interest*, 22 August 2017, https://nationalinterest.org/feature/why-the-russian-navy-more-capable-adversary-it-appears-22009?page=0%2C1 (accessed 7 October 2022).

49   The tension between innovative design and problems is well illustrated by the K-278 Komsomolets, a Soviet nuclear-powered attack submarine with a unique design including a double hull with an inner hull of titanium. This allowed it an operating depth much greater than US

submarines. It achieved a record depth of 1,020m in the Norwegian Sea in 1984, but on its third patrol a serious fire broke out, leading to the loss of the submarine and the death of forty-two of its crew.

50 B. Watson, *Red Navy at Sea: Soviet Naval Operations on the High Seas, 1956–1980*. London: Arms & Armour Press/RUSI, 1982.

51 Kofman and Edmonds, 'A More Capable Adversary'.

52 For an overview of this debate, and the debate about whether the Russian leadership has a strategy, see Monaghan, *Power in Modern Russia*.

Part I

Maritime strategies in historical context

1
Russia and some principles of maritime strategy

Andrew Lambert

Maritime states and sea power

If we are to interpret Russia's strategy at sea, we must begin by disentangling two concepts that are generally conflated or misused. The first is that of a "seapower", the Greek word *thalassokratia* that Herodotus and Thucydides used to describe states dominated by the sea, where the ocean was central to their prosperity and power, ultimately a question of identity and culture.[1] Being a cultural seapower did not require a state to possess a powerful navy, although they often did, but that they prioritised the navy over other forms of defence. While the first seapower was Periclean Athens, it was not the greatest naval power of the age. That status belonged to the Persian Empire.[2] A vast multinational empire stretching from western Greece to Egypt, Arabia, and the borders of India, Persia harnessed the naval and maritime skills of subject peoples to move armies and support campaigns of conquest. Its capital was a long way from the sea, an element that Persian rulers found alien and alarming. A continental imperial power with a powerful fleet, Persia was the precursor of Rome and Byzantium – and modern Russia.

These hegemonic empires used sea power, a phrase coined by Captain Alfred Thayer Mahan in his book *The Influence of Sea Power upon History, 1660–1783*, which examined the strategic use of the sea for political ends, broadly defined.[3] Mahan split the Greek word *thalassokratia* into a new phrase, because he could not use the examples of Athens, Venice, or Britain as precursors for his strategic argument that the United States needed a large navy. Those states were too small, weak, and above all *maritime* to inform the identity of an emerging continental superpower.

Instead, he emphasised the strategic use of the sea by Republican Rome, a continental military empire bent on hemispheric dominion. His classical model was not the rise of a Carthaginian seapower state, but its annihilation by Roman military power. Similarly, his modern example was not the rise of Britain, but the failure of continental France to achieve the naval hegemony it needed to crush feeble seapower opponents and become a new Roman Empire. Mahan wanted his countrymen to understand that the root causes of French failure lay in poor strategic choices, not a continental identity. He recognised that his country would inherit the Roman mantle, not the British.

The distinction between having naval power and being a seapower matters because navies are profoundly shaped by the nations they serve to a far greater degree than is the case for armies or air forces. The basic tasks of land and air forces are obvious and scalable: border defence, support for internal security, the conquest and control of adjacent territory. States have a far wider range of options at sea, because the open ocean is not subject to the territorial jurisdiction of any power and in war can be used by the dominant navy.

Some navies have been configured for this mission: the Athenian, Venetian, Dutch, and British are obvious examples. All four were small states dependent on maritime trade, imperial possessions, and insular or quasi-insular strategies of limited war. By contrast, the navies of continental hegemons, Persia, Rome, the Ottoman Empire, imperial Germany, and Russia, were shaped for "decisive battle". They would achieve diplomatic or strategic effect by threatening or defeating the fleets of maritime-dependent seapowers. Naval success would clear the path for an invasion, followed by a final battle on land. The Punic Wars exemplify this model, while Russia used similar methods to bring Sweden to terms at the end of the Great Northern War.

Continental powers often economise on naval power, focus on land forces, and rely on strategies of coast defence and commerce predation to distract and weaken their maritime rivals. These strategies were consistently deployed by France during the Second Hundred Years' War (1688–1815). Unable to focus the national effort at sea, France ceded command of the sea to Britain, using economic methods to hamper the exploitation of that command. Occasional French battlefleet challenges to British command were driven by terrestrial strategic issues, not maritime priorities. Very few succeeded.

But France, like Russia, was a great power with regional neighbours. It needed a sea control fleet of battleships to deter or coerce those neighbours. The primary function of Russian sea-going forces from 1700 onwards has been regional control, the dominance of local powers, linked to seizing or controlling critical choke points, especially the Bosphorus and the Danish Narrows. The intention was to deny superior naval forces access to enclosed sea areas on Russia's coasts. This ambition can be traced through the history of Russo-Danish relations between 1700 and 1914. Russia's Baltic Fleet was built to coerce Sweden and Denmark, not engage the Royal Navy if it entered the Baltic. That role was left to costly fortresses and defensive flotillas.

The distinction between seapower and continental navies was reinforced by the introduction of industrial technology in the mid-nineteenth century. Iron, steam, and underwater weapons facilitated greater naval role specialisation, allowing nations to choose bespoke naval forces to satisfy specific strategic needs, ranging from local coast defence to oceanic sea control. Russia's interest in defensive mine warfare – which began when large fields were laid off Kronstadt in 1855 – has persisted, as has the Royal Navy's expertise in offensive mine counter-measures, which also began off Kronstadt.[4]

While Western naval analysts have often misread the purpose of Russian naval activity, and even basic design features, creating alarm, anxiety, and increased naval budgets, subsequent historical analysis has consistently demonstrated the primacy of defensive strategies in Russian thinking. A working command of the sea, of the type the British sought across several centuries, was needed to secure the global empire of trade. This had little attraction for a continental empire with widely separated and largely constrained coastal zones. Russian strategy has always been dominated by terrestrial concerns and powerful land forces.

This matters because maritime strategy, as Sir Julian Corbett (1854–1922) explained in 1911, is a policy option that follows the conscious decision to focus the entire national effort on the sea, for trade, security, culture, and identity. It is only relevant to seapowers: relatively small, weak states. Maritime strategy integrates land, sea, air, and space assets, military and civilian, into a policy that has as its primary strategic mission securing command of the sea as the basis for defensive and offensive action. Corbett's friend Admiral Lord Fisher, a Crimean War veteran, explained the concept in a telling aphorism: '[T]he [British] Army is a projectile to be fired by the Navy!'[5]

Maritime strategy necessarily privileges the application of resources to sea-related missions. It is only possible for insular or quasi-insular powers and only appropriate to relatively small states that depend on the sea. Such states necessarily rely on the defensive power of sea control to conduct limited wars of economic exhaustion and strategic raiding, the basis of maritime strategy. As long as they are able to prevent the hegemonic continental military power from staging an invasion of the home islands, this method can produce positive results. It is a strategy of the (relatively) weak, relying on naval command. It is not an option for powers that share borders with significant rivals. The obvious modern example would be Britain between 1713 and 1945, a maritime trading power that used its command of the sea and sea-based wealth to act as a great power, without creating a mass army. Such states had oceanic empires and fought largely for trade, not land. The decision to become a maritime power was conscious and calculated.

It is important to emphasise that maritime strategy is a product of that choice, and that it has only ever been exercised by maritime states, which chose to emphasise oceanic issues, trade, culture, and strategy, over the normal terrestrial priorities of human society. Furthermore, only maritime powers can use maritime strategy: however large their naval resources, terrestrial powers are restricted to naval strategies because their primary interests remain ashore. The consequences of choosing to become a seapower form the central pillar of Thucydides' account of the Peloponnesian War, which pitted maritime Athens against continental Sparta. Pericles adopted a maritime strategy, relying on economic exhaustion and forms of insularity to counter Sparta's superior military power. Fortifying Athens and connecting it to the port at Piraeus with the "Long Walls" transformed the city into a virtual island. It survived Spartan sieges and only surrendered after the Athenian fleet had been destroyed.

The issue at stake here is Russia's relationship with the sea. That relationship is critical to any understanding of how Russia may use naval force in the future. Russia has always faced external terrestrial threats, from the Mongols, Poland, Ottoman Turkey, France, and Germany. The Soviet Union and post-Soviet Russia have consistently claimed that NATO poses an offensive threat, if only to sustain a rhetoric of victimisation and danger that has been deployed by all Russian regimes. No Russian state has been overthrown by sea-based invaders; the real danger had always been terrestrial.

Russia has never been a seapower. It has used naval power in much the same way as Xerxes – to hasten the advance of the army and conquer territory, not control maritime space or support economic activity. Russia's cultural engagement with the sea, as in Ivan Aivazovsky's nineteenth-century art, has been a space for frustrated dreams of naval glory and apocalyptic visions of the last wave, a final divine judgement. The sea is not, and never has been, a powerful or positive element in Russian culture. The navy has never been Russia's primary strategic system and has always been the first casualty of economic failure, domestic turmoil, and defeat. Its primary missions have consistently been defensive, and its assets, human and material, have been sacrificed to terrestrial concerns in every major war Russia has fought since the days of Peter the Great. During the Cold War, some Western analysts, transfixed by new ships and large missile tubes, were convinced the Red Fleet was preparing to challenge for command of the sea. It was not. In previous eras, British analysts recognised the local and defensive priorities of large Russian fleets. And so did the Russians.

A version of Corbett's *Some Principles of Maritime Strategy* based on a serious assessment of Russian experience would conclude that Russia has no history of maritime strategy. This suggests that Russia's present and future naval capabilities and challenges will be shaped by the same old realities. Mahan's famous check list of what constitutes a seapower remains valid. Russia failed the test in 1890, and still does. It lacks the coasts, seafarers, maritime culture, government, and focus to become truly *maritime*. This is an observation, not a criticism: Russia is simply too large and too deeply committed to terrestrial issues to follow a small island out to sea.

The only question, therefore, is how far Russia has been able to sustain a high-quality professional naval force. The United States, for instance, which has not been a seapower for around two hundred years, has maintained such a force for long periods, even though it was never the primary national defence force. It has been the dominant sea power for the past seventy years, despite not being a seapower state. Cold War-era Soviet naval ambitions reflected the need to defend the Soviet Union and its Warsaw Pact allies against attack from the sea, by amphibious forces, carrier strike, or submarine-launched ballistic missiles. Even now, terrestrial defence remains the dominant maritime concern for the contemporary Russian state.

Russia's use of strategic sea power

If we accept that Russia has never been a seapower, then the enquiry is restricted to its use of strategic sea power. This emphasises the reality that Russia's options at and about the sea have been limited, and largely defensive. The sea has been one of the many directions from which invasions and threats have come. The Russian response has been to extend borders, fortify frontiers, and emphasise military power, part of a wider cultural obsession with invasion, lately manifested in the cinema.[6] No amount of naval force would have stopped the major invasions of Russia, least of all that of the Mongols. A great fleet might have prevented the invasion of the Crimea in 1854, but the fleet had been cut back after 1841 when a new treaty guaranteed the Turkish Narrows would be closed to non-riparian warships. When Russia violated that treaty by invading Turkey, Britain and France were at liberty to sail into the Euxine.

As Corbett emphasised, principles of maritime strategy are enduring only if they are understood through long-term analysis of the experience of an individual state.[7] Between 1898 and 1922, Corbett's research and teaching focused on analysing the evolution of English/British strategic practice since the 1550s, which he developed as lecture courses for the Royal Naval War Course, 1902–14, and in high-profile Cabinet, Admiralty, and Committee of Imperial Defence memoranda from 1904 to 1919. Having mastered his brief, he published a systematic account of the underlying principles, which retain considerable utility over a century later, but only for maritime powers. His chosen themes were the major conflicts for command of the sea, wars with Spain, the

Dutch Republic, and then France providing case studies to inform strategy and planning for another such conflict, with Germany. Intending to update the message before his sudden death, he also analysed the strategic practice of the first two years of the First World War. He did not focus on Anglo-Russian conflicts, where command of the sea had never been in doubt, though he began teaching the Crimean War to the Naval War Course in 1910, just as Anglo-Russian relations began to deteriorate. He recognised that Russia, as it always had in wars with Britain, conceded sea control at the outset, avoided fleet action, and relied on coast defences, cannon, and minefields.

Corbett had lectured the War Course on the Russo-Japanese War from 1904 and began work on a confidential history of the conflict in 1912 for the Committee of Imperial Defence to support the education of senior naval officers. The resulting text, which cross-referenced the Crimean War of 1854–56, should be essential reading for all students of Russian strategy. Corbett's book demonstrated that Japan had defeated Russia by using a form of maritime strategy and encouraged his readers to assess how far such methods would be useful the next time Britain went to war.[8] He stressed that Japan was a very different state from Britain, one dominated by the army, not the navy.[9]

When the leading Russian general of the era set out his preferred strategy on the eve of war, it was both strikingly simple and wholly continental. General Kuropatkin anticipated Japanese army operations in Manchuria and Korea would be defeated by the mobilisation of superior Russian military resources, and the conflict resolved by the invasion of Japan, the defeat of the Japanese army, and the subjugation of its people. The plan opened with the fleets contesting command of the sea, a contest he assumed Russia would win.

As Corbett observed, everything depended on using the unlimited, continental form of war to ensure Russia's superior resources were decisive. But he also observed that the region in question was not part of the Russian Empire, nor one of the border regions in the west that had occupied Russian strategists since Peter's day. It 'could never arouse the national spirit to a degree necessary for the effort required'. For Japan, however, the situation was effectively the opposite: the issue was fundamental, the populace was behind the war effort, the resources to fight were all at hand in the Home Islands, and Japan had no hope of overthrowing the Russian Empire.[10] Japan sought strictly limited, regional aims and waged a limited war to secure them, exploiting its insularity to choose a strategy that had little attraction for a major continental power with potentially hostile neighbours. If Japan secured command of the sea, it could choose the form the war would take and ensure the unlimited Russian counter-stroke could not be delivered. This strategy required the Russian Pacific Fleet to be blockaded and ultimately destroyed, and to that end Japan deployed and largely expended a powerful army, in what was almost a re-run of the Crimean Campaign. The Japanese were also compelled to drive the Russians back along their strategic communications, crippling their ability to sustain large armies in the critical region.[11] Here, the operations would be direct and military, in contrast to the indirect naval action in the Sea of Azov that had cut the logistics of Russia's Crimean Army in the summer of 1855. In 1904–5, the cost of waging war would break the Russian economy, Japan being in no position to blockade Russian external trade.[12]

Corbett did not see Russia as a primary naval/maritime threat, even though he recognised it was an aggressive, expansive power that challenged the status quo in several continental areas of great significance for Britain while possessing the world's third largest battlefleet in 1900 and being allied to France, which owned the second. The problem for Britain then, and a wider Western collective now, is how to bring the strategic weight of seapower to bear on Russia.

The answer has always been limited economic war, linked with targeted attacks on naval assets and infrastructure.

Maritime strategy has long been a viable Western option against authoritarian continental empires. Finally, as Pericles explained, the greatest weapon of the seapower state was democracy, or any other form of progressive, inclusive government subject to the will of the people and the rule of law. Democracy was the cutting edge of Athens' war against Sparta, and as Thucydides emphasised, it was Athenian ideology that really frightened Sparta, as it threatened to empower the helots, undermining the regime's economic and political basis. The Russian state has consistently blocked the inward flow of similar ideas.

It remains deeply symbolic, therefore, that when Peter the Great began his startling project to create a new imperial capital at St Petersburg, replacing the old national centre at Moscow, he began with a massive fortress on Kotlin Island. Specifically designed to keep the Royal Navy at a safe distance, Kronstadt commanded the only deep-water channel to the new city with several hundred cannon. He would not have built the city without it. Kronstadt reflected Peter's view of maritime strategy: the Royal Navy posed a serious threat to his regime, one that Russia could only counter with a fortress, not a battlefleet.

Peter's response to the challenge of responsible government was equally clear. He retained the centralised economy of his ancestors and blocked the emergence of a Russian maritime economy, because that would have required the autocrat to share power with a new commercial class. Having seen how this political model worked in London and Amsterdam, Peter preferred to leave Russian trade in foreign hands.

Nor should his decision to create a Russian navy be read from Western maritime perspectives. Peter had no desire to make Russia into a seapower state. Over a thirty-year period, he created enough naval might, in a variety of forms, to serve the national interest, but nothing more. While his engagement with the sea remained emotional and personal, the vision that drove his naval policy was strategic and functional. Logic and opportunity, not personal enthusiasm for ships and sailing, led Peter to create naval forces. He recognised the need for naval assets in 1695, when his army failed to capture the Ottoman fortress of Azov, because the Russian army could not cut its maritime supply lines. In 1696, hastily built ships isolated the fortress, which surrendered.

This pragmatic approach dominated Peter's naval project.[13] He rejected critical elements of Western progress, elements associated with seapower identity and maritime strategy, inclusive politics, an open economy, a seafaring national identity, and the curiosity to see a world beyond the national frontier. Dressing up as seapower was not the same as becoming one. Peter brought many Western technologies to his country, including warships, navigational equipment, printing presses, globes, and telescopes, but he imposed them on an older reality. Petrine Russia did not become a seapower but merely acquired the strategic sea power necessary to defeat a range of enemies. Peter rejected the underlying political model as unsuited to Russian conditions and strategic requirements. None of his successors ever thought of reversing that decision.

Historian Lindsey Hughes posed the key question: 'Did Peter set much store by his Navy?' Her answers were more clear-sighted and incisive than those of contemporary analysts and historians working for Western navies. The Russian Navy served a higher, essentially terrestrial purpose: naval resources were shifted from theatre to theatre as required, from the Sea of Azov to the Baltic, and finally the Caspian Sea, supporting Russia's imperial expansion. Peter's new fleets were abandoned as quickly as they were built. Naval power was merely a useful addition to the arsenal of an expansive continental state.[14] The possession of a navy did not indicate that Russia was moving towards a maritime strategy in Peter's reign, or at any time since.

Critically, Peter's navy served continental strategic agendas: it was not configured for sea control, economic warfare, or personal interest. Peter did not build his navy solely to gratify his vanity.

He understood the mutual relationship of sea and land power more completely than did most other statesmen of his time; and he indicated this with the crude but striking image that 'any potentate who has only an army has one hand, but whoever has a fleet as well has both of his hands'.

After the Azov Campaign of 1696, 'the value of combined land and sea operations was rarely far from Peter's mind'.[15] He used the sea to enhance terrestrial strategy, a mirror-image of maritime strategy. A sophisticated strategist, Peter countered the superior tactical power of his enemies with mass, movement, and strategic combination.[16] The sea gave his armies mobility. He had a very clear understanding of the strategic role of naval power in Russian strategy, one that did not require Russia to become a seapower state or adopt a maritime strategy. Russia would be the third Roman Empire, not a revived Carthage, Venice, or Holland. When Peter's propagandist, cleric Feofan Prokopovich, sought a suitable analogy for the great victory at Poltava, he turned to the Second Punic War. Poltava was the modern Zama, making Peter the modern Scipio Africanus, emphasising the continental military nature of his imperial ambition and his naval project.[17]

The importance of history in understanding Russia's maritime and sea power

It is worth reflecting on Vladimir Putin's origins in Leningrad and how far the influence of his upbringing has influenced Russia's naval rhetoric and ambition, including the veneration of Peter the Great. Peter did not expect his battlefleet to fight the Royal Navy in the 1710s. He built it instead to overawe regional powers, Sweden and Turkey, while coastal forces provided logistical lift, moving heavy cannon and other bulky stores, along with fire support, for an all-conquering army marching along the coast. This strategy was repeated in many of Russia's subsequent wars. There are powerful echoes, for instance, of Petrine naval activity in the

Second World War career of Sergei Gorshkov, an expert in coastal and riverine warfare and in the war against Ukraine in 2022.

The threat maritime strategy posed to Russia was countered asymmetrically, by fortresses, treaties, and influence beyond the empire's boundaries. In 1914, Russian strategy in the Baltic was built around "Peter the Great's Naval Fortress", a combination of coastal artillery batteries, minefields, and battleships designed to secure the entrance to the Gulf of Finland against a superior naval force. In 1914, that force belonged to imperial Germany, but in 1919 British warships attacked Kronstadt and bombarded key shore defences.

The seas that Russia looks to have remained local: the Baltic, Arctic, Black Sea, and Eastern Pacific. The seizure of the Crimean Peninsula and Sevastopol in 2014 is a case in point, a prestigious city rendered heroic by two great sieges and the loss of countless Russian lives. For Moscow, it could not be allowed to fall into the hands of NATO. Again, there is ample precedent. In 1907, Russia tried to ban British warships from the Baltic, despite the Anglo-Russian Entente effectively making the two countries partners in resisting the rise of imperial Germany. In the event, Denmark refused to be in the firing line for a third Battle of Copenhagen, but the Treaty of Björkö remains deeply significant.[18] The treaty emphasised Russia's preference for access denial and closed seas as the most effective method of preventing or reducing the strategic impact of maritime power on the state. The legal regime in place for the Northern Sea Route is the obvious contemporary example of this approach.

Russia, like other continental powers, has consistently attempted to restrict access to and through oceanic space. The closure of the Straits of Kerch and the transit regime in the North Eastern Passage are only the latest iterations of an approach antithetical to trade, exchange, and progress. Russia has long waged what is known as "lawfare", trying to limit the impact of maritime power by international agreement. In 1800, Tsar Paul challenged

Britain's right to use sea control as the basis of a maritime strategy of economic blockade, an approach that threatened Russian interests. His mother Catherine II had used a similar approach during the American War of Independence, trying to leverage Britain into concessions.[19] Paul, acting in concert with France, wanted to disarm Britain and extend Russia's frontiers. To make his point clear, he seized British shipping in Russian ports.

Recognising an existential threat – the loss of their primary strategic weapon, along with access to Baltic naval stores and grain, and diplomatic isolation – the British government sent a fleet to the Baltic. When Nelson forced the Tsar's Danish allies to abandon the "Armed Neutrality" at Copenhagen, the Russian project collapsed. Paul had been murdered days earlier by aristocrats who feared for their profits. His son Alexander quickly reversed the policy. In 1807, Alexander was forced into Napoleon's "Continental System", an economic counter-blockade of Britain that impoverished the whole continent in French interests. Within four years, the consequent conflict with Britain had broken the Russian economy. As Dominic Lieven has demonstrated, Alexander chose to fight Napoleon, the military colossus of the epoch, rather than endure another year of British economic warfare.[20] Although the Anglo-Russian war cost very few lives, it shattered a Russian economy that depended on selling bulky produce into British markets. These limited economic methods, the core of maritime strategy, were always Britain's primary strategy against Russia: combat operations were necessarily secondary when Russia cared little for the sea, or the navy, and had no overseas colonies or trade worth fighting for. Between 1807 and 1812, Britain deployed its largest fleet to the Baltic to ensure the flow of vital naval stores from the region while developing alternative sources outside Russia.[21]

In the Crimean War of 1854–56, the Russian Empire tried to bully Ottoman Turkey into crippling concessions. Britain and France chose to act. The military operations of the war were limited – because Russia had no means of hitting back at Britain or France. This allowed the Western powers to use a limited war maritime strategy to defeat Russia. Locked in by Austro-Prussian neutrality, including the Austrian occupation of modern Romania, naval weakness, and insurgency in the Caucasus, Russia was forced to wait on the defensive.

The Western allies attacked from the sea, avoiding inland incursions. Instead of marching on Moscow, allied soldiers remained on the coast of the Crimea and a few Baltic islands. The attack on Sevastopol was a classic maritime strategic option, a grand raid intended to destroy a hostile fleet and naval base – to guarantee sea control. This defeat humiliated a Russian Empire that had rested on the laurels won defeating Napoleon in 1814. The old state could not defend the city once the logistics link across the Sea of Azov had been cut. The Army failed in battle, and the navy was scuttled without a fight. Despite the heroic efforts of naval personnel, Russia's second naval base had been destroyed along with the entire Black Sea Fleet. The third naval base, outside Helsinki, was burnt to the water's edge by a high-tech bombardment without the loss of a single allied life. In the Baltic, Russia lost political control of Sweden, while the Tsar's costly fleet was left to rot: it had not even tried to contest command of the sea.[22] Nicholas I had made the navy larger and more effective than it had ever been, even under Peter, but he had no intention of fighting the British at sea. Instead, he deployed the first large-scale minefields in an attempt to deny access to vital areas.

These operations, however, were only a secondary strategy. The primary allied target was the Russian economy. Once they had taken delivery of pre-purchased Russian goods, grain, timber, iron, hemp, and flax that had been ordered in the autumn of 1853, the allies imposed a targeted economic blockade. Within six months, Russia was bankrupt. It lacked access to foreign capital, fiscal reserves, alternative export markets, and access to other purchasers. It could not diversify and, by late 1855, bread and conscription riots openly challenged imperial authority.

The military colossus had feet of clay, lacking the ability to stop the enemy landing at will anywhere on its extensive coast other than under the guns of Kronstadt. It is hard to avoid the conclusion that Tsar Nicholas I had been bluffing, parading large forces and posing as an all-powerful hegemon to hide the profound weakness of a backward economy that could not modernise without fundamental social and economic change. Abolishing serfdom, which happened in 1861, was essential for economic development, industrialisation, and attempts to follow Western military professionalism. The result was a new economic order – which would ultimately challenge imperial authority.

After 1856, Russia began to rebuild, a long, slow process that could only be contemplated by a dynasty or an autocracy. The process of defeat, retreat, introversion, and reconstruction forms a pattern in Russian history. Today, the Russian economy has some of the same old limitations, bulky exports, low liquidity, and dependence on overseas markets. The use of pipelines may negate naval blockade, but even in 1855 the economic war was primarily handled by banks and stock markets, or by diplomatic pressure on potential neutral lenders like the Dutch. It is often argued by Western observers and officials alike that the modern loopholes are obvious: states that buy Russian oil and gas might not vote for sanctions, the modern incarnation of economic warfare. Indeed, it might be said that Russia has always bought influence and stolen technology. In the eighteenth century, Russia acquired the plans of HMS *Victory* and built four replicas, and in the nineteenth century almost every new British warship design reached St Petersburg.[23] But copying and using require very different skills. The end of the Cold War exposed the limits of a far stronger Soviet Union, which missed the move to microprocessors because it relied on copying American computers.

The lack of a recognisable maritime strategy becomes obvious when we turn to the basic naval functions. The Russian Navy has never been able to secure the export of Russian produce. In 1911,

Italy blockaded the Dardanelles during a short war with Ottoman Turkey, inadvertently crippling Russian grain exports in the process and causing serious economic harm to the empire. In 1941–45, the Royal Navy escorted massive supply convoys to Archangel and Murmansk, not the Soviet fleet. In the Indian Ocean and the Eastern Pacific, British and American ships did all the work. The Russian Navy has never been connected with trade. It is the seagoing arm of the military rather than the maritime security force of a dynamic sea-based economy.

Russian thinking about maritime strategy reflects a long tradition of focusing on hostile threats. When the Russian Navy began teaching naval strategy in the late nineteenth century, it translated a British textbook, Admiral Philip Colomb's 1891 book *Naval Warfare*. Colomb's text explained how England/Britain had acquired, maintained, and exploited command of the sea to defeat continental powers. As if to highlight the role it would play in Russian thinking, Colomb's book ended with a discussion of British power projection during the Crimean War.[24] Having learnt a salutary lesson in that conflict, Russia exploited the technological revolution of the 1860s to create a new navy built around coast defence ships and ocean-going cruisers. No longer obliged to create a standard ocean-going battlefleet, which had been the only form of strategic naval strength, Russia abandoned the open seas to the British and reinforced its coastal defences with mobile fortresses.

This has important implications for understanding Russian naval power. The Russian Navy's primary mission has always been territorial defence. The main victories were close to the shore: Gangut, Chesme, and Sinope were not battles for sea control, or power projection. The battlefleet idea was only revived in the 1890s to support terrestrial expansion in East Asia. In 1900, Russia's fleet was thus well provided with coastal defence ships, some of which limped all the way to its destruction at Tsushima. The sacrifice of entire fleets to help defend Sevastopol and Port Arthur was a critical demonstration of Russian sea power in action, naval forces used up as ground troops. This is wholly alien to the thinking of a seapower state: historically, Britain was happy to risk armies to secure sea control, sailors being far more important than soldiers.

Conclusion

In the foreseeable future, Russia will continue to bully weak neighbours, try to extend its defensive perimeter, close down oceanic space, and recruit allies from among those who also fear democracy, the rule of law, free speech, and progress. Disruption and uncertainty remain Russia's chosen weapons; they work best against the ignorant, divided, and ill-prepared. There is tremendous continuity between current practice and past precedent. In the mid-nineteenth century, a great British prime minister described the Russian Empire as akin to a gout-ridden, arthritic giant, forever stretching out its hands to grab territory, classic continental military behaviour. He advised stamping on Russia's fingers every now and again to remind it of its weakness and deny Russia any significant strategic gains. Lord Palmerston ran the Crimean War for this purpose and purchased twenty-five years of peace in the process.

Rather than over-focusing on Kalibr missiles and Russian assertiveness, therefore, we should step back and recognise an empire of anxiety, one that has been invaded by everyone, one that relies on a weak economic base, burdened with heavy defence spending, and an aging population. The greatest dangers are internal instability leading to irrational behaviour and limited prestige operations getting out of diplomatic control. The latter is the best explanation for the Crimean War. For all the visual drama of a long-range precision-strike, Kalibr's strategic function remains the same as the Petrine cannon at Kronstadt.

The purpose of recovering, understanding, and integrating some principles of maritime strategy is to avoid being surprised by old behaviour and old ambitions. Furthermore, as Corbett understood, having been a practising barrister, the legal basis for any future action must be secure. While modern liberal democracies tend to be reluctant to resort to force and unwilling to weaponise moral outrage, sanctions, legally based targeted economic pressure administered by courts of law, remain an attractive modern version of the classic maritime strategy that Russia signally failed to counter between 1807 and 1811, and again in 1854–55.[25] It is the obvious pressure point.

In sum, Russia has no history of employing maritime strategy, because it is not a small, agile, liberal seapower state. Instead, it has long experience of the impact of maritime strategy, as applied by seapower states, or more effective naval powers, like Great Britain in the nineteenth century, imperial Japan in 1904–5, and the United States in the second half of the twentieth century. Russia's strategic focus has been on reducing the risk and extending terrestrial control as far beyond the littoral as possible while exploiting technology, alliances, and legal practice. Russia is an anti-seapower state, but the geostrategic advantages held out by the "Heartland" thesis of Corbett's friend and fellow Edwardian intellectual Halford Mackinder have never materialised.[26]

On this issue, Mahan was right. Russia still depends on the rest of the world, as a market and a source of technology. It remains out of step with the liberal West, unwilling to trust the people with real choice, a surveillance state that Nicholas I would recognise, relying on old-fashioned nationalism and manipulating fears of the other that date back to the Golden Horde to justify repressive approaches to peaceful protest. As Tsar Alexander II recognised in December 1855, and Mikhail Gorbachev more recently, the Russian state had to be rebuilt before it could recover the necessary sense of greatness to underpin the project.

Going to sea was a luxury until the 1950s, when the emergence of strategic nuclear weapons made it necessary to Soviet security. By the 1990s, technology had progressed, and the utility of commanding the seas beyond the horizon had evaporated. Today, the Russian Navy emphasises the operation and security of ballistic missile submarines. These assets are critical to a national strategy based on credible deterrence but have no role in the maritime sphere. Russia has no interest in conducting a maritime strategy. It remains a profoundly continental state, strikingly vulnerable to maritime strategies based on sea control and economic embargo.

Notes

1 In cultural terms, it is significant that the *Aurora*, the hero ship of Russia, the equivalent of HMS *Victory*, is a small cruiser that ran away from Tsushima and fired a few blanks in the October Revolution.

2 A. Lambert, *Seapower States*. London: Yale University Press, 2018. See Chapter 6 for a discussion of Russia and seapower.

3 A. T. Mahan, *The Influence of Sea Power upon History 1660–1783*. Boston: Little, Brown, 1890. Chapter 1, pp. 25–89, contains the core of Mahan's sea power argument.

4 For the beginning of British policy, see R. Dunley, *Britain and the Mine 1900–1915: Culture, Strategy and International Law*. London: Palgrave Macmillan, 2018, pp. 24–7.

5 A. D. Lambert, '"The Army Is a Projectile to Be Fired by the Navy": Securing the Empire 1815–1914', in P. Dennis (ed.), *Armies and Maritime Strategy: The 2013 Chief of Army History Conference*. N.p.: Big Sky Publishing, 2014, pp. 29–47.

6 In many ways, this again reinforces the impression of naval power being secondary. Most of the films reflect on the Great Patriotic War (as the Second World War is known in Russia) on land. An exception to this is the 2008 film *Admiral*, a biopic of Imperial Russian Navy and Russian Civil War Admiral Kolchak.

7 Corbett, *Some Principles of Maritime Strategy*. Corbett only qualified his title as 'Some Principles' as he completed the manuscript, emphasising the inherent British exceptionalism of his argument.

8 J. S. Corbett, *Maritime Operations in the Russo-Japanese War, 1904–1905*. Edited by J. Hattendorf and D. M. Schurman. Annapolis: USNIP, 1994. Only a few copies of the book were printed, and it was finally published in 1994. Volume I appeared in the spring of 1914, volume II in 1915. Few naval officers had the time to read them.

9 Corbett, *Maritime Operations*, I, pp. 1–3.

10 Ibid., pp. 63–4, 359.

11 Ibid., pp. 65–6.

12 Corbett, *Maritime Operations*, I, pp. 13, 15, 67, 171.

13 For an incisive assessment of the role of naval power in Petrine strategy, see W. C. Fuller, *Strategy and Power in Russia 1600–1914*. New York: Free Press, 1992, pp. 69–71.

14 L. Hughes, *Russia in the Age of Peter the Great*. New Haven: Yale University Press, 1998, pp. 83–6.

15 Fuller, *Strategy and Power*, p. 69.

16 Ibid., pp. 70–1.

17 Hughes, *Age of Peter the Great*, p. 207.

18 A. Lambert, '"This Is All We Want': Great Britain and the Baltic Approaches 1815–1914', in J. Sevaldsen (ed.), *Britain and Denmark: Political, Economic and Cultural Relations in the 19th and 20th Centuries*. Copenhagen: Museum Tusculanum Press, 2003, pp. 147–69.

19 I. de Madariaga, *Britain, Russia and the Armed Neutrality of 1780*. London: Hollis and Carter, 1962.

20 D. Lieven, *Russia against Napoleon*. New York: Viking, 2010, pp. 51–2, 335, 524.

21 J. Davey, *The Transformation of British Naval Strategy: Seapower and Supply in Northern Europe, 1808–1812*. Woodbridge: Boydell, 2012.

22 A. Lambert, *The Crimean War: British Grand Strategy against Russia, 1853–1856*. 2nd edn. Aldershot: Ashgate, 2011.

23 J. Tredrea and E. Sozaev, *Russian Warships in the Age of Sail, 1696–1860: Design, Construction, Careers and Fates*. Barnsley: Seaforth, 2010, pp. 153–6.

24 P. H. Colomb, *Naval Warfare: Its Ruling Principles and Practice Historically Treated*. London: W. H. Allen, 1891; R. W. Herrick, *Soviet Naval Strategy*. 2nd edn. Annapolis: Naval Institute Press, 1988 [1968].

25 For a case study of more recent practice, see J. R. Ferris, 'The War Trade Intelligence Department and British Economic Warfare during the First World War', in T. Otte (ed.), *British World Policy and the Projection of Global Power, c.1830–1960*. Cambridge: Cambridge University Press, 2020, pp. 24–45.

26 A. T. Mahan, *The Problem of Asia*. Boston: Little, Brown, 1900; H. J. Mackinder, 'The Geographical Pivot of History', *Geographical Journal*, Vol. 18 (1904), pp. 421–37; H. J. Mackinder, *Democratic Ideals and Reality: A Study in the Politics of Reconstruction*. London: Constable, 1919.

2

Russia: a sea power of a sort?

Geoffrey Till

In many ways, Russia does not conform to the usual pattern of conventional seapower. But for all that, it still needs to be taken seriously as such. Our reactions to the nature and activities of the Russian Navy should be informed by an understanding of what is special to Russia, as well as by our own assumptions about what is "normal" about great power behaviour at sea. The dangers of "mirror-imaging" demand no less. But first it is necessary to clarify how the necessary words are being used in this chapter.

Seapower, broadly, is the capacity to affect the behaviour of other people by what is done at or from the sea. Making use of Julian Corbett's approach,[1] a country for which the sea 'is … a substantial factor' and a country that can exercise seapower strategically may be considered a 'sea power' (two words!). But Corbett emphasises the point that what happens, or may happen, on land is the ultimate decider of strategic outcomes, even for the most maritime of states. This means that being a sea power rather than a notionally "purely" continental one totally preoccupied with territorial concerns is essentially a matter of degree – or would be if such a thing existed.

Geographical considerations

Making rough use of Alfred Thayer Mahan's analysis of the broad characteristics of seapower should help us navigate this definitional minefield. A glance at a map shows that Russia's geography is distinctly unhelpful to its maritime aspirations. Even after the great improvements effected by Peter the Great and his successors, access to the open ocean was and remains divided between the four fleet areas, climatically challenging and dominated by possible adversaries. Moreover, most people wanting to attack Russia have walked, ridden, or driven there. That Russia has a host of unfriendly neighbours, no natural topographical frontiers, and a spotty record of military endeavour combine to give the Russians an acute sense of their own vulnerability and often a ground forces-, and, increasingly, an aerospace forces-centred way of looking at things. These days, for example, Moscow points to the combination of NATO missile shields and the US withdrawal from the Anti-Ballistic Missile (ABM) and Intermediate Range Nuclear Forces (INF) treaties as an existential threat.

Such geographical considerations are critical because they help mould conceptions of national identity and can determine national aspirations and behaviour. Particularly for the Russians,

> [t]erritory ... is a parameter that determines the country's status in world politics. It outlines state frontiers and limits the sphere of influence of a country's culture, traditions, and way of life. The territory influences economic and international relations ... territory is an inalienable part of national self-awareness and condition of shaping or healing national identity.[2]

Such views echo through Russian thinking today, reflected in large part by the work of the Russian Geographical Society. Addressing the congress of this organisation in November 2009, then Prime Minister Vladimir Putin stated that

[t]he scale, the *territory*, the population and the natural resources are inalienable components of a Great Power. Had we seen the meaning of this phrase better ... we would probably have been more careful with what we inherited from previous generations of Russians who lived in this territory and worked hard to accumulate the wealth which we are using now and which we must protect.[3]

Nowhere is the linkage between national identity and territory more apparent than in Russia's attitudes towards Asia. Thus, in 1811, Fyodor Dostoyevsky, answering the question 'What is Asia to us?', stated that

Russia is not only in Europe, but also in Asia, and a Russian is not only a European but also an Asian. Moreover, perhaps we have more of our high hopes fulfilled in Asia rather than in Europe ... Asia, our Russian Asia, is also our root that needs to be rejuvenated and resurrected.

We pleased them in every way, we shared our "European" views and ideas with admiration of Europe, but they gave us a superior look and did not listen to us ... In Europe, we were dependants and slaves, but we would enter Asia as masters. In Europe we have been Tatars, but in Asia even we are Europeans. The mission, our civilizing mission in Asia, will bribe our spirit and attract us there, as soon as the movement begins.[4]

Even if this was not the main reason for the initial forays into Asia, it certainly explains Russia's subsequent attitudes to the other end of its continent. From the start, it was clear that there would need to be a significant maritime component to this surge to the East and that it could not stop at the water's edge once the Pacific was reached. Recognising this, Peter the Great encouraged the development of a group of Japanese linguists to facilitate further expansions overseas, which eventually led to the establishment of bases and ports in California in 1812 and Fort Elizabeth on the Hawai'ian island of Kaua'i in 1817 and, of course, to significant encounters with imperial Japan, most notably in 1904–05 and 1907, 1917, and between 1939 and 1945.[5] The to-and-fro between imperial Japan and Russia involved Russian military defeat in 1905, converted almost immediately into a more friendly relationship in the 1907 agreement. This agreement ended with the Japanese intervention in Siberia in the Russian maritime provinces during the Russian Civil War and began a new to-and-fro over the next generation before the Soviet Union's defeat of Japan in Manchuria in 1945 resolved the issue in Soviet favour (though a peace treaty has still not been signed).

Again, this echoes through the discussion about Russia's place in the world today. Officials including Putin point to Russia's reorientation towards the Pacific as a priority task for the twenty-first century, and official documents emphasise Moscow's intention to strengthen Russia's economic presence in Asia and build a security architecture there. Moscow's pivot to Asia, some suggest, reflects the Russian leadership's replacement of the idea of a "Greater Europe from Lisbon to Vladivostok" by one of a "Greater Asia from Shanghai to St Petersburg".[6]

The same impulses drove the Russians north, into the Arctic. Early seventeenth- and eighteenth-century explorations led to a growing interest in its economic possibilities, its potential as a route to the Pacific with its manifold scientific interests and eventually to the acquisition of Alaska. In Stalin's time, the Arctic was Russia's new frontier, the novel and exciting place where Soviet Man could conquer the future.[7] Its strategic significance became apparent in the Great Patriotic War, but even more during the Cold War when, after the Central Front, it became the second most important theatre of military operations.

Since the end of the Cold War and especially with climate change, the Arctic has become a major maritime preoccupation for Moscow. The Russian leadership has sought to advance its claims in the region, with renewed discussion in 2021 emerging about a further territorial claim well beyond previous ones.[8] Despite all its climatic and environmental challenges, the combination of the vast resources there – especially oil and gas – and transit in the shape of the Northern Sea Route (NSR) make it a strategic priority for Moscow. The NSR, which promises to cut passage times to Asia by 20 per cent, could become a significant trade artery,[9] yield substantial transit fees, and stimulate development of Russia's northern coastal areas, and its utilisation is slowly rising.[10] For all these reasons, the Northern Fleet's administrative status has been upgraded twice within a decade – first in 2014 to the Arctic Joint Strategic Command and then in 2021 to a Military District, consolidating capabilities. Plainly, "Russia" is not confined to the water's edge.

But the amorphous nature of Russia's boundaries contributes to a historically persistent sense of vulnerability motivated by the 'the insecurity of a land power that had to keep attacking and exploring in all directions or itself be vanquished'.[11] At the same time, the country's proximity to areas such as the Arctic and the Asia-Pacific may be thought to offer opportunities for the country to break out of its challenging and in many ways disadvantageous geographic confines.

Such geographic considerations and the potential vulnerabilities they entail can certainly have naval and strategic consequences. A sense of the country's vulnerability to what used to be called the "arc of crisis" to its south also surely helps explain Russia's policy in Syria and the presence of its naval forces in the Eastern Mediterranean – not only to advance operations in Syria, but also to act as a forward-deployed strategic deterrent to the Euro-Atlantic community. Similarly, the expanding opportunities of the NSR in an age where the Arctic is objectively changing in consequence of global warming, inevitably given its past vulnerabilities, encourages the country to look to its defences in that area too. Moscow refers to the NSR as its own internal waterway and has introduced restrictive legislation and substantial military capabilities along the passage to control it.

These geographic considerations encourage a tendency to over-insure and to spend more on defence than defence would seem to warrant in the eyes of other people. More narrowly, such anxieties seem likely to be behind a rethink about the role of precision-guided conventional and nuclear weapons that envisages their sub-strategic use for pre-emption and escalation dominance. This works to the relative benefit of the Russian Navy in giving it a "new" role in precision strikes against economic and governance targets and reinforces the importance of its second-strike capability.[12]

Russia's unique geographic circumstances combine to shape conceptions of seapower that will obviously not be the same as countries like Japan, Britain, or the United States. It has led Russians to be more regional and less oceanic in outlook, and perhaps to be more worried about incoming threats. But it is easy to find instances when such priorities afflicted these countries too. Moreover, from time to time, Russia has also exhibited oceanic tendencies, and certainly does now. For such reasons, the differences between Russian strategic approaches to seapower and those of more conventional seapowers are indeed matters of degree not kind. Geographic considerations certainly do not justify the conclusion that Russia is not a sea power.

Government, society, culture, and the economy: maritime power between attention and neglect

Mahan also closely linked seapower with particular forms of economic activity that were more than just agrarian. Seapower, he thought, was intimately connected with trade, and the advantages of the sea as a means of its conduct would produce a natural synergy between mercantile power and naval power. The latter would protect the former against everything from pirates to malign states, while the former would help provide the sailors, ships, dockyards, and financial infrastructure from which great fleets could be built and, importantly, maintained. Not surprisingly, the maritime interest would become significant in terms of domestic politics and global in terms of its engagement with others. Some would go further, arguing that sea consciousness would lead to the adoption of trading values about freedom and the rule of law that underlie Western concepts of democracy. Seapower and liberalism, in other words, go hand-in-hand.[13]

Clearly, not much of this applies to Russia, or has ever done so. Putin's claim that Western democracy has clearly passed its sell-by date simply underlines the point.[14] Historically, Russian seapower was much more the result of the passing whim of its rulers than of an organic growth welling up naturally from its merchant classes. Russia's social sea-mindedness was very limited when compared to that in the UK, for instance, or the Netherlands. Most of its people lived far, far away from the sea. Peter the Great and Catherine II did what they could to develop the sea-mindedness of their country but were confronted by the autocratic nature of the state for which they were responsible. Indeed, conventional seapower theorists present the illiberal nature of the state as a great source of weakness for Russia's maritime aspirations, and so in many ways it is, and always has been.

To the extent that Russia is considered a naturally autocratic state, the resultant maritime deficiencies can be considered at two levels. The first is the tactical and operational. Out in the Far East, Vladimir Semenov lamented the passive inactivity of the Russian Fleet in Port Arthur in 1905, attributing much of it to poor leadership (except when the "Little Uncle" Admiral Stepan Makarov was in command), neglect, and a lumbering, top-heavy stultifying bureaucracy, insufficiently aware of its deficiencies: 'The maxim "be careful and risk nothing", once more had the upper hand. Under the hypnotic effect which ... [resulted from the loss of Admiral Makarov], ... a new maxim was added: "Never do anything without orders or without previously asking permission."'[15] This shines important light on the Russian Navy, to be sure, both in terms of its commanders and how they implemented the concepts that underpinned its activities and, indeed, more broadly, those of the Russian armed forces. While some of Russia's naval commanders (and in the army) were competent and dynamic, not only Makarov but also those such as Alexander Kolchak, who later became an admiral in the imperial navy, caution was a besetting characteristic more generally. Admiral Wilgelm Vitgeft, who succeeded Makarov after the latter's death, was less dynamic, though some argue that his more passive approach coincided with the intent to maintain a "fleet in being", build up strength, and support land operations. Only when he was directly instructed by Emperor Nicholas II did Vitgeft sortie from Port Arthur to meet the Japanese in the Battle of the Yellow Sea.[16]

The October 1917 Revolution created an ambiguous atmosphere for initiative. In the wake of the Kronstadt rebellion in 1921, purges affected not only investment in the navy, but also morale and competent innovation. By the late 1920s, a significant percentage of the officers and sailors were drawn from the Komsomol, rather than experienced or qualified seamen. In the 1930s under Stalin, it was easy for naval officers to conclude that the reward for innovative thinking was a bullet in the back of the head. This does much to explain the mediocre performance of the Soviet submarine force in the Great Patriotic War, for instance, and its sometimes limited effectiveness in the Black and Baltic Seas due to the prevalence of 'exactingness' – or the habit of doing things 'by the book'.[17] The depressing effect of the political officers – the *zampolits* – added yet another layer of restraint on the development of tactical initiative at sea.

Second, such restraints were also apparent at the strategic level. Because of the nature of Russian society, rulers with a maritime vision like Peter the Great had to start effectively from scratch, relying heavily on the maritime experience of foreigners and building state-owned and operated shipyards and general maritime infrastructure. Through much of the nineteenth century, the deficiencies of Russia's industrial base forced its sailors to shop heavily in Western shipyards. Worse still, naval procurement was conducted in such a piecemeal fashion that it produced a heterogeneous fleet that was difficult to operate as a cohesive whole. In 1904–5, for example, the result was 'no fleet, but a chance concourse of vessels',[18] and this played an important part in Russia's defeat by the Japanese. Because, in both the construction and the deployment of their fleets, the Russians were thus often fatally dependent on foreigners, the sea all too often was thus seen as something not quite Russian.

The sea was important to the Russian economy because of exports, but unlike the Dutch in the seventeenth century, the Americans at the time of the Revolutionary War, or the British prior to the Revolutionary and Napoleonic Wars, the Russians did not have a vibrant, private maritime defence-industrial base to exploit. Worse still, a constitutional aversion to free enterprise imposed real limits on their prospects of economic growth. In turn, this made the building of a first-class fleet, and more particularly its continued maintenance, much more difficult. At a time of endlessly expanding military expenditure and industrial effort, this played a major part in the final collapse of the Soviet Union.[19]

Additionally, too much depended on the priorities of particular leaders – Russia's maritime and naval capacity was greatly affected by the dynamics of leaders who showed interest or who were not interested or whose wider political activity had negative consequences for the navy. Though Peter the Great dedicated considerable effort to maritime and naval affairs, all too often the navy was seen as little more than an imperial caprice. As one British ambassador put it in the 1830s:

> In this light is the Russian navy considered by almost every official person with whom I have conversed on the subject. They all declare it to be a "toy", and a very expensive toy, with which the Emperor delights to occupy himself, but not one of them … anticipates the possibility of its ever being made use of as a means of attack or defence, and all openly deplore the expense which it occasions, as weakening their financial resources, and withdrawing large sums annually from the more useful national purposes.[20]

Deprived of the top-down pressure from an active and committed ruler, the navy all too often languished in neglect. Such was the fate of its Far East squadron in 1905 and of its relieving squadron under Admiral Zinovy Rozhestvensky, both forces suffering from fragile morale, poor training, ill-maintained ships, and inadequate supplies.[21] And as we have seen, top-down pressure of a different kind can cause serious damage: in the late 1930s, Stalinist autocracy had even more dire consequences, with the purging of many of the navy's most professional officers.[22]

Nevertheless, a few caveats need to be entered against this – in some ways comforting – Western-centric view of Russian maritime development. The first is the obvious point that some distinctly undemocratic and illiberal states have still managed to field first-class naval forces, including Wilhelmine and Nazi Germany, imperial Japan in the past, or as China might in the future. That such navies have usually "lost" does not mean they always will, especially given the often-narrow margins of their eventual past defeats.

First, even with its inherent deficiencies, the Soviet Navy *was* the navy of a superpower and could command the resources to match. For example, the Soviet Ministry of Shipbuilding of the Cold War era provided about fifty significant shipyards, thirty of them very large indeed. Despite the climate, the construction yard at Severodvinsk on the White Sea produced more submarines than the rest of the world put together. The Soviet Union also took about 70 per cent of the shipbuilding capacity of Eastern Europe and Finland. Nor was this merely a question of quantity. Where the Soviet leadership chose to concentrate its resources, its achievements were impressive. By the 1970s, the Soviet Union produced about seven thousand naval architects a year; people from its prestigious Institute of Welding contributed to levels of expertise in certain aspects of construction – like welding titanium hulls for submarines – that were operationally highly advantageous and perhaps ten years ahead of the Americans.[23]

Second, the assumption that navies can only be built in times of economic prosperity is just that – an assumption. Some interesting studies have shown that the rise and fall of the Russian Navy did not always correlate with the rise and fall of the country's economy. Indeed, as discussed in later chapters in this volume, Russia is currently proceeding with a naval modernisation programme that warrants respect, despite the less than sparkling state of the country's economy.

More generally, the fact that a country is not noted for its liberal characteristics does not mean that it has no sense of historic mission or of its own importance. Its Asian empire is not just an aspect of Russian history, it is Russian history: 'Russia's national identity as empire has been rooted in "the people, the land, and the church" since the beginning.'[24] Expansion into the new territories became a part of Russia's value system and ideological conviction, a Russian version of the United States' Manifest Destiny with the twin aims of spreading civilisation and enlarging its dominions. Central to that is the concept of *derzhavnost* ("great powerness").[25] Whether such a conception is justified or not is beside the point – what matters is what Russians *think* is true. And there is some truth in the current if cynical observation that 'Putin has failed to build us a great future, so he has built us a great past.'[26]

Following the 1917 Revolution, the sense of mission remained, although its substance changed considerably as concepts of Russia as a historic powerhouse of a new ideology came to sit alongside its existence as a major multinational empire. Whether as Svyataya Rus (Holy Russia), or as the fount of Marxism, or as an empire, or just as a *velikaya derzhava* (a great power-state), Russia expects to command respect, and its behaviour has nearly always reflected that expectation. And, of course, this helps frame its naval conceptions. A great navy both illustrates, and is a means of becoming or remaining, a great power. Hence the continuing aspiration for a great fleet – come what may.

However, there were, and remain, sceptics. Indeed, General Kuropatkin himself warned the Tsar just before the Russo-Japanese War that concentrating too many resources on the navy and imperial adventures in the East, far from earning credibility in Europe, could make Russia dangerously vulnerable in the West.[27] Navalism could reasonably be seen not just as strategically counter-productive but as a threat to the regime itself. Such diversity of view also needs to be factored into assessments of Russia as a seapower.

Again, it should be noted that historic patterns of neglect and doubt over the necessity of maintaining a large navy have afflicted more conventional sea powers too. There is nothing distinctive about this aspect of Russian experience, except, perhaps, issues of scale and frequency. But that experience does result from often very different circumstances. This needs to be recognised and, perhaps, taken into real consideration when it comes to determining responses to what Russia does, at sea or anywhere else.[28]

Consequent naval conceptions

These sometimes competing characteristics plainly have consequences for what Russians conceive their naval tasks to be and how those tasks might be carried out. To that extent, they are likely to be distinctive, helping to explain why the Soviet Navy, and the Russian Navy before and after it, in many ways steered a different course from conventional Western navies. Immediately after the Revolution, for example, two points were made.

The first is conceptual. In the 1920s, Russia was a new kind of state, a Marxist one in a hostile capitalist world. Because its society and ideology were radically distinctive, it could not be expected to follow the strategic and doctrinal precepts that derived from an earlier and very different time. There needed to be new strategic ideas more in keeping with Russia's revolutionary nature. It was not wise for them to ape the concepts of capitalist navies.

As Admiral Vyacheslav Zof, Commander in Chief of Soviet naval forces between 1924 and 1926, stated:

> We often ... identify with the classical sea powers and try to operate like they do. The battle of Jutland is our model which we study and attempt to imitate. Admirals Beatty and Spee – they are our role models. That which we learn from foreigners is good ... But to try to transplant all that directly into our conditions is not correct. We have other forces, other means, and we operate under different conditions. Consequently, it is necessary to work out the tactics for a small navy which acts together with the Army according to a single strategic plan.[29]

The second is more pragmatic. The old Tsarist navy was in a pitiable state, its shipyards in ruins. The new Soviet Navy could not have built the battleships and aircraft carriers that characterised Western navies even if it had wanted to, nor could it sail the World Ocean. The "Old School" who hoped that the new Soviet Navy could eventually carry on where its Tsarist predecessor had left off attracted the exasperated scorn of Zof, who complained that they seemed completely to ignore economic and technical reality, and the fact that 'perhaps tomorrow, or the day after, we will be called upon to fight. And with what shall we fight? We will fight with those ships and personnel that we have already.'[30]

These two factors shaped the ideas of the "New School" in which the navy became ever more the handmaiden to the ground forces, and where its operational focus was on the provision of a networked system of defence of local waters characterised by small combatants, coastal submarines, mines, land-based batteries, and airpower. It was almost as though the Soviet Union's near waters were territorialised, becoming just demarcated areas designed to keep intruding Western naval forces away. This focus on sea denial is often said to be the chief characteristic of the navy of a continental rather than a free-wheeling maritime state preoccupied with the open ocean.

In this, the New School recognised that they were both helped and threatened by new technology, first in the hope, pushed by many in the West too, that submarines, torpedoes, and land-based aircraft would make mincemeat of large and lumbering battleships and carriers. Equally, the increasing range of the enemy's means of strike would require them to push those maritime defensive frontiers further and further forward – as far away from the Motherland as possible. Just like any other navy, in fact, technology had a big role in shaping policy, in this case driving the Soviet Navy from narrow coastal approaches to sea denial towards more oceanic versions of the concept verging on sea control.

Such possibilities encouraged heavy investment in, and reliance on, transformative military technology. These same impulses are evident today, in Russia's military deployment in the Eastern Mediterranean, the Arctic, the Baltic, and the Black Sea, and also of course in Putin's recent public display of chilling new cutting-edge technologies ranging from the Poseidon doomsday torpedo to nuclear-powered cruise missiles. 'Nobody has anything like this' said Putin of the Poseidon in June 2019.[31]

But, despite all this, there have been periods where conventional rather than unconventional attitudes towards seapower have made themselves felt. One example would be the way in which Peter the Great, enthused by his latest visit to British shipyards, would bore William III rigid over dinner about the delights of seapower. Another was the activity of Admiral Fyodor Ushakov later in the eighteenth century, who could, claimed the Soviet Admiral Sergei Gorshkov, have taught Nelson. The wars against the Swedes and Turks in the eighteenth century and then the Turks again in the nineteenth century demonstrated that the Russian Navy was as aware as any other of the advantages of sea control rather than simply sea denial, even in the confined waters of the Baltic and Black Seas.

The heroic but fateful voyage of the Baltic Fleet into the Pacific in the early years of the twentieth century showed similar but grander aspirations, although that particular endeavour did not end well. The building of the new and admired Catherine

II-class battleships that followed soon after showed a desire to get such things right next time. The "New School" had fallen into disfavour by the mid-1930s, and Stalin showed his preference for big ships and big ideas with an ambitious construction programme, and by shooting admirals who disagreed. In more recent times, Gorshkov himself admitted publicly and to a roomful of Americans that Mahan and everything he stood for was largely sensible.[32] Despite everything, the Soviet Navy became steadily more effective, more "normal", and began to sail the oceans of the world, disconcertingly turning up where the Americans least wanted them.[33]

The current mix of conventional and unconventional, the new and the unfamiliar, can also be seen in the latest iterations of Russia's maritime and naval thinking.[34] The Maritime Doctrine of the Russian Federation has distinct echoes of Admiral Sergei Gorshkov's book *Seapower of the State* (1979), most obviously in its richly maritime rather than narrowly naval-military scope. Plainly the intention is once more to rectify the country's historic deficiencies in the provision of a broad maritime base for Russia's Navy and economy. This, and the subsequent document Fundamentals of the State Policy of the Russian Federation in the Field of Naval Operations, both emphasise the increased importance of the World Ocean and the Arctic and Pacific Oceans in particular: 'The significance of the Pacific Ocean regional priority area is enormous and continues to grow.'[35]

Underlying it all is the assumption that such is the potential of this and other parts of the World Ocean that the navy's aspirations cannot simply be limited to local waters and sea denial. In terms of responding to the threat of US "Global Strike" capabilities, effective deterrence requires the credible threat of punishment as well as denial. For this, cutting edge and innovative technology in the shape, for example, of long-range high-precision weapons, sub-strategic nuclear weapons, and a forward submarine presence, will be required.

Russia: a sea power of a sort?

All the same such aspirations in the past were constantly impeded by the weights of adverse geography, societal restrictions, and resource constraints, which could not simply be shaken off. While in many ways Russia acts as a perfectly normal sea power, its leadership faces some distinctively difficult challenges. So how, given all these near permanent constraints, has the navy coped and done its best to field comparable capabilities and achieve sufficient strategic effect at sea?

Five Russian paths to seapower

First and foremost in understanding how the Russian Navy has coped with these challenges must be Russia's tendency to regard geography not as something fixed, but instead more as something that is negotiable and can be altered by political or military action. There were plenty of examples of this at the end of the Second World War when their military performance put the Russians in a position of strength. Stalin put pressure on the Norwegians and the Turks to be rather more positively accommodating and bid for some substantial holdings along the North African shoreline.

More recently, the move against Georgia in 2008 and then Crimea and Ukraine in 2014 and in 2022 has utterly transformed the situation in the Black Sea to Russia's advantage. Now over half of its exclusive economic zone is claimed and supervised by Russia. Nor have they shown themselves slow in making the best use of the geography they have. Their construction of a bridge across the straits into the Sea of Azov greatly disadvantages Ukraine, creates a kind of escalation dominance, and facilitates Russian control of the area. To this could also be added Russia's (renewed) permanent naval presence in the Eastern Mediterranean and increasingly in the Central Mediterranean, which, if it does not alter physical geography, shifts the cognitive maritime and security maps and geography of the Euro-Atlantic region. At the other end of the Eurasian landmass, the Russian acquisition and determined retention of the North Kuril Islands helps their strategic position in the Sea of Okhotsk, makes their ballistic missile submarine bastion there more secure, and facilitates access to the open ocean.

Second, Russia perhaps more than most has a track record in making the best and often most innovative and asymmetric use of new technology. In the nineteenth century, Admiral Stepan Makarov was regarded as *the* authority on torpedoes. It was entirely in that spirit that the idea of firing nuclear torpedoes into places like New York harbour bubbled up when confronted by a US Navy better able to wield a nuclear deterrent. These ideas and claims often seem far-fetched and overblown to Western commentators but subsequently prove to have some substance. The high-speed Shkval torpedo and Brahmos hypersonic missile are good examples. This may also prove to be the case regarding at least some of the new weapons announced by President Putin in 2018.

More immediately, the Russians have shown themselves to be constructively innovative in their recent displays of the combined effect of relatively small craft and powerful missiles, such as the "distributed lethality" concept of the Kalibr cruise missile innovatively combined with the Buyan-M corvette. In the Syrian campaign, powerful corvettes/light frigates like the Stereguschchiy (Project 20380) and the new Gremyashchiy (Project 20385) with their Kalibr land-attack (3M-14) missiles with a 2,500 km range have impressed observers. The Russian Navy is expected to have some fifty of these by the mid-2020s. Their Bastion and Bal coastal defence systems also command respect. Their latest submarines such as the *Severodvinsk* SSGN and the subsequent Yasen-M-class SSGNs suggest near parity in performance with NATO submarines. Moreover, with new weapons like the Poseidon now apparently coming on stream, Russia's capacity to surprise through "military-technical means" seems alive and well despite setbacks in the war in 2022. Their continuing problem, however, is that, as discussed in detail in subsequent chapters, the Russian capacity to bring their ideas to technological fruition has frequently been undermined or at least made more difficult by the limitations of their industry and general economy.

Third, the Russians have proved adept at securing control at sea by means other than extensive investment in big and expensive ships. The overland advance of the Russian army in the last years of the Great Patriotic War immeasurably improved their strategic position in the Baltic, and the strength of their shore-based sensors, Iskanders, and air-forces makes it seem an unwelcoming place to this day. Much the same could be said of the Black Sea and parts of the Eastern Mediterranean. This famously led Admiral Chernavin to declare, in positively Corbettian terms, that there was no such thing as naval strategy, but only a general maritime strategy to which navies make their contribution.[36] Not only did this echo the views of early Soviet military thinkers such as Alexander Svechin, but it is the sort of thing that most admirals would say in these days of joint and multi-domain operations. Perhaps the key difference is that Russian admirals actually believed it probably much earlier than their Western counterparts.

Fourth, and related to this, Russians seem especially good at thinking about power at sea "in the round", holistically, as part of a much wider package of the ways in which one state can influence another – including diplomatic, economic, and other tools of the state. On his way to the Far East, for example, Vladimir Semenov was warned by a superior, 'war does not always begin only with the firing of guns. In my opinion, the war has begun long ago. Only those who are blind fail to see this.'[37] Today, Western observers and officials often point out that Russia's current Chief of the General Staff, Valeriy Gerasimov, stated that the role of non-military means in achieving political and strategic goals has grown, and, in many cases, even exceeded the power of force of weapons in their effectiveness. This holistic approach envisages a whole mix of devices that operate alongside conventional kinetic means of securing state objectives.[38] Since contemporary Russia appears to have taken to such manoeuvres with some relish,[39] these "other means" can make limited seapower, as part of the package, more effective than it perhaps deserves to be simply on its own merits.

Russia's interpretation and use of sea-related international law is a good example. By its assertive presence in waters of contention and a strong sense that its task is to defend the country's rights and sovereignty, the Russian Navy arguably affects the cognitive maritime maps of other nations and navies. Requiring a forty-five-day notice period for ships intending to pass through the NSR, if unchallenged, would have this effect. Building a bridge across the Kerch Strait is not considered by them to constrain free access to the Sea of Azov but certainly has that effect on the Ukrainians.[40] The seizure of the Crimean Peninsula results in considerable extensions to the de facto if not de jure Exclusive Economic Zones in the Black Sea, a point underlined by the militarisation of some of their oil rigs in those waters.[41] Of course, such differences of view are neither new nor particularly Russian; fishing disputes in international waters near Russia's territorial seas were a major stumbling block in negotiations between the UK and Soviet Russia in 1922–23, for example.[42] Nor is Russia by any means alone in making the most of international law when that seems a promising way forwards.

Fifth and finally, a country's power at sea – or anywhere else for that matter – is only really measurable in relation to that of other countries. Accordingly, the realties and vulnerabilities of the strategic environment in which the Russian Navy currently operates is a very relevant factor in assessing its effectiveness. The point here hardly needs labouring that trans-Atlantic relations are not at their most united and effective, and that its manifest sea dependencies could easily become a major source of strategic vulnerability.[43] Moreover, if the future is always distressingly complex and hard to predict, this seems particularly so at the moment. Especially perhaps, in that when responding to current Chinese and Russian challenges, the West is facing climate change and bad weather at the same time.[44]

All this suggests that although Putin's claim that the Russian Navy is and must remain the world's second most powerful navy seems less than totally credible,[45] we would be wise not to dismiss it too readily simply because Russia's approach to seapower is not quite the same as ours. For all its past and present difficulties and failures, there is, after all, some basic truth in Admiral Gorshkov's claim that 'the fleet wrote into the history of our homeland many remarkable heroic pages and played an important role in the history of the development of Russia'.[46] Even if we choose to dismiss or ignore this claim and the aspirations it leads to, it is fairly clear that, presiding as he does over 'a great maritime power ... a great sea and land power', Putin will not.[47]

Notes

1 J. Corbett, *Some Principles of Maritime Strategy*. 2nd edn. London: Longmans, Green, 1911 – reprinted with introduction by Eric Grove, Annapolis: Naval Institute Press, 1988, p. 1.

2 S. V. Kortunov, 'Russia's National Identity: Foreign Policy Dimension', *International Affairs: A Russian Journal of World Politics, Diplomacy & International Relations*, Vol. 49, No. 4 (2003), p. 105. I would like to acknowledge the extensive help afforded me in this chapter by Anna Borisova Davis, of the Russian Maritime Studies Institute, US Naval War College, in the provision and translation of this and following material.

3 'Vystuplenie V. V. Putina na syezde RGO', Website of the Russian Government, 18 November 2009, www.archive.premier.gov.ru/events/news/8292 (no longer active). Emphasis added. Here, "scale" ("masshtab") is also an important word.

4 F. M. Dostoyevsky, *Dnevnik pisatelya za 1881 god*. [Writer's Diary, 1881], Complete Collection in Thirty Volumes. Vol. 27. Leningrad: Nauka, 1984, p. 33, line 10; p. 36, line 40; Dostoyevsky, *Dnevnik Pisatelya za 1877 god. Yanvar'–Avgust* [Writer's Diary, 1877, January –August], Complete Collection in Thirty Volumes. Vol. 25. Leningrad: Nauka, 1983, p. 22. Trans. Anna Borisova Davis.

5 J. R. Gibson, 'Russian Expansion in Siberia and America', *Geographical Review*, Vol. 70, No. 2 (April 1980), pp. 127–36, at p. 132, http://www.jstor.org/stable/214435 (accessed 7 October 2022).

6 See, for instance, A. Korolev, 'Russia's Reorientation to Asia: Causes and Strategic Implications', *Pacific Affairs*, Vol. 89, No. 1 (2016),

pp. 53–73, who refers to these more recent developments and also quotes Dostoyevsky.

7   J. McCannon, *Red Arctic: Polar Exploration and the Myth of the North in the Soviet Union, 1932–1939.* Oxford: Oxford University Press, 1998, Chapter 5.

8   'Russia Considers Extended Claim to the Arctic Seabed', High North News, 1 February 2021, www.highnorthnews.com/en/russia-consid ers-extended-claim-arctic-seabed#:~:text=Two%20Russian%20vessels %20have%20collected,far%20from%20Russia's%20existing%20claim. &text=It%20happened%20between%20August%20and%20October%20 last%20year (accessed 7 October 2022).

9   Moscow again touted this in 2021 when the Suez Canal was blocked. 'As Suez Canal Remains Blocked, Russia Promotes Northern Sea Route', Maritime Executive, 26 March 2021, www.maritime-executive.com/arti cle/as-suez-canal-remains-blocked-russia-promotes-northern-sea-route (accessed 7 October 2022).

10 C. Paris, 'Russia's Siberian Waters See Record Ship Traffic as Ice Melt Accelerates', *Wall Street Journal*, 8 October 2020, www.wsj.com/arti cles/russias-siberian-waters-see-record-ship-traffic-as-ice-melt-accelerat es-11602180850 (accessed 7 October 2022).

11 R. D. Kaplan, *The Revenge of Geography: What the Map Tells Us about Coming Conflicts and the Battle against Fate.* New York: Random House, 2012, p. 168; K. I. Zubkov, 'Vliyanie vostochnykh regionov na sotsial'no-politicheskoe i kul'turnoe razvitie Rossii' [The influence of the Eastern regions on the socio-political and cultural development of Russia], in V. V. Alekseev, E. V. Alekseeva, K. E. Zubkov, and I. V. Poberezhnikov (eds), *Aziatskaya Rossiya v geopoliticheskoi i tsivilizatsionnoi: dinamike XVI–XX veka* [Asian Russia in geopolitical and civilisational dynamics in XVI–XX centuries]. Moscow: Nauka 2004, pp. 560–1, trans. Anna Davis.

12 K. Zysk, 'Escalation and Nuclear Weapons in Russia's Military Strategy', *Journal of the RUSI*, Vol. 163, No. 2 (April/May 2018), pp. 4–15 (A).

13 For example, N. A. M. Rodger, *The Safeguard of the Sea: A Naval History of Britain 1660–1649.* London: HarperCollins, 1997, pp. 433–4; P. Padfield, *Maritime Supremacy and the Opening of the Western Mind.* Woodstock and New York: The Overlook Press, 1999, esp. Chapter 1; A. Lambert, *Seapower States: Maritime Culture, Continental Empires and the Conflict that Made the Modern World.* New Haven and London: Yale University Press, 2018.

14 'Plenarnoe zasedanie Peterburgskovo Mezhdunarodnovo ekonomich- eskovo foruma', Website of the Presidential Administration, 7 June 2019, http://kremlin.ru/events/president/news/60707 (accessed 7 October 2022).

15 V. Semenoff, *Rasplata (The Reckoning)*. London: John Murray, 1913, p. 122.
16 The Japanese won the battle, and Vitgeft himself was killed – another example of the high casualty rate suffered by senior Russian officers in battle both in this war and many others.
17 B. Ranft and G. Till, *The Sea in Soviet Strategy*. 2nd edn. London: Macmillan, 1989, pp. 142–4.
18 V. Semenoff, *The Battle of Tsushima*. London: John Murray, 1906, p. 10.
19 J. Lehman, *Oceans Ventured: Winning the Cold War at Sea*. New York: W. W. Norton, 2018, pp. 212–74.
20 See C. J. Bartlett, *Great Britain and Seapower 1815–1853*. Oxford: University Press, 1963, p. 106.
21 Semenoff, *Rasplata*, pp. 112–14, 360–77.
22 N. Polmar, T. A. Brooks, and G. Fedoroff, *Admiral Gorshkov: The Man Who Challenged the U.S. Navy*. Annapolis, MD: Naval Institute Press, 2019, pp. 31–3.
23 B. S. Butman, *Soviet Ship-Building and Ship Repair: An Overview*. Arlington, VA: Spectrum Associates, 1986. See also *Understanding Soviet Naval Developments*. Washington, DC: Office of the CNO, Dept of the Navy, 1985, p. 79.
24 G. Hosking, *Russia: People and Empire; 1552–1917*. Cambridge, MA: Harvard University Press, 1997, pp. 6, 9.
25 M. Urnov, '"Greatpowerness" as the Key Element of Russian Self-consciousness under Erosion', *Communist and Post-Communist Studies*, Vol. 47, Nos. 3–4 (September–December 2014), pp. 305–22.
26 N. Khrushcheva and J. Tayler, *In Putin's Footsteps: Searching for the Soul of an Empire across Russia's Eleven Time Zones*. New York: St. Martin's Press, 2019, p. 271.
27 W. C. Fuller, *Strategy and Power in Russia 1600–1914*. New York: The Free Press, 1992, p. 378.
28 T. Graham, 'Let Russia Be Russia: The Case for a More Pragmatic Approach to Moscow', *Foreign Affairs*, November–December 2019, pp. 134–46.
29 Quoted in R. Herrick, *Soviet Naval Theory and Policy*. Washington, DC: US Government Printing Office, 1988, p. 10.
30 Quoted in ibid., p. 7.
31 Among the famous new weapons announced in Putin's June 2019 speech were the Tsirkon cruise missiles, the 9M730 Burevestnik nuclear cruise missile – SSCx9 'Skyfall' – and the Poseidon 'doomsday torpedo' with apparently limitless range. 'Briefing: Russian Defence Modernisation', *Jane's Defence Weekly*, 17 April 2019 (A).
32 J. B. Hattendorf, *The Influence of History on Mahan*. Newport, RI: Naval War College Press, 1991, p. 4.

33 J. Trevithick, 'Admiral Warns America's East Coast Is No Longer a "Safe Haven" Thanks to Russian Subs', The War Zone, 4 February 2020, www.thedrive.com/the-war-zone/32087/admiral-warns-americas-east-coast-is-no-longer-a-safe-haven-thanks-to-russian-subs (accessed 13 November 2022). More generally, Polmar, Brooks, and Fedoroff, *Admiral Gorshkov*, pp. 152–71.

34 See Maritime Doctrine of the Russian Federation, 2015, and Fundamentals of the State Policy of the Russian Federation in the Field of Naval Operations for the Period until 2030, signed by President Putin 20 July 2017. Both of these key documents have been translated by Anna Davis of the Russian Maritime Studies Institute 2017 of the US Naval War College. Also S. Gorshkov, *The Sea Power of the State*. London: Brassey's, 1979, Chapter 1.

35 *Maritime Doctrine*, p. 26.

36 V. Chernavin, 'On Naval Theory', *Morskoi sbornik*, No. 1 (January 1982).

37 Semenoff, *Rasplata*, p. 3.

38 V. Gerasimov, 'Tsennost nauki v predvidenii', *Voenno-promyshlenniy kurier*, 26 February 2013, www.vpk-news.ru/articles/14632 (no longer active). At the same time, we should not overlook the point that Gerasimov has repeated ever since that such non-military measures are only implemented on the basis of armed force.

39 E. Schmitt, 'Russia Applies Pressure on US in Syrian Posts', *New York Times*, 15 February 2020.

40 J. Marson, 'Russia Hinders Ukraine in Vital Waterway', *Wall Street Journal*, 28 November 2018, (A).

41 D. Axe, 'Blame Game after Near Miss, of USS *Chancellorsville* and RFS *Admiral Vinogradov*', *International Fleet Review*, August 2019; Office of the Under Secretary of Defence for Policy, 'Report to Congress: Department of Defense Arctic Strategy' (Washington, DC: June 2019), https://media.defense.gov/2019/Jun/06/2002141657/-1/-1/1/2019-DOD-ARCTIC-STRATEGY.PDF (accessed 13 November 2022).

42 C. Keeble, *Britain, the Soviet Union and Russia*. London: Macmillan, 2000, pp. 95–6.

43 N. Youssef, 'New Threats Alter Trans-Atlantic Ties', *Wall Street Journal*, 19 February 2020. "Westlessness" was the theme of the Munich Security Conference, February 2020.

44 Especially when those two challengers are operating together, cooperating on a new nuclear-powered Arctic icebreaker, naval exercises, or on China's Belt and Road Initiative. See N. Rolland, 'A China–Russia Condominium over Eurasia', *Survival*, Vol. 61, No. 1 (February–March 2019), pp. 7–22.

45 D. Axe, 'US Navy Still Outguns Fleets of China and Russia', *International Fleet Review*, August 2019.

46 Gorshkov, *Sea Power of the State*, pp. 68–9, 70–1.

47 Fundamentals, paragraph 8, p. 3, and paragraph 52, p. 16.

Part II

Russia's maritime strategies and capabilities today and tomorrow

3

Russian strategy and power at sea: should we care?

Vice Admiral Sir Clive Johnstone, KBE, CB

During the latter part of my time in the Royal Navy, I found myself increasingly thinking about what constituted the "threat": first, trying to decode the real nature of the "threat", and then how we could be best placed to meet it. One of the enduring threads of unease was that while I had sophisticated technical knowledge at my fingertips and could command a ship, task group, or headquarters, I was always less sure about my true level of understanding of the surrounding context that forms part of military success. This unease has only amplified now that I am thinking and writing about strategy from outside the Armed Forces.

Is it really possible to prepare to fight an adversary, or train to do so, without understanding the foundations of their capability and world view? In some senses, the learning of tactics and doctrine suffices, but I think it becomes ever more important to learn anew how the "competitor" thinks and the factors that will shape the decisions that they make under pressure. While there is considerable tension between the Euro-Atlantic community and Russia, this is not a return to the Cold War, no backward look. Times have changed, and not only is the international "geography" very different in terms of the balance of power and main trading routes, but societies, economies, and politics have all substantially changed. This requires digging deeper into the history, economy, geography, anthropology, society, technical, and then cultural education, indeed the way individuals and teams think and why they do so in that way.

Though prominent Western politicians quote from Russian literature or refer to Russian history, or lace discussion with relevant-sounding terms – the term *maskirovka*, referring to a form of deception, is a frequent example – it is not clear to me that we understand Russia well. There is much surface chatter, but little depth and nuance. This, perhaps, is not a uniquely British or Western failing: in the Black Sea in 2017 and 2018, it seemed to us that few Russian admirals or generals had had much, if any, interaction with the West and NATO beyond TV, reading, and perhaps a common Afghanistan experience. Consequently, we were cautious about whether our counterparts could really read our messages about deterrence, let alone understand the precise meaning of our actions. At best, it seems that West and East speak in different dialects.

We need to be clear as well as thoughtful. This is a dynamic, interactive process. Not only do we need to see the actions of others. We need to understand the reality of our actions and how these in turn are understood by others. How can we understand our options and quantify them if we do not know what our adversary thinks or how they see and hear us? Equally, as we so often learn to our cost, how do we quantify the consequences and costs of our actions in the short, medium, and long term?

In my experience, though, analysis of Russian naval capabilities tends to portray the Russian Navy in black or white terms, either as a terrifyingly powerful force or as though it were on the verge of collapse. But such binary caricatures exaggerate certain specific features and profoundly distort our understanding of the overall picture. They are too comfortable and often pander to self-interest or the vagaries of the latest funding review. While it is easier to have a caricature of an enemy than a more sophisticated appreciation, such simple images often mean we do not strive to understand ourselves let alone the enemy, and the misunderstanding becomes reinforced. It is worth noting, for instance, that the Russians have a very different understanding of the value of "command of the sea" and how to achieve it. Moreover, the place of the navy in strategy is very different – there is no specifically "naval strategy" as a separate function: the navy plays a role in military strategy, supporting the wider activity. We have seen this in Russia's invasion of Ukraine and its "Special Military Operation", in which the navy has served as a contributary player. This also leads us into danger because it prevents us from accurately decoding and then declaring what we really value: liberty, the freedom to have liberal values, and the confidence and ability to be prepared to fight and protect them.

Certainly, following what feels like a prolonged absence after the Cold War, the Russian Navy is in the news again. But why should we care about it? The simple answer is that it has become, alongside China, a major feature of a fast-evolving twenty-first-century international economic and maritime horizon. More specifically, it is an agent of Moscow's strategy, one that is diverging rapidly from – and increasingly in dissonance with – our own.

There are various ways to understand and describe Russian foreign policy – through the last decade, Russia has been described by senior officials and observers alike as both a power in long-term decline and as a great power resurrected, as both "only" a regional power and as a global power.[1] There can be little doubt, though, that Russia's relationship with the Euro-Atlantic community, and especially the United States and the United Kingdom, has become ever more tense and adversarial. From a Western point of view, debate will continue about whether this began in the 1990s with NATO enlargement, or in the mid-2000s as Russia began to transition towards more obvious authoritarianism and due to disagreements over arms control treaties, the US-led invasion of Iraq in 2003, the gas disputes between Russia and Ukraine with their impact on European energy security, and the Russo-Georgia war in 2008.

But the wide range of policy and value differences and disagreements are there for all to see – and have been emphasised with Moscow's annexation of Crimea and the attempted murder of Sergei Skripal in 2018, among many other examples. Dissonance became structural, even systemic, during the 2010s as engagement was frozen, and talk of a Great Power Competition was crystallised in the Euro-Atlantic community's official documents by the end of the decade. Moscow's invasion of Ukraine in February 2022 has driven discussion about NATO intervention against Russia whether through the imposition of a no-fly zone over Ukraine or breaking the Russian blockade of Ukraine in the Black Sea. With the imposition of heavy sanctions on Russia, the reciprocal expulsions of diplomats, and the war of words, it is hard to see not just how relations might improve, but how they could deteriorate any further without war breaking out.

If Washington, London, and Brussels are emphatic that Russian behaviour is intolerable, Moscow vociferously asserts that the West is both a destabilising actor in international affairs with its repeated interventions and even a challenge to Russia itself. Indeed, Moscow came to the conclusion that a Great Power Competition was emerging a decade before the Euro-Atlantic community did, one that would intensify into the 2020s. In many ways, this would not be a return to the Cold War-style competition, even if it bore many of the same characteristics as the twentieth-century confrontation, but instead would be a twenty-first-century geo-economic competition over resources, access to trade routes, and access to markets. These views, explicitly stated by the Russian leadership, were echoed also by the military leadership.[2]

This means that – for Moscow – the war in Ukraine represents the Great Power Competition made real,[3] and in many ways it is what its strategy of the last fifteen years has been intended to prepare it for. Although the Russian military has taken heavy losses in personnel and material (including the *Moskva*), its global horizon remains. Indeed, Moscow appears to think that this is part of a longer-term struggle and shift in the global architecture. Though there are debates about the role of the navy, the strategic water-ways remain an essential feature of Russian thinking.

This is important, because despite our clash, we share all the strategic waterways across the world with the Russian Navy, from the Arctic North, the Baltic, the Atlantic, Mediterranean, Black Seas through to the Persian Gulf and Indian Ocean, and all the way from the icy waters of Antarctica to those of the North Pacific. Senior NATO officials point to the highest Russian activity in the North Atlantic for thirty years, while senior Russian officials have themselves pointed out that the activity of the Russian Navy has increased in all the key areas of the Global Ocean, with hundreds of missions, port calls, and (joint) exercises. We need, therefore, a sophisticated view of Russian strategy and power at sea, includ-ing the Russian Navy and where it fits in this strategy, one that blends the obvious strengths and weaknesses into a coherent and nuanced picture. At the national level, as just noted, Moscow has made persistent efforts to generate strategy, shaping an archi-tecture to enhance planning and implementation, for instance through increasing the authority of the Security Council. In terms of defence and security, Moscow conducted both an extensive re-equipment of its armed forces alongside a major re-structuring and reform programme. In part, these reforms were driven by the rather poor performance of the Russian armed forces in the Russo-Georgia war in 2008 and the attempt to reform away from a Soviet-style military.

At the broader level, there were a number of reorganisations of command through the 2010s. The National Defence Management Centre, which was established in 2014, for instance, was intended to upgrade central control of the armed forces, unifying existing command and monitoring systems across Russia. At the heart of a system of such information centres across Russia, it is intended to play a central role in providing decision-making coherence, as well as coordination and management. Other re-structuring included, for example, the merging in 2015 of the air force and aerospace defence forces to form the Aerospace Forces, and a major re-organisation of internal security forces in 2016 by establishing a National Guard, also called Rosgvardiya.[4]

This is the broader context in which the navy has been oper-ating: a somewhat shifting landscape. And although the ground forces have remained dominant overall, the first point to make is that the navy has benefitted from this wider restructuring and modernisation process. As discussed elsewhere in this volume, the navy was the recipient of a substantial chunk of the funding devoted to the modernisation of equipment through the 2010s. It has also become more prominent in the structures of command and administration. In a series of changes as the leadership re-arranged its Military Districts and Unified Strategic Commands, the Northern Fleet was first detached from the Western Military District to become part of a new northern joint strategic command in 2015, and then accorded the status of a Military District in 2021.

Within this, we must note that the capability of the Russian Navy is not uniform across all fleets and flotillas. The marks of years of underinvestment that preceded the current modernisation programme are still visible, and some fleets are not yet equipped with emergent new weapons systems. There are also questions about the training and professionalism of the crews: some have commented, for instance, on the negligence and poor damage control measures on the guided-missile cruiser *Moskva*.[5]

Equally, the navy's purposes are multidimensional. The modern Russian Navy is not designed to compete with a US-led NATO, for instance. Instead, it is to counter it and to disrupt Western confidence, systems, and authority, as well as to support the strat-egy of a twenty-first-century Eurasian power seeking to assert its interests and act in an increasingly maritime international context. One example of this is how Moscow uses its maritime forces for re-supply, local defence, and strategic disruption, especially with the establishment of grey zones or waters of uncertain threat and access. And at the strategic level, Russia possesses a substantial nuclear deterrent together with conventional armed forces strong enough to impose substantial costs in a conflict. The Russian Navy plays an important role in Moscow's strategy and cannot be over-looked despite its shortcomings.

So, this very presence demands attention and respect. More than the Chinese, or any other non-NATO nation, as the Russian Navy operates in global waters, it creates an array of difficulties, from the simple challenge of sharing water space through to the more complex challenge of denying freedom of navigation and persistent presence. To our sailors and commanders at sea, therefore, the Russian Navy is an endless and intriguing maritime neighbour.

It is not just the Russian challenge we should be concerned about, but the *range* of challenges that simultaneously test us, also including terrorists and state instability, refugees (migration, its causes and impact), and political challenges and the pressures of social media and the new "truth". This is important because we have seen these threats repeat in all regions of NATO's interest. This picture has been complicated still further by China's emerging maritime presence in our waters, questions of climate change, the blurring of the boundaries in the military operational space and in our appreciation of the problems we face, and, most recently, the COVID-19 pandemic.

But as we think specifically about Russia and the Russian Navy, I would emphasise that the nature of the threat – indeed the whole battlespace – is changing. The principal conclusion from my time in command is that the sea, the maritime battlespace, feels different. Threats are not just binary; not just to the East or to the South, the Atlantic or Pacific, not just "Russia", anti-submarine warfare, or migration. Threats are now multi-faceted and are both persistent and fleeting; several are emerging simul-taneously. Threats might be in areas we have thought of as our back yard. Threats – all the threats – are positioned like counters on a three-dimensional chess board. This image, the chessboard, with events popping up and surprises becoming the norm, should define our thinking.

The threats posed by missiles and hybrid activity (or non-military aggression) are now driving conventional naval thinking, not just in terms of how to manage task group blue-water operations, but how to cope with "swarm" or "wasp" fleets, even alongside disruption at home. Indeed, in their routine assessments, allied joint and maritime planners should consider the security of "safe" port infrastructure and logistics as well as the fighting competence of units. Resupply and respite are as important as lethality. To extend this attempt for a more sophisticated appreciation, I suggest we need to understand better how military and maritime escalation might develop. I suggest we need to think through NATO Treaty Articles 3 and 4 (crisis and tension) rather than a single-minded focus on NATO Treaty Article 5 (the commitment to collective armed defence).

As mentioned above, this is no simple return to the Cold War. It is too easy to see the situation as some form of a return to the past, but this is merely comfortable mental furniture. There are new risks in a more complex geopolitical climate that is set in a fiercely competitive arena and an environment of limited elasticity. Indeed, for me, like space and cyber-security, the seas and oceans are the alliance's new frontier. Although the sea has always been an essential feature of Euro-Atlantic security, it is now evolving into something new and different, as a changing climate opens up the High North, threatens our coastlines and infrastructure, and will likely bring widespread social instability. Indeed, the operational environment does not have an edge or a boundary but is all encompassing and permanent. We cannot talk about the North or the Atlantic in isolation or as though it is the only sector of interest or import. Maritime challenges will come from many locations – perhaps at the same time. The need to be looking for indicators everywhere is critical – a "360 approach", if we are to be colloquial. Successful balance, posture, and messaging depends on it.

And these are also questions the Russian Navy must face. The development of the High North, and particularly the opening up of the Northern Sea Route, is a priority for Moscow. But what does this mean for the Russian Navy? And how does that navy cope with the evolving twenty-first-century operational environment, divided geographically as it is across its four fleets and the Caspian flotilla? How does the Russian Navy see and plan to cope with the multiplicity of challenges from different locations, perhaps at the same time? Indeed, the Russian Navy is the first to experience a swarm attack (by unmanned vehicles) against the Black Sea Fleet in its base in Sevastopol, and many will seek to draw lessons from this experience. We have to understand better the Russian view of this complex web of challenges and their responses to this dynamically evolving context.

I emphasise this because this competition (at sea and beyond) is not theoretical – it is real, and it crosses uncomfortably with our lack of comprehension of how maritime warfare is changing and where it might be heading. Our competitors, including the Russian Navy, are mobilising to maximise their chances in an increasingly congested world. Recently signed official strategic documents with a horizon to 2030 (and even 2035) indicate Russia's desire to maintain the status of the world's second naval power, and various presidential and other announcements hint at ambitious capability and technology leaps including submarine and missile technology, AI, and cyber.

There does not appear to be a shipbuilding plan to turn the Russian Navy into a global competitor with the United States or China,[6] and the depth of technology development suggests that focus will be in particular areas and capability, not a total generational shift. But Moscow's maritime strategic agenda, as set out in its planning documents, amounts to an ambitious and tough warfighting narrative, and the creation of a substantial force and an agent for disruption and also for asserting and maintaining Russian interests.

The ambitious declarations looking out to 2030 reflect the tradition of Russian leaders looking to the navy for status projection on the international arena. More prosaically, the Russian Navy is coalescing around four principal missions: defence of Russia's maritime approaches and littorals, long-range precision strike with conventional and nuclear weapons, power projection via the submarine force, and defence of the sea-based nuclear deterrent carried onboard Russia nuclear submarines. Alongside these missions is the traditional requirement for naval diplomacy, arms sales, and national self-promotion (especially for the domestic audience). The dogged deployment into the Mediterranean by the aging aircraft carrier *Kuznetsov* was one rather tired example of this, even if the interaction with other Russian elements in Syria and in the Eastern Mediterranean was more of a success than some have argued.

The Russian vision is to build a navy that can successfully impose Moscow's will in its neighbourhood, extend its reach where necessary, and keep the United States (and NATO as a whole) at arm's length through integrating layers of defences, long-range anti-ship missiles, ground-based aviation, submarines, coastal cruise-missile batteries, and mines. In this manner, Russia wishes to ensure it can deny NATO access from the sea and make costly any forced entry operations.

Next, the Russian Navy is increasingly positioned, especially by the deployment of the Kalibr family of missiles, to conduct long-range attacks with conventional weapons against fixed infrastructure targets, and this plays an important role in nuclear escalation if called upon.

I noted at the outset that we should consider the Russian Navy with respect and learn from their development. We should acknowledge the capability of the Russian Yasen-class submarine programme and note the impressive early deployment of the first of class, the RS *Severodvinsk*. Equally, the Russian Kilo (Paltus)-class diesel-electric attack submarine, especially the Improved-Kilo with the Kalibr missile firing capability, is a formidable adversary, particularly in littoral or brown (noisy) water. There is a fascinating focus on training of the crews and the re-structuring of crews around being fit for task or readiness. This suggests a maturing of deeper capability and was one area that I pressed to understand better when commanding in the Royal Navy and in NATO.

While we have seen Russia fail to build large, complex warships of late, its decision to develop a corvette and frigate construction programme, with all platforms Kalibr missile capable, is notable – even if grown out of necessity. This is a logical approach to reviving the shipbuilding industry, perhaps the worst sub-sector of the Russian defence industry. The Russians have learned that you do not need much tonnage to pack a potent missile system. The surface combat force is not being organised around platforms but around an integrated family of missile or other capabilities. These include vertical launching system (VLS) cells with Oniks (SS-N-26), Kalibr (SS-N-27A/30), Pantsir-M for point defences, Redut VLS cells for air defence, and Paket-NK anti-torpedo systems. In the future, the Tsirkon hypersonic missile is also expected to play an important role.

This development is interesting because it is so different from the thinking that results in NATO navies building fewer, impressively expensive, super-frigates/destroyers that are becoming almost too precious to consider forward deployment unless under a very extensive (US or UK) protective umbrella. While the Russian platforms lack endurance and sustainability, and task groups always sail with a maintenance platform or recovery tug, their firepower and number allow them to threaten Western infrastructure in an agile way that demands early intervention to stop.

Russia's shipbuilding programme made some progress through the worst of the delays caused by the first rounds of sanctions in the 2010s and the breakdown of defence cooperation with Ukraine after 2014. As discussed in other chapters in this volume, the ship-building industry as a whole has been going through a difficult recovery period, having suffered from many years of neglect and underfunding. But it would be wrong to assess this problematic past as inherently representative of the future. For example, Russia has been building a large new shipyard in the east, called Zvezda, with the assistance of the Chinese. Intended for commercial production, this shipyard just installed a 1,200-ton crane, vital for modular construction and no small leap for Russian warship building.

The routinely expressed view that the Russian Navy is about to collapse is misplaced. Indeed, with activity in the Black Sea and Mediterranean (Syria) as well as the High North, Atlantic, and Far East, it has probably not seen operational tempo and readiness levels like this since the mid-1990s. Russian ships, including their elder platforms like the Sovremenny-class destroyers, are conducting successively longer voyages, while the force as a whole is spending much more time at sea than in the two preceding decades. While the surface combatant force remains an eclectic mix of legacy Soviet platforms serving alongside new frigates and corvettes, over 30 per cent of the Soviet-era ships are receiving major modernisation programs, and their deployment and employment is changing.

We should be very wary of the competing challenges that are besetting our planet and the security implications that may drive either a dash for resources, including protein and water, or simply a conflict drawn out of misadventure or misunderstanding. These include the various aspects of Russian strategy and power at sea: not only in terms of its naval combat power, but in the wider ramifications of how that is deployed, including when it is deployed against nations that are not NATO allies. As we are seeing, Russia's invasion of Ukraine in 2022 is having a significant impact on the wider global economy through the Russian Navy's blockade of Ukraine's ports. Russia's assertion in its neighbourhood has wider consequences, even as Moscow attempts to position Russia as a ubiquitous power with a global horizon. It is not just the fire-power aspects of Russian strategy at sea, but the implications of Moscow's actions in geo-economic competition. We in the UK and NATO should be bolder at re-writing and investing in our doctrine so we think and speak clearly to defend our interests and avoid conflict. At the same time, we should think hard about the Russian Navy and understand who they are, their function, and role in Russian strategy – how the navy will really be used.

Notes

1   For overviews of these debates, see A. Stent, *Putin's World: Russia against the West and with the Rest*. New York: Twelve, 2019; K. Stoner, *Russia Resurrected: Its Power and Purpose in a New Global Order*. Oxford: Oxford University Press, 2021.

2   For discussion, see A. Monaghan (ed.), *Russian Grand Strategy in the Era of Global Power Competition*. Manchester: Manchester University Press, 2022.

3   See Putin's speech at the Victory Day Parade on 9 May 2022. Website of the Presidential Administration, 9 May, http://en.kremlin.ru/events/president/news/68366 (accessed 13 November 2022).

4   This wider re-structuring is beyond the scope of this volume, but it is given a thorough examination in A. Monaghan, *Power in Modern Russia: Strategy and Mobilisation*. Manchester: Manchester University Press, 2017.

5   T. Ozberk, 'Analysis: Chain of Negligence Caused the Loss of the *Moskva* Cruiser', Naval News, 17 April 2022, https://www.navalnews.com/naval-news/2022/04/analysis-chain-of-negligence-caused-the-loss-of-the-moskva-cruiser (accessed 13 November 2022).

6   See the chapters by Richard Connolly and Dmitry Gorenburg in this volume for more on the strengths and weaknesses of Russian shipbuilding.

4

Evolution of Russian naval strategy

Michael Kofman

Although commonly thought of a continental land power, Russia is also a country with a rich naval tradition. For centuries, the Russian leadership had purposefully invested in a navy. The country was the third largest naval power in the world in the late nineteenth century, to say nothing of its sizable commercial maritime fleet. As Peter the Great has been quoted as saying, 'any ruler that has but ground troops has one hand, but one that has a navy has both'.[1] Since then, Russia's naval power has gone through cycles of diminution and resurrection, with the late Soviet period being its last greatest incarnation. The modern Russian Navy is smaller, but nonetheless a potent force that underwrites Russian naval policy and military strategy. This chapter will explore the evolution of contemporary Russian naval strategy, key aspects of naval policy, and operational concepts for the employment of naval power in wartime.

The concept of a "naval strategy" is somewhat of a misnomer in the Russian sense, since it represents a degree of mirror-imaging from Western thinking. Russia does not formally have a naval strategy: unlike Western counterparts, the Russian military system is not one where services independently develop their own strategies. Doctrine and strategy development are integrated within the General Staff, rather than characterised by a trade union approach common among individual service strategies in other countries. Consequently, there is a military doctrine, national security strategies, and defence plans, but the navy does not have its own and distinct formulation of these ideas.[2] So-called Russian naval strategy is therefore more a discussion on operational art in the maritime domain, roles, and missions of naval forces in strategic operations, and the purpose of military actions at sea in achieving political goals in peacetime.

Military strategy offers general tenets on the theory and practice of warfare, to include the maritime domain. It is considered the highest form of military art. Naval discussions are more operational-strategic, or operational-tactical in focus, with emphasis on opera-tional art, and the navy's role in military strategy. It is the job of military strategy to marry operations with political objectives, or interim goals, delineate theatres, strategic directions, and priori-tise between them, to include the maritime domain. However, the Russian Navy has its own distinct missions, tasks, and conceptual mental maps that form foundation blocks for understanding its role. These will be discussed throughout the chapter to establish terms of reference, and the relevant concepts for understanding Russian military thought specific to operations at sea.

The Russian Navy has four principal missions: first, defence of critical infrastructure in the homeland against long-range strikes from the sea with conventional or nuclear weapons, implemented via a damage limitation approach and layered defences. Second, conducting long-range precision strikes against an opponent's critically important targets on land, either for the purpose of warfighting or escalation management. Third, strategic nuclear deterrence, by maintaining a sea-based second-strike capability that ensures unacceptable levels of damage are inflicted upon any opponent, and fourth, naval diplomacy to pursue international engagement and project Russia's status as a great power outside its region. The navy also supports land operations and defends mari-time approaches or littorals as part of its routine set of missions and tasks. However, its more significant contribution is reflected in the navy's role within Russian strategic operations, and military concepts like strategic deterrence, which make use of calibrated precision strikes with conventional and nuclear weapons.

The Soviet inheritance: theatres, echelonment, and strategic-operations

The Soviet navy looked at the world through oceanic theatres of military action (OTVDs), breaking it down into four theatres: Atlantic, Pacific, Arctic, and Indian.[3] Military actions were a more specific term, speaking to naval activity that took place in peacetime or wartime with the potential to be of strategic significance. Combat actions were another form of military activity, referencing the conduct of combat operations in a specific maritime area. Many of these distinctions and theatre divisions remain today. There were also sea theatres of military action, which appear to have largely disappeared from common reference.

Historically, a strategic operation in the OTVD simply described coordinated military operations by the navy in conjunction with other forces. The navy would lead a joint operation, executed under a single plan devised within the high command.[4] In 1987, the strategic operation in an OTVD was eliminated from military planning as a distinct operation, but one can find general references to strategic operations in the maritime theatre today, although no such operation exists in practice.[5] These references speak to naval operational art, tasks, and missions and considerations specific to maritime theatres.

A theatre typically had strategic- and operational-level directions, along with strategic regions that serve as notable subdivisions.[6] Thinking in this manner helps divide tasks and explain echelonment of responsibility between tactical, operational, and operational-strategic-level military commands. Presently, the Russian military segments the country into five military districts (West, South, Central, East, Arctic). Force employment in these districts is managed by Joint Strategic Commands. They are the operational-strategic-level commands responsible for strategic directions, most of the units based within their respective military district, and the conduct of combat operations. The General Staff can delineate theatres and carve out operational-level sectors within a strategic direction, but most importantly retains command over strategic-operations, which combine action across multiple theatres or strategic directions. Historically, a strategic operation could be a campaign encompassing 1,200–1,800 km in depth, involving twenty-five to thirty days of military action.[7]

The Soviet navy's primary missions included repelling massed aerospace attack via missile and aircraft means, which according to Milan Vego involved 'searching for and destroying the carriers of strategic weapons in the maritime TVDs', including missile submarines, surface combatants carrying land-attack cruise missiles, and aircraft carriers.[8] The second mission consisted of suppressing the opponent's military-economic potential. This involved destroying critically important military and economic objects, along with administrative-political centres. However, this was primarily a nuclear mission, to be carried out by ballistic missile submarines and theatre nuclear strike capabilities. The third was to provide support to the ground troops in their operations, destroying major enemy formations in the continental theatre of military action.[9]

Within these strategic operations, the Soviet navy's mission was to repel aerospace attacks from the sea, destroy key installations on land, eliminate large surface action groups or carrier strike groups, support ground force operations along the littorals, and interfere with sea lines of communications when possible.[10] There was a desire to attain naval superiority in near seas, or maritime spaces adjacent to the continental theatre, but not much beyond. The Soviet navy expected to conduct these operations in combination with fleets, land-based long-range aviation, and in some cases alongside strikes being made by strategic nuclear forces.[11]

Soviet operational challenges and concerns continue to influence Russian naval missions and tasks today. For example, the Soviet Union's Pechora exercise demonstrated that strategic anti-submarine warfare was not a viable mission for the Soviet navy, and in practice going after US ballistic missile submarines proved an unsolvable problem outside of select cases where they patrolled close to Soviet waters.[12] By the 1970s, however, it was also clear to the Soviet Union that its submarines were easily detectable in the Atlantic due to US sound surveillance sonar networks, which meant that forward deploying ballistic missile submarines was risky in wartime, and naval operations to interdict sea lines of communications equally challenging. This relegated interdiction missions to a tertiary status, and consequently there would not be a Soviet attempt at a "Third Battle of the Atlantic" in wartime.

Thus, when it came to the Soviet Union's vast submarine force, strategy and material constraints yielded a naval withholding strategy to defend ballistic missile submarine patrol areas close to Soviet waters in these "protected maritime regions". In the West, these came to be nicknamed "bastions", a moniker still in use today. Soviet ballistic missile submarines would deploy within these bastions, protected by the rest of the Soviet navy and land-based aviation. The Soviet navy was responsible for maintaining the "combat stability" or survivability of the nuclear deterrent at sea, whose job it was to deter aggression by being able credibly to inflict unacceptable levels of damage. These missions, and the importance of "bastion defence", remain today.

The Soviet approach featured an anti-carrier triad of strike assets, composed of guided-missile submarines, guided-missile surface combatants, and land-based anti-ship bombers. Soviet naval squadrons would play a game of cat and mouse with US fleets in peacetime, seeking to keep their anti-ship missiles within range of likely targets. Soviet tactics and techniques in the maritime domain featured a layered defence to protect littorals and maritime approaches. However, the more significant component was a damage limitation strategy, designed to attrit US naval assets at sea prior to them being put to use, that is, Soviet naval forces had to shoot first at extended ranges from their own bases, because they were the conventionally inferior force.[13] A close-in defence was not viable given the long-range strike potential of NATO forces at sea – operational realities that continue to shape Russian naval missions and tasks.

Contemporary Russian military doctrine, military strategy, and deterrence concepts

Russian military doctrine is an important guide to the system's understanding of the political and military dimensions that inform military policy on organisation, training, capability development, and defence-industrial policy.[14] The doctrine defines the military-political environment and a typology of conflicts. First, a state of military danger in which relations between states could lead to the appearance of a military threat under certain conditions. Second, a period of military threat, when the military-political situation is characterised by the heightened possibility of armed conflict and raised degree of readiness among states or separatist organisations to use force.

Contemporary Russian military strategy has its roots in the doctrinal evolution of the late Soviet period. For much of the Cold War, Soviet military doctrine was offensive in character, envisioning a strategic offensive to displace the conflict on to an opponent's territory, together with a strategic aerospace offensive to attack adversary forces in depth. Military strategy reflected this predisposition, emphasising offensive ground and air operations. This formulation changed in 1986 when the political dimension of doctrine acquired a defensive character, predicated on defensive-defence and reasonable sufficiency.[15] Soviet forces concentrated on the task of repelling an enemy's offensive, then conducting operations to restore the status quo, thereby planning for a defensive war fought primarily from their own or allied territory.[16]

Yet a defensive doctrine should not be confused with a defensive military strategy. Indeed, the military-technical aspects of doctrinal debates in the late 1980s reflected that a strategic defensive required sustained counterattack, and a counter-offensive to neutralise an opponent's gains. Military strategy would thereby come to be composed of defensive and offensive strategic operations, which began to meld, with the offensive/defensive distinctions eliminated over time. The formulation that emerged at the end of the Cold War was "active defence operations".[17] The emphasis within these operations began to shift towards air and space and penetrating strikes against critical objects in depth. This significantly reduced the expected benefits of ground offensives or the utility of seizing terrain.[18] That evolution set the stage for a revamped naval role in post-Soviet Russian military strategy, even as the Russian Navy itself was undergoing a precipitous collapse in terms of force size, capability, and operational readiness during the 1990s.

Military strategy in Russia represents the highest form of military art, providing key tenets for the theory and practice of war, defining strategic missions, theatres of military operations, preparation of the armed forces, organisation, and understanding of the character of armed conflict.[19] It links operational-level concepts, and strategic operations, with political objectives. Strategy informs the critical choices made regarding the structure, posture, and capabilities of the armed forces along with deterrence actions to be taken in both peacetime and wartime.[20]

Russia's military leadership describes its military strategy as "active defence", defining a set of preventive measures intended to deflect, reduce, or neutralise threats to Russia or attempts at forceful coercion.[21] Significantly, while the military strategy carries a defensive character, it is composed of offensive and defensive operations. It is not a strategy premised on area denial, or anti-access capabilities, or the efficacy of defensive capabilities at the operational level. This of course has profound implications for our understanding of the role of the Russian Navy and other maritime forces, including maritime aviation. There is considerable confusion over Russian operational concepts, because in an effort to generalise military problems, defence planners will often group capabilities into a singular functional problem set. Yet Russian operational concepts have never fallen along the rubric of anti-access, or area denial, even if the tactical capabilities could be interpreted as such.

The "defensive" aspect speaks to the expectation that Russian forces will be conducting defensive manoeuvre and sustained counterattacks from their territory, or adjacent seas, rather than an initial offensive to seize an opponent's territory. This is consistent with late Soviet period military strategy, using the same term and conceptual underpinnings. Russian military strategy transitioned from offence, to defensive defence, and then active defence, but none of the core components of military thought can be interpreted as a theatre anti-access or area denial approach. As subsequent sections highlight, military technology and operational concepts are not conducive to such thinking.

In wartime, the term "active" in Russian military strategy signifies persistent engagement with an opponent via sustained strikes with long-range conventional systems against critical enablers, infrastructure, command and control, and logistics. Rather than a denial, it is a disorganisation- and attrition-based concept of operations. Active defence signifies a strategy premised on attrition via fires and long-range strikes across the theatre of military action, designed to set the conditions for a successful counter-offensive that would neutralise an opponent's gains.[22] Its precepts include "surprise, decisiveness, and continuity of action" to retain strategic initiative, with emphasis placed on fires, decisive action by flanking formations, and preserving the force.[23] The goal is to prevent an opponent from achieving a decisive outcome during the initial period of war, forcing them into a conflict of attrition, and inflicting costs to military and economic potential such that they will seek war termination on acceptable terms.

Military strategy also incorporates the national security concept "strategic deterrence", which is a complex of measures to be taken during a period of danger, military threat, and in conflict. These breakdown activities along military (forceful) and non-military (non-forceful) categories, with emphasis placed on the former.[24] During a period of military threat, forceful activities use the principle of deterrence by intimidation or fear-inducement. Once hostilities have begun, these concepts translate into an escalation management strategy, which operates under the principle of deterrence through limited use of force.[25] The term "active" speaks to a set of actions designed to deter an opponent and neutralise threats. These include demonstrative actions, demonstrative use of force, and inflicting "deterrent damage" with single or grouped strikes. Strikes may be pre-emptive. The goal is to communicate to an opponent that their costs will exceed any gains sought from the conflict.

Russian military strategy appreciates that their general-purpose forces will be militarily inferior against a technologically superior opponent like the United States. It therefore places considerable weight upon the employment of strategic conventional capabilities within strategic deterrence concepts (i.e. non-nuclear deterrence). Non-nuclear deterrence is predicated on long-range precision-guided weapons as its offensive component.[26] These are employed for demonstration purposes, or coercively via single and grouped strikes against an adversary's critically important objects. These capabilities are intended to destroy or disorganise an opponent's long-range strike potential, and to inflict calibrated damage against their critical infrastructure.[27]

Nevertheless, nuclear weapons retain a strong deterrence role in Russian military thinking on regional and large-scale war, even as strategic conventional capability continues to grow. It is unlikely that Russian military concepts will abandon the presently strong role that nuclear weapons have in larger-scope conflicts. Non-strategic nuclear weapons are reserved for escalation management in a regional-war context, after conventional strike means have proven unsuccessful or expended, and nuclear warfighting in a large-scale war. The latter refers to limited or strategic nuclear use in theatre against an opponent's forces, for the purpose of warfighting rather than escalation management.

The Russian Navy attained a strong role within current strategic deterrence concepts and associated missions. The service is not only responsible for the strategic sea-based nuclear deterrent, but provides for the strategic conventional component of the aforementioned deterrence concepts via long-range strike land-attack cruise missiles. The navy also fields a substantial percentage of Russia's non-strategic nuclear weapons, able to employ them demonstratively or against military or economic targets. While the Russian Navy may be conventionally inferior in most respects to potential opponents in the United States, NATO, or even China, rather than return to a secondary role supporting the Russian ground troops in continental operations, it has instead evolved into a major component of the strategic deterrence forces at sea. Thus, the Russian Navy had prioritised the capabilities and the effects they can contribute to strategic operations, and strategic deterrence concepts, more so than naval combat operations against what will invariably be superior naval opponents.

Formal policy frameworks: the linkage between maritime goals and naval policy

Russian naval policy provides the linkage between naval means and political or economic objectives in the maritime domain, along with prioritisation among key regions and maritime theatres. The guiding frameworks include the 2015 Maritime Doctrine, the 2017 Fundamentals of State Policy in the Field of Naval Activity through 2030, and an updated version of the Maritime Doctrine, published in August 2022.[28] The maritime doctrine frames the purpose of the navy as defence of national interests, maintaining political stability at global and regional levels and repelling aggression from the sea.[29] Showing the Russian flag in the "World Ocean" (Mirovoi Okean) is often referenced in such policy frameworks, essentially a status projection mission, to demonstrate Russian interests further afield and the country's status as a great power with ubiquitous interests. The "World Ocean" is more a policy than military term for the maritime domain, representing a general political reference for distant maritime theatres.[30]

The maritime doctrine offers a useful regional prioritisation for investing in naval capability and non-military maritime infrastructure, asserting that the quality and quantity of fleets will be maintained at levels that correspond to the threat to Russian interests in those regions. This is a good indicator that the principle of reasonable sufficiency or defensive sufficiency is still in vogue. The regions include Atlantic, Arctic, Pacific, Caspian, Indian, and Antarctic. Four of these align with former Soviet OTVDs (Atlantic, Arctic, Pacific, Indian), whereas the Caspian and Antarctic appear less important contemporary additions as maritime regions of interest.

In the Atlantic, the main threat drivers are defined as NATO military activity and encroaching in infrastructure, to which the declared solution is a strengthened military potential and increased naval presence. Added significance is placed on maintaining a permanent naval presence in the Mediterranean.[31] In the Arctic, the doctrine defines Russian goals as securing strategic stability and freedom of access to other oceans. The region is seen as an area of potential competition and conflict, while strategic stability refers to the survivability of Russia's sea-based nuclear deterrent. In the Pacific, resources are front and centre. Relations with China are posited as friendly, but there is a desire to build up naval capability in this region: expanding the Russian Pacific Fleet. In the

Indian Ocean, the Russian goal is to further develop ties with India and maintain a periodic naval presence. This region has the lowest priority relative to other maritime theatres.

Russian maritime goals consist of defending national interests, strengthening the country's overall position among maritime powers, retaining sovereignty over its own waters, defending economic and resource extraction rights, and providing for defence from military aggression. The doctrine speaks more specifically to means, with some explanation of interests at stake, but treats investment in naval capability as an end in and of itself rather than articulating a clear thesis for the ways in which political goals will be achieved with naval means. Like many such documents, the goals are unspecific, while the framework is there to underpin the arguments on infrastructure investment and procurement. The doctrine also provides for mobilisation of maritime transport, fishing fleets, and scientific-research or specialised fleets in support of the navy. This conveys the intent to surge Russia's civilian maritime capacity in support of military operations during wartime.

Perhaps the more significant document in this pantheon is the 2017 state policy on naval activity through 2030, which declares that Russia is a great maritime power and that naval power is an important component of strategic deterrence, enabling Russia to conduct an independent naval policy.[32] In this document, naval presence in the "World Ocean" is better defined against the backdrop of a competition for access to resources, keeping sea lines of communication open, and reducing military-political pressure against Russian interests. Although presence is portrayed as an end in and of itself, Russian state policy never explains how presence is supposed to achieve positive outcomes, except by garnering media attention and showing the Russian flag abroad. This is not dissimilar from Western strategies that treat presence as a salve, or a magical totem able to generate deterrence effects (to be clear, Russian documents assign no deterrence missions to presence operations).

The "ways" in Russian naval policy include maintaining naval power sufficient to deter aggression, keeping forces at a high state of readiness, and retaining the capability to inflict unacceptable damage, measures that reduce the level of threat to Russia in the World Ocean. Unacceptable damage in this context refers to Russia's sea-based strategic nuclear deterrent, while "complex of measures" speaks to military actions, deployments, and demonstrations designed to deter opponents in peacetime. This is consistent with a military strategy of active defence and its vision of preventive peacetime measures to neutralise threats and deter or contain adversaries.

The policy on naval activity is more specific than the maritime doctrine in defining the threat environment, and prescriptions for how naval power can help address challenges or security grievances. The text accuses the United States and its allies of attempting to establish dominance in the World Ocean, by seeking overwhelming naval superiority and limiting Russia's access to resources or sea lines of communication. There are specific references to territorial claims against Russia, with emphasis placed on Atlantic and Arctic maritime regions. Within these, the document prioritises the Black and Mediterranean Seas, defining the military challenge as strategic offensive conventional weapons and missile defences being based at sea near Russia's borders. This once again represents an important strand in Russian military thought regarding the significance of certain conventional capabilities, such as long-range cruise missiles and the strategic impact of theatre missile defences aboard upgraded US ships.

Significantly, a theatre prioritisation begins to emerge, placing Atlantic and Arctic as first, Pacific as second, and Indian as third. Thus, the policy is more specific in identifying the types of threats in the maritime domain that Russian naval power must address. These are primarily capabilities that can threaten Russian infrastructure on land, or those that can affect the strategic stability (viability) of Russia's nuclear forces.[33] The policy states that demonstrating the readiness and resolve to use conventional and non-strategic nuclear weapons will have an important deterring effect on opponents. In terms of means, Russian policy pursues long-range conventional and nuclear strike capabilities, a balanced development of the navy to prevent other powers from attaining superiority, and the capacity for prolonged naval presence in strategic maritime regions.

Both documents frame the role of naval power along policy objectives that can be broadly defined as status, economic interests, sovereignty, and military requirements for deterrence or defence. They reflect an outlook or logic of a land power with interests at sea, and a maritime component to its strategic thinking. Russian economic interests are much closer to home, tied to resource extraction. The military threats are better defined than the opportunities or goals of maritime activity. Beyond status projection and naval diplomacy, the role of the Russian Navy as a policy instrument in the World Ocean remains vague, but status as a leading naval power remains an end in and of itself. Nonetheless, the principle of defensive sufficiency and prioritisation based on threats in particular oceanic theatres seems well established.

Russian policy documents succeed at defining the rationale for investing in naval means, prioritising regions, and making a bureaucratic case for Russian naval power. They are therefore less useful as statements on naval strategy, and more reflective of strategy as a process, seeking to galvanise resources in order to build up Russian naval power and explain its role within broader national security concepts like strategic deterrence. Their central impact is organising different elements of the state relevant to Russian maritime power, investment in infrastructure, and shipbuilding. They formally enshrine a role for the Russian Navy in non-nuclear deterrence, limited nuclear escalation, and maintaining strategic capabilities to inflict unacceptable damage. This is a significant coup, allowing the Russian Navy to position itself on the central axis of important missions within Russian military doctrine.

Russian naval tasks, missions, and operational art

In the 1970s, Admiral Sergei Gorshkov took the Soviet navy from a secondary role in Russian military strategy to organising around the task of neutralising the US Navy in the initial period of war.[34] This to some extent untethered the Soviet navy from supporting the ground forces. After the 1990s, one might expect the present Russian Navy to return to its supporting role, given its lack of warfighting viability against contemporary adversaries, but that is not what has transpired. The Russian Navy held on to a damage limitation approach at sea, inherited from the USSR, but then added a central role in strategic deterrence concepts and wove itself into current strategic operations. These include strategic aerospace operation, strategic operation for the destruction of critically important objects, strategic nuclear forces operation, and strategic operation in a continental theatre of military activity. With nuclear and conventional means, the navy participates in nuclear forces operations or destruction of critically important objects and is also central in deflecting an adversary's aerospace attack in the initial period of war, which is a component of the strategic aerospace operation.

The Russian Navy divides the maritime domain into coastal (*pribrezhnaya*), near sea (*blizkaya*), far sea (*dalnaya*), and oceanic zone (*okeanskaya zona*). These are not clear-cut divisions, but the coastal defence zone is approximately within 200 km of the coastline. The near sea zone includes seas that are 600–1,000 km from the coast. The far sea zone takes this distance out further towards the 1,000–2,000 km mark, beyond which lies the oceanic zone. These zones are not only defined by ranges from Russia's coast, or naval bases, but also sea states, and the classes of ships that can operate in these areas. In particular, they are delineated by missions and tasks. A vessel that can fire its weapons in the sea state of one maritime zone may have dramatically reduced performance in another.

Perhaps the simplest way to conceive of these zones is that the near sea zone is one where the Russian Navy seeks to establish sea control and intends to fight for naval superiority. The far sea zone is where the navy intends to pursue sea denial, contesting its use for the purpose of launching strikes against the Russian homeland, but not attempt to attain superiority or sea control. The oceanic zone is primarily for presence operations, illustrating status and interests, and interdiction of sea lines of communication if at all practicable. Russian nuclear-powered submarines represent the main combat element in distant waters, conducting out of area patrols in the oceanic zone. Russian surface combatants typically venture out into it in small groups for exercises or presence operations but focus on the near sea and far sea zones in terms of missions and tasks.

Russia uses a ship-ranking system that structures roles for vessels along these maritime divisions. The ranks themselves are assigned based on a combination of ship features or factors. First-rank ships include nuclear-powered submarines, carriers, cruisers, destroyers, large landing ships, and larger frigates. They are destined for the oceanic and far sea zone. Second rank are diesel electric submarines, frigates, heavy corvettes, and medium landing craft. These vessels operate primarily in the far sea zone. Third rank consists of corvettes, missile boats, and minesweepers. These ships are destined for the near sea zone, but some can deploy and operate further with limited endurance. In the fourth and final rank are coastal vessels, small landing craft, or patrol boats, which work the coastal defence zone, patrol naval bases, or inland waterways.

Although at times described as layered defence, the Russian Navy's operational concepts reflect a plan to attrit opponent forces at longer ranges, such that they do not have the freedom of action to strike the Russian homeland. Defence against such strikes is often impossible, or cost prohibitive, whether layered or not. Indeed, since the 1960s, the range of carrier-based aviation has made coastal defence or layered defence an increasingly dubious proposition. Hence the Russian Navy's value is in destroying the launchers or platforms that carry long-range strike capabilities, and helping to absorb or deflect the blow (i.e. damage limitation). This requires sallying forth and contesting the far sea zone, which may be done with long-range anti-ship weapons, although the current capabilities for realising such a concept remain constrained, as discussed below.

The navy's role in strategic deterrence and subordinate concepts is more easily achieved since deterrence in this case requires an accessible level of conventional and nuclear capability. The requirements of deterrence are much lower than those of warfighting and defence. Perhaps the most challenging mission is establishing a protected maritime region for Russian ballistic missile submarines to patrol, whether in the Sea of Okhotsk or east of the Barents Sea. The reason is straightforward: Russia no longer fields the kind of navy capable of offering effective protection against NATO submarines in these regions and has major deficiencies in providing defence in the near sea zone.

Russia's main operational problem in the near sea zone is a lack of effective anti-submarine warfare means or capacity for counter-mine warfare.[35] The capabilities are very dated, and their availability is low. The missions they have to conduct include anti-submarine defence, counter-mine warfare, anti-saboteur operations, air defence, reconnaissance, and maritime domain awareness. Of these, the navy is able to conduct the less important operations, but on the whole it has dramatically reduced capacity to secure Russia's ballistic missile submarines or address the threat of mine warfare.[36]

Their primary mission, however, is to ensure that the ballistic missile submarines are able to deploy and cannot be intercepted in the near sea zone by enemy attack submarines, hence the obvious gap in capability. This may be surprising, given most Russian ships built over the past ten to twenty years have been corvettes and light frigates, primarily aimed at the near sea zone (to the dissatisfaction of Russian Navy analysts).[37] At the same time, Russia has insufficiently invested in anti-submarine warfare capability and not enough in minesweeping technology. Therefore, there is both a shortage of technical ability and force availability to provide effective coverage and sustained protection.

The inability of Russian naval forces to provide for the protection of the sea-based nuclear deterrent is an openly discussed subject in Russian military analytical circles. There is thus a dissonance between the major investment in Russia's latest generation of Borei-class ballistic missile submarines (SSBNs) and the navy's ability to provide for their combat effectiveness. In 2020, Russia had ten operational ballistic missile submarines in service. According to experts Hans Kristensen and Matt Korda, these could field a combined maximum load of 816 warheads, but the likely deployed warhead count in practice is somewhere in the six hundred range given constraints imposed by arms control agreements and other limitations.[38] Thus, the submarine force fields close to a third of the country's strategic nuclear warheads, forming a substantial component of Russia's second-strike nuclear deterrent.

However, in the later 1980s the Soviet navy fielded 270 general-purpose nuclear-powered submarines (not including more than sixty SSBNs), a force that by 2021 has been reduced to about twenty-one nuclear-powered submarines of various types.[39] Hence in the 2020s the Russian Navy will be fielding about ten SSBNs, in two maritime "bastions", with perhaps twenty or so nuclear-powered submarines to defend them. Russia has a miniscule fraction of the submarine, surface combatant, and naval aviation capability of its Soviet predecessor yet retains the same operational deployment strategy for its modernised ballistic missile submarine force. The gap between ends and means is near self-evident, raising fair questions about whether these patrol areas can in truth be considered protected maritime regions.

In the far sea zone, the navy's task is to weaken the striking power of enemy forces, reduce the military and economic potential of the opponent, disorganise their systems of political administration or military command and control, and threaten their sea lines of communication.[40] The operating assumption is that in the initial period of war, the bulk of enemy naval power will be concentrated in the far sea zone, even in the Arctic where the operating conditions are exceedingly difficult. The Russian Navy faces its most daunting challenges in this zone (far sea), which some argue ultimately require the use of nuclear weapons, that is, the tasks cannot be resolved via non-nuclear means alone.[41] According to Russian analysts, offensive strike capabilities have to have such standoff range as to provide safety for the forces deploying them, and the missiles must be able autonomously to find their targets given the expected inaccuracy of available targeting data. In the medium term, the Russian Navy has a low chance of attaining effective reconnaissance and targeting capability in the far sea zone.[42] Assuming a contested electromagnetic spectrum – the presence of strong electronic warfare – the range for detecting targets is far too short to meet current requirements.

Russian military analysts are equally frank about the difficulty of coordinating strikes by ships, submarines, and land-based aviation against moving naval targets. Long-range strike capabilities mean US carrier strike groups or surface action groups can operate at the outer-range limits of Russian Tu-22M3 bombers, and while they may be reached by Russian surface action groups, the Russian Navy's problem is their combat stability (i.e. survivability prior to getting within range).[43] Russian analysts write that the opponent can essentially command the terms of the engagement and retain the initiative. Russian forces will not have the ability to destroy capital ships such as carriers or amphibious assault ships until they are able to clear the screen of destroyers and other defending ships. The United States can leverage its complete superiority in naval aviation to deploy airborne warning and control systems, detecting Russian forces early on and eliminating any chance of a surprise missile attack. Meanwhile, the technical characteristics of US command and control or navigation systems are such that Russian ships will not have suitable options to jam them. There is also the challenge posed by false targets (decoys), the prospect for surface action groups hiding in obscuring terrain like Norwegian fjords, or using electronic warfare to mask their signature.

Despite these challenges, degrading a US strike remains the top priority for the Russian military. The Russian military alternatively frames this as a sustained prompt global strike operation or massed missile-aviation strike, which can only be parried or deterred with select conventional capabilities. Increasingly, Russian views nestle this operation within the US multi-domain operations concept as an integrated massed air strike (see Figure 4.1).[44] This challenge constitutes a strategic conventional attack that cannot be deterred by general purpose forces. According to some analyst estimates, the US navy could deploy three thousand cruise missiles at sea circa 2016 and will have six thousand by 2025.[45] The naval component is only one element of the strike, featuring long-range aviation, land-based precision fires, drones, hypersonic and cruise missiles. The Russian Navy's task, as technically difficult as it may appear, is to survive an initial air attack, assist in deflecting such a strike, and degrade opponent naval forces fielding said capabilities.

But Russian thinking about the contribution of naval power to military strategy has also shifted the accent from the defensive, destroying combat groupings at sea, to offensive operations targeting objects on land.[46] As part of Russian strategic operations that target critical infrastructure of military, economic, and political significance, the Russian Navy's most significant mission, outside of strategic nuclear deterrence, is to inflict high costs on the opponent and disrupt their combat operations. The goal is to destroy the military-economic potential of an opponent and substantially degrade their command and control. Current and emerging capabilities allow the Russian Navy to leverage precision weapons in

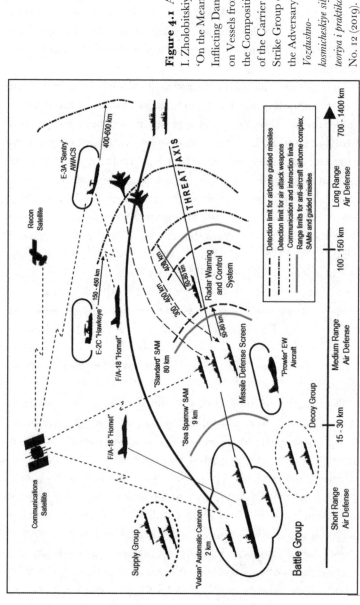

Figure 4.1 A. I. Zholobitskiy, 'On the Means of Inflicting Damage on Vessels from the Composition of the Carrier Strike Group of the Adversary', *Vozdushno-kosmicheskiye sily: teoriya i praktika*, No. 12 (2019).

realising such an operation and to contribute effectively to the so-called "system of non-nuclear deterrence".[47]

The mission requirements for conventional and nuclear strikes against land targets appear permissive. While the Russian Navy may struggle with the practical tasks of intercepting US strike groups and destroying them at range before they are able to strike, such attacks can be deterred in part through Russian offensive conventional capability if turned to critically important targets on land.[48] Furthermore, selective employment of these capabilities would allow control over escalation and a series of iterative strikes against the target to dose or steadily increase the pain. Therefore, where defence seems difficult, or prohibitive, Russian naval operations are intended to realise a strategy based on cost imposition to deter would be opponents from conducting large-scale strikes against the Russian homeland.

Capability development: from non-nuclear deterrence to the balanced fleet

At first blush, it may appear that Russia is building a green-water navy with long-range strike capabilities. Most senior official statements suggest that Russia is prioritising building "near sea zone" ships with advanced anti-ship and land-attack cruise missiles.[49] But this is simply a steppingstone due to the severe limitations in the defence industrial complex demonstrated during the first state armament programme that lasted from 2011 to 2020 and as equally displayed in the follow-on state armament programme of 2018–27. In truth, the Russian Navy has consistently advocated a "balanced fleet" concept, which means fleets with distribution of different classes of ships and ability to conduct operations in the coastal, near sea, and far sea zone. This includes more distant operations in the oceanic zone. Consequently, the current force structure reflects not the strategy, but what is achievable from shipbuilding in the interim. In practice, Russia has far more money invested in submarine construction, and nuclear-powered submarines are considered to be first-rank ships that are slated for the far sea zone and operations in the World Oceans. In practice, naval procurement has matched the balanced fleet construct to the extent it maximally could.

Operational requirements drive these investments. While smaller vessels may be able to conduct land-attack strikes at great ranges, they ultimately lack the magazine capacity for massed attacks, and they do not have the endurance to maintain presence in the far sea zone. They also cannot operate in difficult sea states. If the Russian Navy is unable to sally forth sufficiently from outside its coastal waters, or the near seas, then it cannot put in practice a damage limitation strategy. That is, it becomes near useless in defending the homeland against long-range strikes and adversary strategic capabilities, since it cannot contest enemy fleets where they are likely to deploy. More to the point, they cannot even see enemy fleets given limitations in land-based surveillance and reconnaissance. Long-range strike capabilities become near useless for a navy that cannot find and fix its desired targets. Hence the Russian Navy had sought to build and deploy a mix of ships, such that it could conduct blue-water operations, but most importantly field vessels able to engage opponents in the far sea zone and prevent them from operating freely within strike range of critical Russian infrastructure.

The Russian Navy has also sought to overcome the Soviet navy's philosophy of overspecialisation and is instead investing in universal systems, families of capabilities, and multipurpose ships.[50] This means an evolution from specialised launchers to universal vertical launch systems (3S14), which allows deployment of families of missiles across different ship classes and submarines. There is a pairing of these systems with long-range land-attack capabilities, or what has been termed the "kalibrisation" of the Russian Navy in reference to the ubiquitous deployment of the Kalibr-NK land-attack cruise missile. These capabilities, along with air defence, radar, and other standardised packages, are being deployed on corvettes, heavy corvettes, light frigates, and even via modifications to legacy Soviet destroyer-class ships. This allows a vessel of any class or tonnage to be viable in certain roles, particularly in effecting non-nuclear deterrence via long-range strike capabilities and being able to destroy critical objects on land. The overriding philosophy behind platform acquisition and weapon procurement is cost-effectiveness.[51]

But this steady modernisation of naval strike capability has been met with a tremendous decline in land-based naval aviation, which at one point formed the largest element in the Soviet Union's anti-carrier triad. Most anti-ship missiles were born by Tu-22 bombers, of which today there are no more than sixty in service and fewer operational.[52] This means that the Russian Navy has to rely on its much-diminished submarine force, and near non-existent land-based naval aviation, to include reduced availability of maritime patrol aviation. Thus, Russia's arsenal of offensive conventional capabilities remains low when it comes to anti-ship maritime strike capability, and while the number of land-attack missiles is growing, it is still considerably short of the need. Russia's modernised fleet of tactical bombers, Su-34s, can fill in for some of the prior missions conducted by the venerable Tu-22M3, but at this stage they appear to largely carry shorter-range subsonic anti-ship missiles.

The Russian Navy is reasonably well positioned to realise a non-nuclear deterrent, investing in quality over quantity, and placing bets on hypersonic weapons. As envisioned, offensive strike elements that comprise the system of non-nuclear deterrence include land-, sea-, and air-based long-range precision-guided weapons: Iskander-M variants, Kalibr-NK, Kh-555, Kh-101, Kh-32, and hypersonic weapons such as Kinzhal or Tsirkon. The Russian military is actively pursuing larger stocks of long-range precision weapons and has numerous new types in development, but as per recent statements by the Minister of Defence Sergei Shoigu, they expect that in the future hypersonic weapons will form the basis of non-nuclear deterrence.[53] This is significant since in the future strategic deterrence concepts will be predicated more on non-nuclear capabilities as opposed to nuclear weapons.[54] This suggests that while existing conventional weapons are unlikely to dramatically displace the role of nuclear capabilities, hypersonic weapons are perceived as having sufficiently greater deterrent potential to induce a further shift towards conventional systems.

Hypersonic weapons have a narrower role in Russian concepts of operations and military strategy beyond being simply faster or perhaps better than current generation cruise missiles. They are seen as able to penetrate missile defence or air defence systems to hit the most important critical objects, or to eliminate missile defence systems and thereby increase the efficacy of Russia's strategic nuclear weapons.[55] They are therefore a specific subset of penetrating weapons against high-value targets. Both Tsirkon and Kinzhal are designated for what are considered to be the conventional phases of warfare, to be used against command and control, military-industrial potential, and operational-level military infrastructure. These targets are broadly identified in standing strategic-operations concepts. Hypersonic weapons are perceived to be more effective than traditional subsonic cruise missiles like Kalibr-NK, and an asymmetric response to US/NATO superiority in conventional precision-guided weapons, able to offset qualitatively Russia's numerical disadvantage in a cost-effective manner.

Conclusion

The Russian Navy has retained a strong role in Russian military strategy, contemporary strategic operations, and deterrence concepts. While there is no formalised naval strategy, separate and distinct from the military doctrine, state policy guides and informs the political or economic purpose of naval activity. Russian naval missions and tasks continue to evolve alongside four central axes: a damage limitation strategy to prevent the homeland from being struck by massed conventional missile attack, destruction of an adversary's critical objects ashore with long-range conventional or nuclear means, maintenance of a strategic nuclear deterrent to ensure unacceptable damage can be inflicted on any adversary, and status projection via presence in the so-called World Ocean or naval diplomacy.

Instead of becoming tied to supporting ground operations, the Russian Navy has evolved a land-attack role against critical infrastructure and a strong role in strategic deterrence concepts. The force is inadequately equipped, however, to conduct primary missions in the near sea or far sea zone, where major deficits endure. Whether ensuring the survivability of the sea-based nuclear deterrent or parrying a blow from enemy surface action groups deployed at some distance from the coast, the Russian Navy is not suitably positioned for these missions – yet. As it stands, naval capability remains a work in progress, which has led to assessments suggesting that the Russian Navy will be primarily a green-water navy, or a dual fleet with legacy Soviet platforms and more modern ships slated for the near sea zone. Neither offers a completely accurate picture of the strategic considerations that drive force structure development.

The Russian Navy's aspiration is to develop balanced fleets, able to conduct operations across the spectrum of sea zones in question, and provide for presence in the more distant waters of the World Ocean. Balance is of course in the eye of the beholder. Here, the guiding principles remain reasonable sufficiency for an active defence, with fleets structured around the specific threats in oceanic theatres of military action, and the mission requirements that they impose. Among these, the Atlantic and Arctic remain top priorities, followed by the Pacific, and then the Indian Ocean as a distant theatre of interest. In the near and medium term, the Russian Navy will be better defined by the capabilities it fields, and the missions it is able to conduct, than the size or classes of ships available. It is a navy whose purpose is defined by its ability to contribute to the overall military strategy premised on active defence, the strategic operations envisioned, and strategic deterrence concepts.

Notes

1 'The Russian Navy: A Historic Transition', Office of Naval Intelligence, December 2015, www.oni.navy.mil/ONI-Reports/Foreign-Naval-Cap abilities/Russia (accessed 13 November 2022).

2 See, for example, the Russian 2015 National Security Strategy, Website of the Presidential Administration, http://static.kremlin.ru/media/events/files/ru/l8iXkR8XLAtxeilX7JK3XXy6YoAsHD5v.pdf (accessed 8 October 2022).

3 G. H. Turbiville Jr (ed.), *The Voroshilov Lectures: Materials from the Soviet General Staff Academy*. Vol. I. Washington, DC: National Defense University Press.

4 V. I. Koriavko, 'Evolutsiya form primeneniya obedinenii VMF', *Voennaya mysl'*, June 2004, pp. 64–7.

5 V. G. Lebedko, 'Eshyo raz o ponyatiyakh "morskoi boi" i "takticheskaya operatsiya"', *Voennaya mysl'*, April 2004, pp. 47–9.

6 For more on OTVDs, see 'Okeanskii teatr voennykh deistvii (OTVD)' in the Russian military encyclopaedia, http://encyclopedia.mil.ru/ency clopedia/dictionary/details.htm?id=7603@morfDictionary (accessed 13 November 2022).

7 Turbiville, *The Voroshilov Lectures*, I.

8 M. Vego, *Soviet Naval Tactics*. Annapolis, MD: Naval Institute Press, 1992, p. 8.

9 Ibid.

10 Ibid., pp. 8–9.

11 Turbiville, *The Voroshilov Lectures*, I, pp. 249–50.

12 G. Kostev, 'Nesostoyavshiesya voiny', *Morskoi sbornik*, No. 6 (June 2011), pp. 42–51; see p. 42 on the evolution of Soviet naval exercises and origins of current missions.

13 There was an enduring dependence on tactical nuclear weapons within the Soviet Navy, and they continue to retain a strong role in the Russian Navy today.

14 'Voennya doktrina Rossiiskoi Federatsii', printed in *Rossiiskaia gazeta*, 30 December 2014, https://rg.ru/2014/12/30/doktrina-dok.html (accessed 8 October 2022).

15 A. A. Kokoshin, *Soviet Strategic Thought, 1917–91*. Cambridge, MA: The MIT Press, 1998, pp. 184–6.

16 Vego, *Soviet Naval Tactics*, p. 6.

17 Kokoshin, *Soviet Strategic Thought*, p. 190.

18 Vego, *Soviet Naval Tactics*, pp. 7–8.

19 D. Glantz, *Soviet Military Operational Art: In Pursuit of Deep Battle*. New York: Frank Cass, 1991, pp. 9–10.

20 A. A. Korabelnikov, 'Vzaimosvyaz voennoyi strategii, operativnogo iskusstva, i taktiki v soveremennyh usloviyah', *Vestnik Akademii Nayk*, No. 2 (67) (2019), pp. 35–41.

21 A. Sviridova, 'Vektory razvitiya voyennoy strategii', *Krasnaya zvezda*, 4 March 2019, http://redstar.ru/vektory-razvitiya-voennoj-strategii (accessed 13 November 2022).

22 See Russian military definitions for active defence, and defence activities: https://encyclopedia.mil.ru/encyclopedia/dictionary/details.htm?id=2750@morfDictionary and http://encyclopedia.mil.ru/encyclopedia/dictionary/details.htm?id=2748@morfDictionary (accessed 8 October 2022).

23 Korabelnikov, 'Vzaimosvyaz voennoyi strategii', pp. 35–41.

24 Entsiklopedia Ministerstva Oborony RF, 'Strategicheskoe sderzhivanie', n.d., http://encyclopedia.mil.ru/encyclopedia/dictionary/details.htm?id=14206@morfDictionary (accessed 8 October 2022).

25 A. L. Khlyapin and V. A. Afanasyev, 'Kontseptualnie osnovy strategicheskovo sderzhivaniya', *Voennaya mysl'*, No. 1 (2005).

26 Not to be confused with VTO, which are simply precision-guided weapons but in tactical-operational roles.

27 These are often paired with weapons based on new physical principles, such as directed energy, electromagnetic pulse, electronic warfare, and other emerging technologies. B. M. Burenok and Y. A. Pechatnov, *Strategicheskoye Sderzhivanye*. Moscow: n.p., 2011, p. 11.

28 There are other policies of relevance, for example Russian policy documents focusing on the Arctic. See N. Mehdiyeva, 'Strategy of Development of the Arctic Zone and the Provision of National Security for the Period to 2030', NATO Defence College Russian Studies Series, 1/21, 25 June 2021, www.ndc.nato.int/research/research.php?icode=703 (accessed 14 November 2022).

29 Morskaya Doktrina Rossiiskoi Federatsii, 2015.

30 For a good in-depth analysis, see R. Connolly, 'Towards a Dual Fleet? The Maritime Doctrine of the Russian Federation and the Modernisation of Russian Naval Capabilities', NATO Defense College, February 2017, www.ndc.nato.int/news/news.php?icode=1061 (accessed 14 November 2022).

31   Maritime subregions include the Baltic, Black, Azov, and Mediterranean Seas.

32   'Osnov gosudarstvennoi politiki Rossiiskoi Federatsii v oblasti voenno-morskoi deyatelnosti na period do 2030 goda', Website of the Presidential Administration, www.kremlin.ru/acts/bank/42117 (accessed 8 October 2022).

33   Richard Connolly offers a good document review in 'Russia's Strategy for the Development of Marine Activities to 2030', NATO Defense College Russian Studies Series, July 2019, www.ndc.nato.int/research/research.php?icode=618 (accessed 8 October 2022).

34   J. W. Kipp, 'The Russian Military and the Revolution in Military Affairs: A Case of the Oracle of Delphi or Cassandra?', MORS Conference paper, June 1995, p. 10.

35   M. Klimov, 'VMF Rossii naporolsya na miny i podlodki', *Nezavisimoe voennoe obozrenie*, 22 November 2018.

36   V. Kryazhev, Otsenka voenno-politicheskoi i operativno-strategicheskoi situatsii v zonakh flotov Rossii', *Morskoi sbornik*, No. 2 (February 2019), pp. 41–5.

37   A. Shishkin, 'Rossiiski VMF prevrashaetsya vo "flot beregovoi oborony"', *Vzgliad*, 4 December 2017, https://vz.ru/society/2017/12/4/897894.html (accessed 8 October 2022). It should be noted here that some effort is being made to address this deficiency. Progress is being made, for example, in producing the Aleksandrit class (Project 12700) minesweeper – four are in service and five under construction. Forty are planned in total. These are designed to detect and destroy mines in naval bases and harbours.

38   Hans Kristensen suggests the net deployed number of warheads on SLBMs in 2021 may be 624. See H. M. Kristensen and M. Korda, 'Russian Nuclear Weapons, 2021', *Bulletin of Atomic Scientists*, Vol. 77 (March 2021).

39   According to Aleksander Shishkin. See his blog for updated listings of Russian naval vessels and their current status at https://navy-korabel.livejournal.com (accessed 8 October 2022).

40   N. Radchikov, 'Razvitie ponyatiinovo apparata primeneniya gruppiro-vok sil flota v dalnykh morskykh zonakh', *Morskoi sbornik*, No. 2 (February 2012), pp. 22–6.

41   I. Spirin and V. Alfyorov, 'Osobennosti porazheniya obektov v dalnei morskoi zone', *Morskoi sbornik*, No. 12 (December 2015), pp. 41–5.

42   Ibid., p. 42.

43   Ibid.

44   V. I. Stuchinskiy and M. V. Korolkov, 'Foundations for Combat Employment of Aviation to Disrupt an Integrated Massed Air Strike

within an Adversary's Multi-domain Operation, Aerospace-Forces', *Theory and Practice*, No. 16 (December 2020).

45 O. V. Alyoshin, A. H. Popov, and V. V. Puchnin, 'Voenno-morskaya mosh Rossii v sovremennykh geopoliticheskykh usloviyakh', *Voennaya mysl'*, No. 7 (July 2016), pp. 12–17.

46 E. Sukalenko, 'Sovremennie printsipy vedeniya vooruzhennoi borby na more', *Morskoi sbornik*, No. 10 (October 2016), pp. 33–9.

47 E. Sukalenko, 'K voprosu o realizatsii sovremennykh printsipov vedevniya: vooruzhennoi borbe na more', *Morskoi sbornik*, No. 3 (March 2017), pp. 40–5.

48 Alyoshin, Popov, and Puchnin, 'Voenno-morskaya mosh', pp. 12–17.

49 'Prioritetom morskoi chasti novoi Gosprogrammy vooruzheniya stanut korabli s vysokotochnymi raketami i atomnie podvodniye lodki', Website of the Russian Ministry of Defence, 29 November 2017, https://function. mil.ru/news_page/world/more.htm?id=12152815@egNews (accessed 14 November 2022).

50 K. Bogdanov and I. Kramnik, 'The Russian Navy in the 21st Century'. CNA Report, October 2018, www.cna.org/reports/2018/10/russian-navy-in-21st-century (accessed 14 November 2022), p. 3.

51 Kryazhev, 'Otsenka', pp. 41–5.

52 Bogdanov and Kramnik, 'The Russian Navy in the 21st Century', p. 3.

53 V. Pavlov, '"Tsirkon" na strazhe: sily neyadernogo sderzhivaniya pereidyt na giperzvyk', Gazeta.ru, 9 February 2021, www.gazeta.ru/ army/2021/02/09/13472240.shtml (accessed 8 October 2022).

54 See Gerasimov's statements at the Ministry of Defence collegium hosted on 7 November 2017, https://function.mil.ru/news_page/person/more. htm?id=12149743@egNews&_print=true (accessed 8 October 2022).

55 A. V. Evsuykov and A. L. Hryapin, 'Rol' novyh system strategicheskih vooryzhenii v obespechenii strategicheskogo sderzhivaniya', *Voennaya mysl'*, No. 12 (December 2020), pp. 26–30.

5

Russia as a maritime power: economic interests and capabilities

Richard Connolly

Introduction

The role the sea plays in Russian efforts to forge a role as a capable, modern, and sovereign actor in a multipolar global order is neglected in most analyses of Russian strategy. For centuries, the general tendency – both in Russia and outside – has been to view Russia primarily as a continental power whose interests in the sea are modest and secondary to its interests on land. While this changed to some degree in the Cold War, the chaotic emergence of a newly independent Russia from the ruins of the Soviet Union was accompanied by a sharp reduction of interest in the sea. Its maritime interests shrank as important ports and trade relationships became the concern of newly independent states like Ukraine and Latvia. Meanwhile, the Russian Navy was starved of funds. What was the world's second most capable military fleet quickly became a source of concern and embarrassment. By the turn of the century, Russia's maritime interests – both in economic and military terms – were seen as an expensive luxury that could not be afforded.

This situation is changing. The sea is rising in importance in Russia's overall grand strategy. As far as interests are concerned, Russia is becoming increasingly focused on the development of its considerable Arctic natural resource base and in facilitating the expansion of the Northern Sea Route (NSR). The focus on the sea will intensify in future as Russia's onshore natural resource base is depleted and liquefied natural gas (LNG) and oil exports from the Arctic become more important. In addition, the sea lies at the heart of Russia's ongoing efforts to pivot to Asia. Traditional trading partners in the West are giving way to countries in Asia and the Middle East, causing sea-based trade to rise in volume. Shipbuilding facilities to support the natural resource sector, as well as the military, are being developed in Russia's Far East, while new logistical and transportation infrastructure is being built to support the expansion of trade with Asia. Russia's partially modernised navy has also played an important role in the projection of Russian military power, most notably in the Black Sea and the Eastern Mediterranean. Strategic planning documents indicate that the navy will play an increasingly important role in strengthening Russian military power, not least because of advances in long-range missile technology.

In short, as Russia's maritime interests have grown, and as they look set to expand even further over the next decade, the need to develop civilian and military maritime capabilities is rising. Considerable effort is being made to do just that. While obstacles have been encountered, it is also true that significant progress is being made. As a result, we should expect to see Russia's interest and capabilities in the sea continue to rise over the next decade. Russia is likely to become the leading power in the Arctic. It will also assert its interests in the Pacific, as well as in traditional areas of interest closer to home. Understanding the role that the sea plays in Russian strategy is thus of crucial importance to a better grasp of Russia's place in contemporary international relations.

This chapter looks beyond purely naval matters to answer three sets of questions relating to the broader question of Russian maritime power. First, what are Russia's principal maritime interests: how have they changed over the past decade, and what is the trajectory for the coming decade? Second, what financial resources are available to the Russian government and to commercial entities with an interest in the sea: what is the scale of resources available for naval modernisation, and what is the nature of demand for Russian civilian shipbuilding? Third, does Russia possess the industrial capabilities necessary to achieve a far-reaching maritime and naval modernisation programme?

Russia's changing maritime interests

The sea is becoming more important to Russia's overall strategic agenda. As part of a broader effort to become more independent and sovereign, Russian policymakers have made a concerted effort to establish closer economic relations with a range of countries beyond traditional trading and investment partners in Europe.[1] While trade with European economies is facilitated by a dense network of roads, railways, and pipelines, for the transportation of hydrocarbons, trade routes with Africa, the Middle East, Latin America, and, most importantly, Asia, are principally maritime in nature. It is the growing importance of sea-based trade that creates the material basis for Russia's re-emergence as a maritime power, in addition to Moscow's interest in naval power.

Several basic facts about the nature of Russia's integration with the global economy illustrate why the sea is so important to Russia's strategic agenda. Russia is, by global standards, an open economy in which trade plays an important role. According to World Bank data, trade accounted for 49 per cent of Russia's GDP in 2019. This is considerably more open than many other large low- and middle-income economies such as Brazil (29 per cent), China (36 per cent), and India (40 per cent). It is also a more open economy than the United States (26 per cent).[2] A large and growing share of Russian trade takes place with Asian economies. In 2019, five of Russia's top-ten trading partners were from Eurasia: China, Turkey, South Korea, Japan, and Kazakhstan.[3] This is projected to rise further over the next decade. Plans to "pivot to Asia" are predicated on exporting large volumes of hydrocarbons – oil, LNG, and coal, much of it extracted from the Arctic – to rapidly growing economies across the Asia-Pacific region.

Moscow also plans to exploit the NSR by transforming it into a strategically important cargo route that will link the Asia-Pacific with Europe.[4] In 2018, President Putin set a benchmark of 80 million tons of traffic through the NSR by 2024, which would represent a tenfold increase on that year.[5] In 2020 and 2022, Moscow published updates to its Arctic strategy that outlined the need for investment in infrastructure and new icebreaking and ice-class ships.[6]

Russia's re-emergence as an agricultural power of global significance has also changed its interest in the sea. After importing large volumes of grains and other foods during the Soviet period, Russia is now the world's largest exporter of grains.[7] Grain exports now account for a larger share of Russia's exports than all products except oil, gas, and weapons.[8] Russia exported grain to nearly 140 countries in 2020.[9] The most important markets (by value) are in the Middle East (Turkey, Iran) and Africa (Egypt, Nigeria, Sudan). Russian grain exports to the likes of Bangladesh and Indonesia are also growing in importance. The overwhelming majority of Russian grain is shipped from Black Sea ports (Novorossiysk, Taman).[10] Because grain exports are growing so rapidly, existing export terminals are undergoing modernisation and new capacity is being added. The Black Sea's role as the gateway to food export markets across the world means that the region will only grow in importance.

It is these large and growing interests in the sea that make Russia's naval modernisation all the more important. As its maritime economic interests grow, and with it the importance of the sea to Russian grand strategy, so does the need to guarantee sea lines of communication and to bolster Russia's military presence abroad. But, as all sea powers throughout history have discovered, the protection and assertion of maritime power is an expensive business. Not only is a large and capable navy needed, but also a wide array of supporting infrastructure and auxiliary vessels. A network of modern shipyards that are able to produce maritime vessels of all shapes and sizes is also a cornerstone of real maritime prowess. All of which requires considerable financial muscle. In liberal economies, like the United States and the United Kingdom, the financial burden has often been shared between the state and the private sector. But in state capitalist-type economies, like China and Russia, the bulk of the financial resources allocated to maritime power comes from the state or state-owned enterprises.[11] As shown below, the Russian state's growing interest in the sea is reflected in the financial resources made available to strengthen its military and civilian fleets.

Resourcing strategy: the financial basis of Russian maritime power

Russia's capacity to use the sea to implement its wider strategic agenda is heavily influenced by the volume of available financial resources. During the 1990s, both the government and the private sector were starved of cash. Consequently, the civilian and military fleets suffered from chronic underinvestment. Indeed, simply maintaining existing assets and paying personnel on time proved difficult. The quantity of ships declined, as did the quality of those left to operate them. Shipyards were left empty, and older vessels remained in desperate need of maintenance and repair. It was not until the beginning of the 2000s that funding for the navy and for the country's commercial fleets began to rise. Since then, expenditure has risen substantially. The country's vast shipbuilding complex has received much-needed capital investment, with a new generation of workers entering the workplace and bringing new skills.

Nevertheless, serious weaknesses remain. Nearly two decades of financial starvation means that it will take at least another decade of sustained investment before the country's shipbuilding industry can be considered complete. Finishing the job will, therefore, be contingent on a steady flow of funding over the 2020s, both from the government and, increasingly, from state-owned or state-linked conglomerates like Rosneft, Gazprom, Novatek, and Rosatom, all of which have their own fleets and corresponding ship acquisition programmes.

There are two principal components that constitute the financial basis of maritime power: the volume of financial resources available for building, maintaining, and operating the navy; and the volume of financial resources available for building, maintaining, and operating the commercial fleets. In Russia, the vast majority of the funding for both the navy and the commercial fleets emanates from the state, either through direct federal government expenditure (in the case of the navy) or through expenditure by state-owned enterprises (in the case of much of the shipping used in the energy industry or for the navigation of the Arctic). Government expenditure on the navy is directed almost exclusively towards domestic shipyards, most of which are owned by the state-owned conglomerate United Shipbuilding Corporation (Ob'yedinonnaya sudostroitel'naya korporatsiya, or OSK). Commercial fleets, by contrast, have tended to use imported vessels, largely due to the inability of domestic shipyards – owned mainly by OSK – to deliver on price, quality, or speed of construction.

Estimating Russian military expenditure

The importance to Moscow of its maritime and naval capabilities is reflected in the scale of the resources the Russian leadership has devoted to this. As discussed below, through the last decade, the navy has been a priority in defence spending: it had the largest share of the funding attached to state defence spending to 2020. To understand more precisely what this means, and to estimate the scale of naval expenditure, we must first start by generating an estimate of overall military expenditure. With this in hand, it is then necessary to estimate the share of total military expenditure that is allocated to naval activities, and, where possible, how naval expenditure is broken down (i.e. the share of spending that is allocated to procurement, operations and maintenance, and personnel). Given the paucity of publicly available information on both the expenditure side (e.g. the composition of government military expenditure) and the supply side (e.g. the financial position of OSK), it is impossible to produce a precise estimate of the volume of expenditure on Russia's maritime network. Nevertheless, a rough approximation of maritime expenditure is possible.

Measuring Russian military expenditure is far from simple. Those measures that seek to place a monetary value on a country's military expenditure, usually in US dollars at market exchange rates, are subject to confusion in relation to choices made over which units of measurement to use. But measuring the defence burden, usually expressed as a proportion of a country's gross domestic product (GDP) or total government spending, is not simple. Although the Russian government does not conceal the scale of its military expenditure to the same degree that its Soviet predecessors did, it remains the case that transparency of federal government spending on the military declined over the 2010s and into the early 2020s. This is compounded by the fact that important items of military expenditure are sometimes funded by chapters of the federal budget outside the one labelled 'national defence'.

For the purposes of simplicity, it is possible to describe three main methods for estimating Russia's defence burden. The first and narrowest definition includes only that expenditure that is included under the 'national defence' chapter of the federal budget.[12] This includes expenditure on procurement, military wages, pensions, housing, training and exercises, operational expenditure, personnel costs, construction, and the development and production of nuclear weapons by Rosatom.

A second and wider definition that corresponds more closely to those employed by NATO and SIPRI is also often used. This includes spending by the Ministry of Defence under other chapters of the budget, such as military pensions (under the 'social policy' chapter), as well as spending under the 'education', 'health', 'culture', and 'mass media' chapters of the budget. The federal budget also finances other forces, such as paramilitary forces that are judged to be trained and equipped for military operations. In Russia, this includes the Russian National Guard (Rosgvardiya), and the border service attached to the Federal Security Service (FSB). This has consequences for our understanding of maritime and naval matters, since the FSB Border Service plays an important role in territorial waters. This was illustrated in the Kerch Straits episode in 2018 when FSB vessels opened fire on and then captured three Ukrainian navy vessels attempting to pass into the Sea of Azov.

Most revealing and relevant for our purposes here, though, is the third and widest definition of Russian military expenditure, which includes additional instruments used to finance military spending. For example, between 2011 and 2015, the government used state guaranteed credits (SGCs), provided via state-owned banks, to augment direct budgetary funding of the annual state defence order (Gosudarstevennyi oboronnyi zakaz, or GOZ), which is used to procure new equipment, modernise and repair existing equipment, and to carry out research and development (R&D). Between 2011 and 2016, SGCs added an additional 1.2 trillion roubles to direct federal government-funded defence procurement. This boosted the real volume of procurement by 25 per cent over the five-year period in question.

Additional military-related expenditure is also provided through a variety of Federal Targeted Programmes (FTsP, or *federalnye tselevye programmy*), which supplement direct procurement spending. For instance, the FTsP for the 'Development of the

Defence-Industrial Complex' is the largest of these programmes.[13] Others include programmes to develop the space launch centres and the electronic components industry, both of which are strongly linked to military activities in Russia. Because other ministries fund these programmes (such as the Ministry for Industry and Trade), and because many programmes have at least partial civilian purposes, expenditure on FTsPs is not usually included in calculations of Russian military spending. But estimates of military expenditure formulated by Vasily Zatsepin, who previously worked at the Gaidar Institute for Economic Policy in Moscow, include these additional items of expenditure. Taken together, these estimates usually represent the upper boundary of the scale of Russia's defence burden.[14]

The methods described above are based on an analysis of publicly available budgetary data. There may, however, be other forms of hidden spending that are not easy to capture through an analysis of federal budget documents. For example, in October 2019, Igor Nuzhdin, a senior manager for Promsvyazbank – which conducts financial operations for the defence industry – revealed that income for the defence industry from the GOZ amounted to 2.4 trillion roubles in 2018.[15] This figure was 900 billion roubles higher than the sum revealed by official statements in that year, suggesting that a substantial volume of procurement funding may be hidden.

As illustrated in Figure 5.1, all three measures show that Russia's defence burden rose steadily between 2005 and 2016 and then declined thereafter to a level closer to the post-Soviet average. The defence burden – as measured by spending under the 'national defence' chapter of the federal budget – has tended to fluctuate within a band of 2.5–3.5 per cent of GDP, with the notable exception of 2016. In fact, the defence burden measured in this way has never dipped below 2.5 per cent of GDP since the collapse of the Soviet Union in 1991, demonstrating that military expenditure in Russia is viewed as relatively inelastic by the political elite,

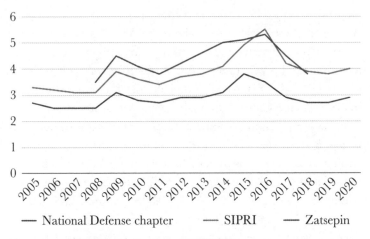

Figure 5.1 Military spending share of GDP (%), 2005–20.

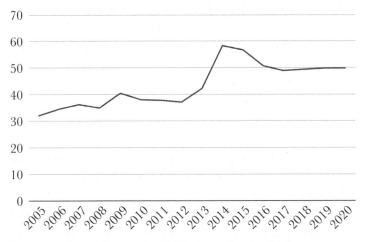

Figure 5.2 State defence order (GOZ) share of 'national defence' expenditure (%), 2005–20.

at least on the downside.[16] As shown in Figure 5.2, the share of procurement in military spending grew sharply after 2012.

The brief discussion presented above highlights the degree to which the share of military expenditure in national output grew after 2010 before declining and then plateauing after 2015–16. But this measure tells us little about the size of Russia's defence effort. Unfortunately, measuring military expenditure across countries (and across time) is fraught with difficulty. This is for two main reasons. First, it is difficult to compare calculations made in each country's national currency. Stating, for example, that the level of military expenditure in Russia is a trillion roubles in a given year and that the level in the same year in Saudi Arabia is a trillion riyals tells us very little. Second, converting military expenditure measured in national currencies to a common currency – usually the US dollar – at market exchange rates conceals important differences in purchasing power across countries. This is because many goods and services have different relative prices within a country, with non-traded goods and services being relatively less expensive in poorer countries. This can result in military expenditure being understated in countries with lower income levels – and correspondingly lower costs – than the United States. Furthermore, measuring changes in military expenditure across time is further complicated by the fact that market exchange rates can be volatile, and this volatility can often be independent of any changes in actual military expenditure.

Figure 5.3 illustrates the difference in results obtained from measuring Russian military expenditure in both roubles and in US dollars at the average market exchange rate. Because the US dollar measure is sensitive to movements in the exchange rate, military expenditure is shown to have declined in 2009 and then again after 2013, the year in which US dollar military expenditure peaked in Russia. This is in contrast to military expenditure measured in roubles, which grew every year between 2005 and 2016. The problem is that the rouble–US dollar exchange rate fluctuated considerably over the period under examination due to changes in the price of oil, Russia's primary export product, as well as changes in the relative rate of

Russia as a maritime power

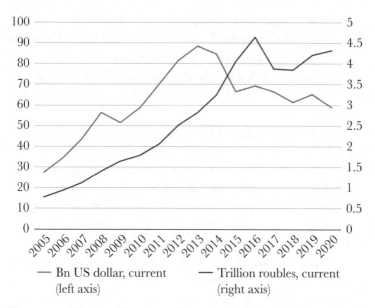

Figure 5.3 Russian military expenditure measured in roubles (current) and US dollars at market exchange rates (current), 2005–20.

inflation and in the Russian authorities' monetary and exchange rate policies. The result is an extremely volatile military expenditure series that bears little relation to the real defence effort. As the rouble weakened after 2016, US dollar military expenditure declined each year, despite the fact that local currency spending continued to rise.

Exchange rate volatility is not the only – or even the most important – problem when using market exchange rate-based measures of military expenditure. More significant still is the fact that many goods and services have different relative prices within a country, with non-traded goods and services being relatively less expensive in poorer countries. This can be very important when calculating relative military expenditure. After all, if the price of goods and services procured by the Russian government for military uses – for instance, the wages of military personnel or workers in the defence-industrial complex, or the price of military equipment – is lower than analogous US goods and services, the market exchange rate-based measure of military expenditure will understate the size of the basket of military goods and services obtained by the Russian government in any given year.

As a result of these problems, a more appropriate method for inferring real relative economic output across countries is therefore to use a purchasing power parity (PPP) exchange rate. PPP "weights" are available that allow analysts to make estimates of the value of economic activity in a country that accounts for differences in relative costs. In October 2020, the IMF calculated an implied PPP exchange rate of 27 roubles to the USD.[17] Given the actual market exchange rate is 60 roubles to the dollar in October 2022, this would suggest that the value of economic activity in Russia is over two and a half times as large as that implied by the prevailing market exchange rate.

In general, market exchange rates are the appropriate choice to measure financial flows across borders. For example, the current account or trade balance represents flows of financial resources across countries. It is appropriate to use the market exchange rate to convert these flows into dollars when aggregating across regions or calculating the global current account discrepancy. But for other variables, it is often more appropriate to use PPP-based exchange rates. For example, while market exchange rates are appropriate for measuring the value of internationally traded goods, non-traded goods and services tend to be cheaper in lower-income countries, especially large, populous countries like Russia. Any analysis that fails to take these differences into account will underestimate the purchasing power of consumers in lower-income countries. This has important implications for assessing the relative level of Russian military expenditure. Because a rouble buys relatively more military output in Russia than a dollar does in the United States, Russia's real level of military expenditure is likely to be considerably higher than a market exchange rate-based estimate would suggest.[18]

The impact of using PPP instead of market exchange rates is striking: the level of expenditure is around 2.5 times higher using PPP exchange rates. Figure 5.4 shows perhaps the most significant difference between Russian military expenditure using market exchange rates and PPP exchange rates. Even in 2005 – well before the rearmament programme began – Russian military expenditure exceeded $80 billion. By 2016, it exceeded $200 billion, although the lump-sum repayment of debt owed by defence-industrial enterprises explains this peak. Nevertheless, even after the reduction in the defence burden from 2016 the level of military expenditure reached just under $160 billion in 2020. As we will see below, this has major consequences for naval spending.

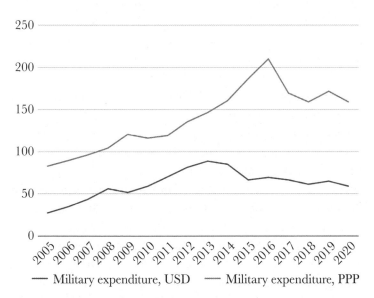

Figure 5.4 Russian military expenditure at market exchange rates and PPP exchange rates, 2005–20 (USD bn, current).

Estimating naval expenditure

The proportion of total military expenditure allocated to the navy is a function of two related variables: (1) the priority assigned by the political leadership to naval activities vis-à-vis other branches of Russia's military services, and (2) the proportion of procurement funding assigned to the production of naval vessels (i.e. the navy's share of GOZ funding).

One way of estimating the navy's share of total military expenditure is by referring to data submitted by the Russian government to the United Nations Office for Disarmament Affairs.[19] Russia supplied reports for the majority of years during the 1990s and has reported annually since 2000. Unfortunately, there are a number of serious problems with the data, with the figures presented not corresponding with other official data on military expenditure in Russia. Data on spending by branch of the armed forces also came to an end in 2017. As a result, the data should be treated with considerable caution. But for the purposes of this exercise, the data submitted to the UN before 2016 do have one useful characteristic: unlike other sources of official Russian data, there is some indication of the *relative share* of total military expenditure assigned to each branch of the armed service even if the absolute sums reported are clearly inaccurate.[20]

Figure 5.5 describes the share of military expenditure allocated to the navy according to the UN data. It averaged 16 per cent between 2005 and 2015, although the annual figure fluctuates considerably, with the lowest share observed in 2011 (7.5 per cent), with a share of around 25 per cent in 2014–15. The large differences suggest either (a) that the data are unreliable, or (b) that the higher shares observed in 2014 and 2015 reflect a surge in naval procurement that accompanied the implementation of the state armament programme to 2020 (GPV 2020) declined over the 2010s and into the early 2020s. The latter explanation is certainly plausible as the navy was estimated to have been assigned the largest share of funding attached to the GPV 2020 of (5 trillion roubles, or 25 per cent of total spending).[21]

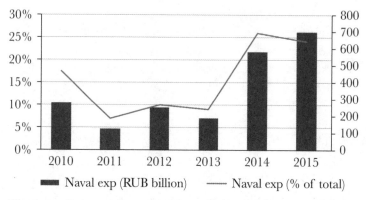

Figure 5.5 Estimated share of naval spending in total Ministry of Defence spending, 2010–15 (constant 2015 roubles).

For illustrative purposes, it is useful to consider the navy's share of reported expenditure in 2015 (i.e. expenditure that took place in 2014). If we proceed on the assumption that GOZ funding totalled 1.2 trillion roubles in 2014 (which in the UN data are reported as 2015), then we might reasonably expect that 25 per cent of that figure (i.e. around 300 billion roubles) was spent on naval procurement (including R&D and repairs), or just under half of all naval expenditure. This would leave a residual of around 400 billion roubles for 2014 that would cover other non-procurement naval expenditure. In 2014, total military expenditure amounted to 3.2 trillion roubles. This would mean that the navy accounted for nearly one quarter (22 per cent) of all military expenditure. Given that this took place at a time when the navy was considered to have been assigned a high priority by the political leadership, we might expect this 22 per cent share to represent an upper bound of naval expenditure.

After 2014, and as naval procurement faced a number of obstacles that prevented the timely delivery of combat vessels, the share of procurement funding allocated to the navy was reportedly reduced. As such, it is reasonable to assume that an average of around 20 per cent of Russian military expenditure will have been

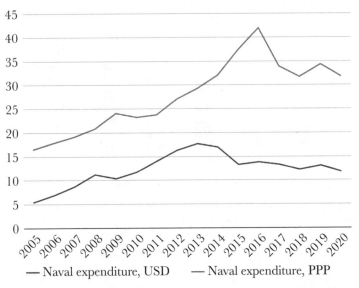

Figure 5.6 Naval expenditure at market exchange rates and PPP exchange rates, 2005–20 (USD bn, current).

allocated to the navy since then. Figure 5.6 shows what this rough approximation of naval spending amounts to in US dollars (at market exchange rates) and PPP. Expressed at market exchange rates, naval expenditure averaged around $13 billion between 2015 and 2020. At PPP, this figure is much higher: averaging $35 billion over the same period. Assuming that the navy was allocated 20 per cent of the procurement budget over the same period, expenditure on shipbuilding, repair and maintenance, and R&D averaged around 300 billion roubles, or $5 billion at market exchange rates and $12.5 billion at PPP. But this could well be an underestimate. In 2020, the CEO of OSK, Alexei Rakhmanov, revealed that OSK generated 450 billion roubles in revenues from Ministry of Defence orders in 2019, a sum that is plausible given that four large warships were laid down in April 2019. Given that OSK accounts for the vast majority, but not all, of Russian naval shipbuilding capacity, this would suggest that total naval procurement in 2019 may have been in the region of 500 billion roubles once orders for other shipbuilders like Tatarstan-based Ak Bars are taken into account.[22]

Measured at PPP, Russian naval expenditure is likely to be the third or fourth highest in the world. This fact alone makes Russia a serious naval power. However, these funds are spread thin. The navy maintains four fleets and a flotilla, including an expensive component of Russia's strategic nuclear deterrent in the form of at least nine nuclear-powered ballistic missile submarines (SSBNs). According to IISS's annual *Military Balance*, the navy employs around 150,000 personnel, as well an additional 31,000 personnel in naval aviation, along with around two hundred fixed-wing combat aircraft and a substantial helicopter fleet.[23] As noted above, these forces are augmented by FSB Border Guard forces. Nevertheless, that the Russian Navy inevitably faces resource constraints due to its wide range of responsibilities should not detract from the fact that Russia is now a naval power of global importance when measured by the volume of financial resources available.

Demand for Russian civilian shipbuilding

Spending on non-naval platforms is much lower, although due to the Russian state's ambitions to develop the NSR and a desire to increase production of vessels used in the oil and gas industry, expenditure is rising at a robust rate. While no overall figure for civilian maritime construction is available, it is possible to reach a rough approximation of the volume of activity in this sphere by examining output in OSK, discussed in more depth below, which accounts for the vast majority of shipbuilding in Russia. In 2020, Rakhmanov, the CEO of OSK, revealed that OSK generated total revenues of 510 billion roubles ($7 billion at average market exchange rates in 2019; $16.8 billion at PPP). Orders for non-military vessels accounted for a mere 17 per cent of this total, amounting to 87 billion roubles ($1.3 billion at average market exchange rates in 2019; $3.3 billion at PPP).

The bulk of the civilian income is likely to be derived from the construction of the Arktika-class nuclear-powered icebreakers (Project 22220) and the Viktor Chernomyrdin-class diesel-electric icebreaker (Project 22600), all at the Baltic Shipyard (Baltzavod) in St Petersburg. These orders were placed by Rosatomflot, a subsidiary of Rosatom, which operates the world's only nuclear-powered icebreaker fleet. A steady flow of new icebreakers is scheduled to take place over the next decade as Soviet-era vessels are replaced with newer and larger vessels. The new icebreakers will play a vital role in Russia's ambitions to exploit the transit potential of the NSR.

The bulk of Russia's civilian fleet is operated by Sovcomflot. Founded in 1988, Sovcomflot is a state-owned entity and is Russia's largest shipping company. The company's fleet (owned and chartered) is concerned principally with the transportation of oil and gas from regions with challenging ice conditions. It also operates ships engaged in seismic offshore exploration. In 2020, it operated over 145 vessels with a combined deadweight of 12.6 million tonnes, with over half of its vessels having an ice class.[24] The company services large-scale energy projects in Russia and abroad, including Yamal LNG, Sakhalin-1, Sakhalin-2, Prirazlomnoye, Novy Port, Varandey, and Tangguh. Although Sovcomflot provides a substantial volume of demand for oil and gas transportation vessels, very few are built in Russia. Of the 145 vessels operated by Sovcomflot, less than 10 per cent were built in Russia, all at Admiralty Shipyards in St Petersburg (part of OSK).

Increasing the share of domestically produced ships in the fleets operated by Sovcomflot, as well as the large oil and gas companies like Rosneft, Gazprom, and Novatek, has been a political priority since 2015.[25] Because OSK has proven unable to meet the requirements of Russian shipping companies, an ambitious plan was formulated to develop the shipbuilding industry in Russia's Far East, at the Zvezda complex at Bol'shoi Kamen', near Vladivostok.[26] At an estimated initial cost of around 200 billion roubles (around \$3.3 billion at the exchange rate in October 2022), it is hoped that Zvezda will manufacture oil and gas transportation ships, as well as offshore equipment, that will be used to develop Russia's Arctic natural resources and to service the emerging NSR.[27] Initially, only Rosneft – the major stakeholder in Zvezda – signalled any real appetite for acquiring vessels made at the shipyard. But determined lobbying by Igor Sechin, Rosneft's CEO, led to the personal intervention of Vladimir Putin, which prompted other carriers to place orders with Zvezda.[28]

It is instructive that the majority of new orders placed by Sovcomflot, which had previously relied overwhelmingly on foreign ships, are for ships built at Zvezda.[29] Promoting the domestic shipbuilding industry has, however, come at a cost. It was reported that the ships built at Zvezda will be a third more expensive than those built in South Korea. As a result, the Russian state has resorted to subsidising activity at Zvezda to compensate domestic buyers.[30] Zvezda, and other Russian shipbuilders, received extra protection from foreign competition when import substitution legislation was enacted that demanded only Russian-made vessels could traverse the NSR.[31] As Russia's oil and gas transportation demands grow larger with the exploitation of LNG facilities and the giant Vostok oil project in the Arctic, the opportunities for Russian shipyards to meet this demand will rise. As is the case with naval construction, there is sufficient demand to keep Russian shipyards busy for years to come. But whether domestic producers are able to meet this demand is less clear.

The industrial basis of Russian maritime power

A common argument made in relation to the Russian Navy is that a lack of funds has prevented fleet modernisation. But, as illustrated above, the volume of funding available to finance Russia's naval ambitions is substantial, so this argument is unsatisfactory. A steady flow of orders has been placed, and a large number of hulls have been laid down since 2011. Nearly every shipyard is operating at full capacity. Moscow initiated an ambitious shipbuilding programme with GPV 2020 in 2011, and generous funds were allocated to load the shipbuilding industry with a large number of orders. It was hoped this injection of cash would kickstart the modernisation of the Russian Navy. Instead, therefore, the key problem lies in the fact that it has taken much longer than officials would like to build naval vessels.

In practical terms, these ambitious plans proved unrealistic. A combination of factors – including the strict demands of building new designs, obsolete production facilities, and an ageing workforce, plus the imposition of Western and Ukrainian sanctions in 2014 – caused progress in warship construction to be much slower than Russian officials had envisaged. Nevertheless, plans to reinvigorate the fleet remain in place, and Russia's shipyards are operating, as noted, at close to full capacity.

What kind of navy is Russia building?

To get a sense for what type of navy the Russian leadership wants to build, it is important to examine the main points made in two key official documents: the Maritime Doctrine (2022) and the State Naval Policy (2017).[32] Together, the two documents reveal the nature of Russia's maritime interests and the capabilities required to defend those interests.

In general, the mission for the Russian Navy is focused on the seas closer to Russia's shores. Russia's system of political economy, based on the export of natural resources and food, has made the sea even more important to Russia than ever. These geo-economic interests mean that the Arctic, the Middle East, and other natural resource-rich regions are identified as maritime zones of strategic importance to Russia, as is the ability to ensure that these resources are safely transported to foreign markets. The NSR and the role it may play in future global trade also prominently features.

To be sure, official documents and statements stress the need for Russia to remain a "great sea power", because a strong navy is required to secure Russia's position as a leading power in a multipolar order. As a result, projecting a presence across the world's oceans is presented as important to Russia's status as a "great power". Yet the emphasis in both documents is weighted towards the protection of geo-economic interests closer to Russia (i.e. the Arctic, the Black Sea, and the Mediterranean). The need to maintain a large blue-water fleet is less urgent. Because Russia's interests lie closer to home, the Russian Navy does not need to be as large as its Soviet-era predecessor, or as large as the modern US or Chinese navies.

Additionally, the navy performs more traditional military functions. While previous naval policy documents emphasised the strategic nuclear deterrence mission, recent statements place greater emphasis on conventional deterrence. This is primarily due to advances made in the development and deployment of long-range precision missiles over the 2010s and early 2020s.

The development of these new capabilities means that in some important areas, the lines between green and blue-water navies are increasingly blurred. For example, during the Soviet era, the largest cruisers could not conduct land-attack strikes ("sea on shore"). Today, even small missile ships displacing up to 800 tons (e.g. the Karakurt- and Buyan M-class vessels) can carry out long-range missile strikes on land targets. As a result, the Russian Navy is emerging as a force that can perform a wider range of missions than it could in the past, and all without building large ocean-going surface vessels.

Together, the statement of interests and capabilities contained in official documents signals the need to: (1) build modern, multirole vessels for use in Russia's littoral waters; (2) upgrade the fleet of icebreakers to facilitate the increase in transit volume across the Arctic; (3) equip as many ships as possible with flexible long-range missile systems suitable for both land-attack and anti-ship missions; and (4) modernise the sea-based nuclear deterrent force. The need to develop a mix of civilian and military vessels is reiterated in Russia's shipbuilding strategy, which also emphasises the need to increase domestic production of vessels and components ("import substitution"), to modernise the production base of industry and to use modular production processes and designs, and to improve the efficiency of the shipbuilding system.[33]

The organisation of Russian shipbuilding

The vast majority of shipbuilding enterprises – ranging from design bureaus to shipyards and repair centres – are owned by the state-owned industrial giant, OSK. OSK was formed in 2007 to bring order to what had become an underfunded and disorganised industry after the collapse of the Soviet Union. Today, most major shipyards are owned by OSK. There are nevertheless several notable examples of shipyards operating outside the OSK umbrella, including the Zelenodolsk Shipyard and Design Bureau near Kazan (Tatarstan), and the Zvezda complex in Bolshoi' Kamen', near Vladivostok.

The facilities under the control of OSK are organised along geographic lines, with four regional clusters of facilities.

The Western Centre for Shipbuilding

Major facilities include:
- Yantar, Kaliningrad;
- Admiralty Shipyards, St Petersburg;
- Sredne-Nevsky Shipbuilding Plant, St Petersburg;
- Severnaya Verf' Shipyard, St Petersburg;
- Pella Shipyard, St Petersburg;
- Baltic Shipyard (Baltzavod), St Petersburg.

The Northern Centre for Shipbuilding and Ship Repair
Major facilities include:
- Northern Machine-Building Enterprise (Sevmash), Severodvinsk;
- Zvyozdochka Ship Repair Centre, Severodvinsk.

The Far Eastern Centre for Shipbuilding and Ship Repair
Major facilities include:
- Amur Shipyard, Komsomolsk-on-Amur;
- Far Eastern Ship Repair Centre (Dalzavod), Vladivostok.

The Southern Centre for Shipbuilding and Ship Repair
In contrast to the rest of the country, the most important production facilities in the Southern cluster are not contained within OSK structures but are instead either privately owned or owned by regional authorities. This is a legacy of the greater degree of regional autonomy enjoyed by Tatarstan as well as the fact that Crimean enterprises have only recently (after 2014) been formally absorbed within the Russian shipbuilding industry. The most important are:

- Zaliv Shipyard, Crimea;
- Zelenodolsk, Tatarstan;
- Morye Shipyard, Crimea.[34]

As many as one hundred thousand people are employed across this vast network of facilities in four regions, enabling Russia to produce a wide range of vessels, including nuclear-powered and diesel-electric submarines, frigates, nuclear-powered icebreakers, small missile ships, and a large number of patrol and auxiliary vessels. In the past, the degree of coordination between the shipbuilding industry on the one hand, and the state on the other (i.e. the Ministry of Defence and the Admiralty), has not always been close, resulting in vessels being produced that suited the preferences of constructors rather than the navy.

147

But in 2020, in an apparent effort to improve coordination between OSK and state, OSK announced plans to relocate its headquarters from Moscow to St Petersburg.[35] If, as is likely, the recently created Centre for the Management of Shipbuilding, Modernisation, and Repair of Warships and Ships of the Russian Navy is also located in St Petersburg, closer coordination between the most important organisations in Russian shipbuilding should be possible. This move should result in a closer alignment of preferences between manufacturers and the navy. The appointment of former commander-in-chief of the Russian Navy, Vladimir Korolyov, to OSK in 2019 offered a further sign of the desire to produce greater alignment between producer and customer.[36]

Capacity and production loads across major shipyards

To illustrate the scale of the naval construction programme, it is worth examining the manufacturing schedule within each of Russia's largest military shipyards. In doing so, it is evident that each is operating at or close to full capacity, confirming that financial constraints are not holding back naval modernisation. Instead, slow build times is a chronic problem across the industry.

The Western Centre for Shipbuilding

The Western Centre for Shipbuilding is the largest cluster of facilities in the Russian shipbuilding industry. Most facilities are based in or near St Petersburg, except for Yantar shipyard, which is based in Kaliningrad. Yantar (Table 5.1) comprises two construction sites – one at Yantar and the other at Petrel – and has capacity to build up to five vessels with launch weights of up to 12,000 tons. During the Soviet period, it built ships of the Udaloy class (Project 1155) as well as a range of other frigate- and destroyer-sized vessels. Three vessels of the Ivan Gren-class amphibious landing craft are currently under construction. The other two remaining

Table 5.1   Principal vessels under construction at Yantar, April 2021

Type	Laid down	Launched	Official estimated commission date
Ivan Gren-class (Project 11711/M)			
– *Pyotr Morgunov*	June 2015	May 2018	2020
– *Vladimir Andreyev* (Pr. 11711M)	April 2019	–	2023
– *Vasily Trushin* (Pr. 11711M)	April 2019	–	2024

Source: Author's calculations from Russian media reports.

construction sites are occupied by Admiral Grigorovich-class frigates, which are currently scheduled to be delivered to India, where they will be fitted with Ukrainian power units. Yantar is currently operating at full capacity. It is not known what, if any, future orders will be placed for ships produced at the facility.

Baltic Shipyard (Baltzavod) has three construction sites – two slipways and a boathouse – as well as a deep-sea outfitting embankment. The slipway "A" is the largest in Russia (length of 350 meters), with capacity to launch ships with a deadweight of up to 100,000 tons. In practice, Baltzavod has capacity to work on two very large hulls simultaneously. Four ships have been launched in the past four years and remain at varying stages of construction. None is a combat ship. Instead, Baltzavod is at the centre of Russian efforts to modernise its icebreaker fleet (Table 5.2). The *Yakutiya* was laid down in May 2020, and the *Chukotka* is scheduled to be laid down in May 2021. As a result, the construction sites are fully occupied, and no further vessels can be laid down until one of the two is launched.

Severnaya Verf' (Northern Shipyard) is the only shipyard that is currently building frigates from the Admiral Gorshkov series (Table 5.3). The existing slipways are able to support the construction of vessels up to a maximum of 170 metres in length and

Table 5.2 Principal vessels under construction at Baltzavod, April 2021

Type	Laid down	Launched	Official estimated commission date
Arktika-class nuclear-powered icebreakers (Project 22200)			
– *Arktika*	November 2013	June 2016	2020
– *Sibir*	May 2015	September 2017	2021
– *Ural*	July 2016	May 2019	2022
– *Yakutiya*	May 2020	–	2024
– *Chukotka*	December 2020	–	2026
Viktor Chernomyrdin-class diesel-electric icebreaker (Project 22600)			
Viktor Chernomyrdin	October 2012	December 2016	2020

Source: Author's calculations from Russian media reports.

Table 5.3   Large surface vessels under construction at Severnaya Verf, April 2021

Type	Laid down	Launched	Official estimated commission date
Admiral Gorshkov-class (Project 22350)			
– *Admiral Golovko*	February 2012	May 2020	2023
– *Admiral Isakov*	November 2013	–	2024
– *Admiral Amelko*	April 2019	–	2024
– *Admiral Chichagov*	April 2019	–	2025
– *Admiral Yumashev*	July 2020	–	2026
– *Admiral Spiridonov*	July 2020	–	2026
Stereguschchiy-class (Project 20380)			
– *Merkuriy*	February 2015	March 2020	2023
– *Strogiy*	February 2015	–	2023
Gremyashchiy-class (Project 20385)			
– *Provornyy*	July 2013	September 2019	2024
Merkuriy-class (Project 20386)			
– *Merkuriy*	October 2016	March 2021	2025

Source: Author's calculations from Russian media reports.

20 metres in breadth. The Russian practice of placing one to two ships on each slipway means that it currently has capacity to build simultaneously a maximum of six to eight ships of the Project 20380 (Stereguschchiy-class) size or larger. Work is underway on a new construction hall that will, once complete, enable the yard to build ships of the Project 22350M class ("Super Gorshkov"). Two further Project 22350 vessels were laid down in 2020. As a result, Severnaya Verf' will be operating at full capacity until the new construction hall is built.[37] This is likely to be in 2023 at the earliest.[38]

Admiralty Shipyard currently has capacity to build two large vessels (up to 70,000 tons) on two open sloping slipways, and a further seven smaller vessels (up to 10,000 tons) in covered berths.

Table 5.4   *Principal vessels under construction at Admiralty Shipyard, April 2021*

Type	Laid down (* est.)	Launched (* est.)	Official estimated commission date
Arktika-class (Project 23550)			
– *Ivan Papanin*	April 2017	October 2019	2023
– *Nikolay Zubov*	November 2019	October 2023*	2024
Lada-class (Project 677)			
– *Kronshtadt*	July 2005	September 2018	2023
– *Velikiye Luki*	November 2006		2023
Varshavyanka-class (Project 636.3)			
– *Ufa*	November 2019	2021*	2022
– *Magadan*	November 2019	2021*	2021
– *Mozhaisk*	2020*	2021*	2023
– *Yakutsk*	2020*	2022*	2024

Source: Author's calculations from Russian media reports.

For most of the post-Soviet period, the shipyard used the large construction sites to build tankers for Sovcomflot. However, both berths are now occupied by two Project 23550 Arctic patrol ships (Table 5.4). These are unlikely to become available for new hulls until the mid-2020s. The seven smaller sites are currently being used to build Lada- and Varshavyanka-class submarines. The average build time for the Varshavyanka-class vessels is around two to three years. As such, while Admiralty is currently operating at close to capacity, it ought to be able to lay down more submarines in the near future, if required. In 2019, it was announced by OSK that a contract has been signed to build a further two Lada-class submarines.[39] However, the hulls have yet to be laid down.

After undergoing substantial modernisation between 2016 and 2018, Srednye Nevsky Shipyard is capable of simultaneously building up to four vessels with a launch weight of up to 2,700 tons. Work is currently underway on four Alexandrit-class (Project 12700)

Table 5.5   Principal vessels under construction at Srednye Nevsky Shipyard, April 2021

Type	Laid down	Launched (* est.)	Official estimated commission date
Alexandrit-class (Project 12700)			
– *Georgyi Kurbatov* (fire damaged 2016)	April 2015	June 2020*	2021
– *Piotr Ilyichev*	July 2018	December 2020	2022
– *Anatoly Shlemov*	July 2019		2022
– *Lev Chernavin*	July 2020		2023

Source: Author's calculations from Russian media reports.

minesweepers (Table 5.5). After making a breakthrough in the use of digital production technologies, as well as a high-tech monolithic fibreglass hull, the average build time is declining. A second stage of modernisation of the production facilities is underway. Once complete, officials believe the shipyard will be able to deliver three Project 12700 vessels per year.

Pella Shipyard specialises in the construction of smaller vessels, including tugboats, research vessels, and patrol ships. It is currently building two ships of the Karakurt class and is fitting out hulls from the same series launched from other shipyards in Russia (Table 5.6). After its production facilities were modernised and expanded over the past decade, Pella has the potential to increase production of Karakurt-class vessels.

The Northern Centre for Shipbuilding and Ship Repair

New construction of vessels in the Northern Centre for Shipbuilding and Ship Repair is concentrated in the Northern Machine-Building Enterprise, or Sevmash, as it is more commonly known. Sevmash is the only facility that produces nuclear-powered submarines (during the Soviet period, Amur Shipyard also built nuclear-powered submarines). It is a huge facility, employing over

Table 5.6   Vessels under construction at Pella, April 2021

Type	Laid down	Launched	Official estimated commission date
Karakurt-class (Project 22800)			
– *Odintsovo* (ex-*Shkval*)	July 2016	May 2018	2020
– *Burya*	December 2016	October 2018	2023

Source: Author's calculations from Russian media reports.

thirty thousand staff. At full capacity, Sevmash is capable of producing up to fourteen large, nuclear-powered submarines. It also functions as a repair facility for large, nuclear-powered vessels.

Sevmash is currently operating at close to capacity (Table 5.7). There are eight submarines that have yet to be launched, with a further five vessels still under construction after being launched. In addition, Sevmash is undertaking the deep refurbishment of the Admiral Nakhimov-class (Project 1144) cruiser and is expected to begin a less extensive refurbishment of *Pyotr Veliky*. Extra capacity will only be available as more ships are launched in the future. Average build time is currently around seven to eight years. Sevmash has introduced a number of new manufacturing processes and is expanding the use of digital production techniques. These are intended to result in a reduction in average build times in the future. Build time is the most important constraint on nuclear-powered submarine production.

The Far Eastern Centre for Shipbuilding and Ship Repair

Ship building in the Far East suffered particularly badly from the absence of orders and investment after the collapse of the Soviet Union. As a result, the most important warship construction facility – Amur Shipyard – remains in very poor shape. After producing a large volume of submarines and surface vessels during the

Table 5.7   Principal vessels under construction at Sevmash, April 2021

Type	Laid down (* est.)	Launched (* est.)	Official estimated commission date
Borei-class SSBN (Project 955A)			
– *Knyaz' Oleg*	July 2014	July 2020	2021
– *Generalissimus Suvorov*	December 2014	2021	2022
– *Imperator Alexsandr III*	December 2015	–	2023
– *Knyaz' Pozharsky*	December 2016	–	2024
– *Knyaz Potemkin*	May 2020*	–	2028
– *Dmitri Donskoy*	May 2020*	–	2029
Yasen-class (Project 885M)			
– *Kazan*	July 2009	March 2017	2021
– *Novosibirsk*	July 2013	December	2021
– *Krasnoyarsk*	July 2014	2021	2023
– *Arkhangel'sk*	March 2015	2023*	2023
– *Perm'*	July 2016	–	2024
– *Ul'yanovsk*	July 2017	–	2025
– *Voronezh*	July 2020	–	2027
– *Vladivostok*	July 2020	–	2028
Special Purpose-class (Project 09851)			
– *Khabarovsk*	July 2014	April 2019	2024
Special Purpose-class (Project 09852)			
– *Belgorod*	December 2012	April 2019	2022

Source: Author's calculations from Russian media reports.

Soviet period, it did not build a warship between 1994 and 2006. Two classes of surface vessels are currently under construction. Although there is capacity at Amur to build larger and more vessels, the poor state of the physical and human capital means that its current workload is as much as the yard can produce (Table 5.8). A modernisation effort is underway, and orders have been placed by the Ministry of Defence to ensure that Amur will enjoy a stable and predictable income to justify the investment in new facilities.

Table 5.8   Principal vessels under construction at Amur, April 2021

Type	Laid down (* est.)	Launched (* est.)	Official estimated commission date
Stereguschchiy-class (Project 20380)			
– *Aldar Tsydenzhapov*	July 2015	September 2019	2020
– *Rezkiy*	July 2016	July 2021	2023
Karakurt-class (Project 22800)			
– *Rzhev*	July 2023*	–	2023
– *Udomlya*	July 2023*	–	2023
– *Ussuriysk*	December 2019	–	2024
– *Pavlovsk*	July 2020	–	2024

Source: Author's calculations from Russian media reports.

Shipbuilding in the south of Russia

The first three clusters examined above are part of the OSK structure. Shipbuilding in Russia's south, by contrast, is not all owned by OSK. Ak Bars, based in Kazan, is a major actor in this area. As in the Far East, shipbuilding in the south suffered from a lack of orders and investment after the collapse of the Soviet Union. The largest warship construction facility – Zaliv Shipyard – has not built a large warship since the 1980s. While part of Ukraine, Zaliv built only commercial vessels. Investment in the production facilities at Zaliv and other southern yards since 2015 has increased production capacity and improved some of the facilities (Tables 5.9–5.11). Nevertheless, given the low level of experience in building large warships at Crimean shipyards, it is likely that average build times will be longer at Zaliv and Morye than in other shipyards across Russia.

Problems in Russian shipbuilding

The Russian shipbuilding programme was afflicted with a number of serious problems throughout the 1990s and the 2000s,

Table 5.9   Principal vessels under construction at Zaliv, April 2021

Type	Laid down	Launched (* est.)	Official estimated commission date
New UDK-class (Project 23900)			
– *Sevastopol*	July 2020	–	2026
– *Vladivostok*	Jul 2020	–	2027
Vasily Bykov-class (Project 22160)			
– *Sergey Kotov*	May 2016	February 2021	2022
Karakurt-class (Project 22800)			
– *Tsiklon*	July 2016	July 2020	2023
– *Askold*	November 2016	September 2021	2023
– *Amur*	July 2017	2023*	2024

Source: Author's calculations from Russian media reports.

Table 5.10   Principal vessels laid down and launched at Morye (fitted out at Pella), April 2021

Type	Laid down	Launched	Official estimated commission date
Karakurt-class (Project 22800)			
– *Kozelsk* (ex-*Shtorm*)	May 2016	October 2019	2023
– *Okhotsk*	March 2017	October 2019	2023
– *Vikhr*	December 2017	November 2019	2023

Source: Author's calculations from Russian media reports.

including a lack of funding; outdated shipbuilding practices; the proliferation of types within classes; the inability to serialise production; and weaknesses in the supply chain of new weapon and electronic systems. The increase of funding for the navy that came with the launch of GPV 2020 did revitalise parts of the

Table 5.11   *Principal vessels under construction at Zelenodolsk, April 2021*

Type	Laid down	Launched	Official estimated commission date
Karakurt-class (Project 22800)			
– *Tucha*	February 2019		2024
– *Taifun*	September 2019		2024
Vasily Bykov-class (Project 22160)			
– *Viktor Veliky*	November 2016	April 2021	2023
– *Nikolai Sepyagin*	January 2018		2023
Buyan M-class (Project 21631)			
– *Graivoron*	April 2015	2020	2021
– *Grad*	April 2017	2020	2022
– *Naro-Fominsk*	February 2018		2023
– *Stavropol*	July 2018		2023

Source: Author's calculations from Russian media reports.

shipbuilding industry. It was envisaged that over fifty new surface vessels and twenty-four submarines would be built by 2020. While a significant number of hulls were laid down, the weaknesses of the shipbuilding industry outlined above, and the impact of Western and Ukrainian sanctions, caused progress to be slower than originally anticipated. These problems were particularly evident in the construction of warships displacing more than 2,500 tonnes.[40]

According to the Russian naval expert Maxim Shepovalenko, the increased funds allocated to naval construction under GPV 2020 were inefficiently used.[41] He calculated that between 2013 and 2017, the shipbuilding industry produced fourteen units with a total tonnage of 127,000 tonnes. By contrast, over the same period China produced thirty-seven units with a total tonnage of 238,600 tonnes and the United States twenty-four units with a total tonnage of 372,000 tonnes. Shepovalenko also noted that Russian shipyards took two to three times longer than foreign yards to produce vessels of frigate size and above. While some of these problems are normal when introducing new designs, the generally poor state of Russian shipyards, many of which were indebted and in need of new investment, was an important factor.

To address these problems, officials from the shipbuilding industry and the Ministry of Defence proposed reducing the cost of borrowing for enterprises in the industry and restructuring OSK's debts that were allegedly accumulated by enterprises before they were taken over by OSK in 2007.[42] It was hoped that this restructuring of debt would result in more internal funds being made available to increase investment in new production facilities and machinery.[43]

One key objective for the modernisation of production within the industry is to create the "Digital Shipyard", a plan to create a digital, synchronised body of information that encompasses the entire supply chain, and builds into what has been called a 'single version of the truth' that governs everything from concept, design, and construction, to upgrades and modifications throughout a vessel's in-service life. Russian shipyards have to date generally lagged Western competitors in the role played by digital processes. But more investment has taken place in the 2010s and early 2020s. One tangible outcome of this investment was the use of digital processes in the successful development of the Alexandrit-class (Project 12700) minesweeper at Srednye-Nevsky shipyard.

Other important weaknesses remain. Russian docks – floating and fixed – are old and, in the case of floating docks, increasingly accident prone. Several accidents involving Soviet-era floating docks – usually imported from Europe in the 1970s and 1980s – have occurred in recent years. The most high-profile case took place in 2018 when PD-50, the Russian Navy's largest floating dry dock at the time, sunk at the 82nd Shipbuilding Plant at Roslyakovo near Murmansk after an electrical malfunction caused its ballast tanks to remain jammed in the open position. Despite a glaring need to modernise docks across the country, foreign-produced docks continue to prove more attractive than those manufactured by Russian firms. In April 2021, an important contract to build a 200-metre-long dry dock for the construction of nuclear-powered icebreakers, such as the Project 22220 Arktika-class vessels, was awarded to a Turkish firm, Kuzey Star Shipyard.[44] Reports suggest that Russian shipyards were ruled out early on by Rosatom on the basis of excessive cost, an inability to meet the stipulated build time, and because Western sanctions on the OSK might delay the supply of key components.

Implications for the future of the Russian Navy

A lack of funds is not the main problem for Russian shipbuilding. A large number of hulls have been laid down since 2011. Nearly every shipyard is operating at full capacity. The key problem is that it has taken much longer to build vessels than was originally planned. This has been due to a combination of reasons, including the standard problems associated with introducing new designs, systems, and production processes; the impact of sanctions and the breakdown of defence-industrial relations with Ukraine; and an outdated production base and workforce. The Russian authorities have taken action to deal with these problems. Investment in shipyards has risen. New production processes are being introduced. And, most importantly, shipyards are overcoming the technical challenges associated with building the lead units of new classes of warship.

What will the likely trajectory of ship construction mean for the Russian Navy in the 2020s? First, despite the weaknesses identified here in Russian shipbuilding, a substantial number of ships is likely to enter service by the middle of the decade. Second, while the quantity of deliveries will probably be the third highest in the world (behind the United States and China) over this period, the composition of those ships will be imbalanced. Larger surface vessels – such as frigates and the new helicopter carriers – are likely to be slower to reach the navy. But submarines and smaller surface vessels – all capable of carrying long-range missiles – are reaching the navy in significant quantities. Finally, the sea-based nuclear deterrent force should be overhauled by the middle of the decade. Crucially, the current shipbuilding programme is largely consistent with the strategic objectives outlined in official statements of Russia's maritime interests.

Conclusion

Russia's maritime interests are growing. This is a result of several trends, including the desire to develop Russia's Arctic resource base and expand the NSR; the economic and political pivot to Asia, which is already underway and is causing the volume of sea-based trade to rise sharply; the annexation and subsequent militarisation of the Crimean Peninsula; and Russia's military involvement in the Middle East. All these trends look set to continue. As these interests grow, greater effort is being made to develop capabilities commensurate with its interests. Sea power – defined to encompass military and non-military dimensions – is a significant component of Russia's wider strategy and is likely to rise in importance.

The sea is seen as vital to domestic industrial and regional development. To develop Russia's Arctic and offshore natural resource base, huge investment is being made in Russia's domestic shipbuilding industry and in building capabilities to extract and transport oil and gas. Infrastructure to support the export of grain and other agricultural products is also growing. These investments are seen as key to regional development in Russia's Far East and High North. As a result, policymakers in Russia acknowledge the importance of developing and then maintaining modern maritime capabilities, including, but not limited to, a capable navy. This emphasis on broad-based maritime interests and capabilities makes Russia's approach to sea power "neo-Gorshkovian" in nature; in other words, it is an expression of Russia's multidimensional interests in the sea.[45]

To date, ambitions to develop Russia's maritime capabilities have been, to some degree, constrained by domestic shipbuilding limitations, both military and civilian. As a result, progress has been slower than policymakers would have liked. Nevertheless, important strengths remain, including in the construction of submarines, small surface warships, and icebreakers. Investment in new shipyards, the modernisation of older shipyards, and the development of new classes of civilian and military ships and naval technologies are all underway. While it is true that significant economic and industrial obstacles to the development of maritime capabilities have been encountered, the determination of policymakers to overcome these difficulties remains strong. The war in Ukraine and the impact of Western sanctions are unlikely to change this. If anything, the elevated state of tensions with an expanded NATO will make it easier for Russia's leadership to justify even higher levels of military expenditure. Consequently, we should expect further progress to be made in the near future.

The Russian Navy is also growing in capability, despite encountering well-documented shortcomings in warship construction. While Russia's naval capabilities are uneven – manifested in the form of a dual fleet comprising larger, Soviet-era vessels undertaking the bulk of blue-water tasks, alongside a newer but smaller fleet of corvettes and small frigates operating closer to shore – the development and wide-scale deployment of long-range missiles is compensating for this imbalance. For example, the ability of smaller ships to conduct "fleet on shore" non-nuclear strike missions is much greater than during the Soviet period, as frequently shown during the war in Ukraine. As industrial constraints are overcome, the weight of Russia's growing maritime interests means that Russia is likely to grow as a sea power. By the middle of the 2030s, we should expect to see a confident, capable, and competitive actor in large parts of the world's oceans, including the Arctic, the Atlantic, the

Indo-Pacific, as well as seas closer to Russia's borders, such as the Baltic, Black, and Caspian Seas. As a result of these trends, maritime and naval capabilities are seen as important instruments to be used in support of achieving Russia's wider strategic objectives.

Notes

1 See, for example: Ukaz of the President of the Russian Federation, 'O strategii ekonomicheskoi bezopasnosti Rossiiskoi Federatsii na period do 2030' [On the strategy for the economic security of the Russian Federation in the period to 2030], 2017, http://publication,pravo.gov. ru/Documents/View/0001201705150001 (no longer active); Ministry of Energy of the Russian Federation, *Energeticheskaya Strategiya Rossiĭskoĭ Federatsii na period do 2035 goda* [Energy strategy of the Russian Federation for the period up to 2035]. Moscow: Ministry of Energy, 2020, https:// minenergo.gov.ru/node/1920 (no longer active).

2 World Bank Development Indicators Database, 2021.

3 World Trade Centre, 2021.

4 N. Mehdiyeva, 'Review of the Document Development Strategy of State Corporation Rosatom to 2030 [Strategiya razvitiya "GK" Rosatom do 2030 goda]', *NATO Defense College Russia Studies Review*, Vol. 3, No. 19 (2019), www. ndc.nato.int/research/research.php?icode=584 (accessed 8 October 2022).

5 A. Staalesen, 'It's an Order from the Kremlin: Shipping on Northern Sea Route to Reach 80 Million Tons by 2024', The Barents Observer, 15 May 2018, https://thebarentsobserver.com/en/arctic/2018/05/ its-order-kremlin-shipping-northern-sea-route-increase-80-million-tons-2024 (accessed 8 October 2022).

6 'Vladimir Putin podpisal Ukaz "Ob osnovakh gosudarstvennoy politiki Rossiyskoy Federatsii v Arktike na period do 2035 goda"' [Vladimir Putin signed the order 'State Policy of the Russian Federation in the Arctic to 2035'], Website of the Presidential Administration, 5 March 2020, http://static.kremlin.ru/media/events/files/ru/f8ZpjhpAaQoW B1zjywNo4OgKiI1mAvaM.pdf (accessed 8 October 2022). Also see E. Buchanan, 'The Overhaul of Russian Strategic Planning for the Arctic Zone to 2035', *NATO Defense College Russian Studies Series*, Vol. 3, No. 20 (19 May 2020), www.ndc.nato.int/research/research.php?icode=641# (accessed 8 October 2022).

7 Y. Gaidar, *Gibel' imperii: uroki dlya sovremenoi Rossii* [Fall of an empire: lessons for contemporary Russia]. Moscow: ROSSPEN, 2006; and S. Wegren, A. Nikulin, and I. Trotsuk, *Russia's Food Revolution: The Transformation of the System*. London and New York: Routledge, 2021.

8 N. Karlova, O. Shik, E. Serova, and R. Yanbykh, 'State-of-the-Art in Russian Agriculture: Production, Farm Structure, Trade, Policy and New Challenges', *Russian Analytical Digest*, 2021.

9 Ministerstvo sel'skogo khoziaistva Rossiiskoi Federatsii, 'Spravochnia informatsiia o rabote po otkrytiiu novykh rynkov po sostoianiiu na 18 Noiabria 2020 goda' [Background information on the work on opening new markets as of 18 November 2020], 23 November. https://mcx.gov. ru/ministry/departments/departament-informatsionnoy-politiki-i-spetsi alnykh-proektov/industry-information/info-otkrytie-zarubezhnykh-ryn kov-dlya-rossiyskoy-produktsii-apk (no longer active).

10 'Novorossiysk-Expansion and Deepening Project', Center for Strategic and International Studies, n.d., https://reconnectingasia.csis.org/data base/projects/novorossiysk-expansion-and-deepening-project/e6a10dc3-dbae-4127-b504-8c177df29485 (accessed 14 November 2022).

11 On China, see T. Yoshihara and J. Holmes, *Red Star over the Pacific*. Annapolis, MD: Naval Institute Press, 2019.

12 The processes relating to Russia's defence budget are described fully in J. Cooper, 'The Russian Budgetary Process and Defence: Finding the "Golden Mean"', *Post-Communist Economies*, Vol. 29, No. 4 (2017), pp. 476–90, www.tandfonline.com/doi/abs/10.1080/14631377.2017.1333 793 (accessed 8 October 2022).

13 For a discussion of dual-use FTsPs, see A. Nikolsky, 'Russian Defence and Dual-Use Technology Programs', *Moscow Defence Brief*, No. 5 (2015), pp. 18–20. Further details of all FTsPs can be found at: http://fcp.econ omy.gov.ru/cgi-bin/cis/fcp.cgi/Fcp/GosProgram/View/2014 (no longer active).

14 An alternative method using National Accounts data, available for only 2015–17, is outlined in O. Ageeva, I. Tkachev, and Y. Starostina, 'Sekretnaya chast' VVP dostigla 4,9 trln rub' [The secret part of GDP reached 4.9 trillion roubles], RBK, 28 August 2019, www.rbc.ru/econom ics/28/08/2019/5d5ff9129a79472cffd85d1a?from=from_main (accessed 8 October 2022).

15 'Predpriyatiya voyenno-promyshlennogo kompleksa nabrali kreditov na 2 trilliona rubley' [Defence-industrial enterprises accumulated 2 trillion roubles in debt], Krasnaya liniya, 21 October 2019, www.rline.tv/ news/2019-10-21-predpriyatiya-voenno-promyshlennogo-kompleksa-na brali-kreditov-na-2-trilliona-rubley (accessed 8 October 2022).

16 The methodological challenges associated with SGCs are discussed in R. Connolly, 'Russian Military Expenditure in Comparative Perspective: A Purchasing Power Parity Estimate', Centre for Naval Analyses Occasional Paper, Arlington, VA: Center for Naval Analyses, 2019.

17 IMF World Economic Outlook, October 2020, www.imf.org/en/Public ations/WEO/weo-database/2020/October/download-entire-database (accessed 8 October 2022).

18 The use of PPP exchange rates to measure military expenditure is not without limitations. They are not necessarily appropriate for comparing military output because they reflect the relative price of an average bundle of all goods and services produced in an economy, usually GDP, and not only military services. The cost of military goods and services could be higher or lower than the economy-wide average of goods and services. The rate of inflation for military goods and services might also differ from the economy-wide average, which might lead to further calculation errors.

19 www.un-arm.org/MilEx/CountryProfile.aspx?CountryId=163 (no longer active).

20 These issues are discussed in greater detail in J. Cooper, *Russia's Military Expenditure: Data and Measurement*. Stockholm: FOI, 2013, p. 39. It is important to note, however, that in Julian Cooper's opinion, the data refer specifically to expenditure by the Ministry of Defence, which in recent years has accounted for around half of total military expenditure.

21 Centre for the Analysis of Strategy and Technology, *Gosudarstvennye programmy vooruzheniia Rossiiskoi Federatsii: problemy ispolneniia i potentsial optimizatsii* [The state armaments program of the Russian Federation: problems of performance and optimisation]. Moscow: Tsentr analiza strategii i tekhnologii, 2015.

22 See 'Meeting with United Shipbuilding Corporation CEO Alexei Rakhmanov', Website of the Presidential Administration, 27 July 2020, http://en.kremlin.ru/events/president/news/63757 (accessed 8 October 2022).

23 IISS, *Military Balance 2020*. London: Routledge, 2020, pp. 199–200.

24 Sovcomflot website: www.scf-group.com/about/profile (accessed 8 October 2022).

25 R. Connolly, *Russia's Response to Sanctions*. Cambridge and New York: Cambridge University Press, 2018.

26 S. Fortescue, 'Zvezda: Shipyard of the Future or Soviet-style Black Hole?', Oxford, Changing Character of War Programme, 7 August 2019, www.ccw.ox.ac.uk/blog/2019/7/22/k3klcyyoaqaif36503w81kb47cyv5x (accessed 8 October 2022).

27 A. Vorobyev, 'Superverf "Zvezda" mozhet vervyye poluchit' subsidii' [Super shipyard 'Zvezda' might receive subsidies for the first time], *Vedomosti*, 24 October 2017, www.vedomosti.ru/business/articles/2017/10/24/739117-zvezda-subsidii (accessed 8 October 2022).

28 I. Safranov, 'Suda vazhneye suda' [Ships are more important than court], *Kommersant*, 17 November 2017, www.kommersant.ru/doc/3468887 (accessed 8 October 2022).

29 Full details of ships currently operated by Sovcomflot, as well as those under construction, are available at http://sovcomflot.ru/fleet/fleetlist (no longer active).

30 V. Petlevoi, 'Verf "Zvezda" mozhet pereyti s zarubezhnoy stali na Rossiyskuyu' [The Zvezda shipyard might go over to foreign steel], *Vedomosti*, 17 February 2019, www.vedomosti.ru/business/articles/2019/02/17/794352-verf-zvezda (accessed 8 October 2022).

31 A. Vorobyev, 'Chinovniki khotyat kontrolirovat' zakazy goskompaniy na inostrannykh verfyakh' [Officials want to regulate the orders of state companies at foreign shipyards], *Vedomosti*, 3 April 2016, www.vedomosti.ru/business/articles/2016/04/03/636228-kontrolirovat-zakazi-goskompanii (accessed 8 October 2022).

32 *Morskaya doktrina Rossiyskoy Federatsii* [Maritime doctrine of the Russian Federation], 2015, www.scrf.gov.ru/documents/18/34.html (no longer active); and 'Ukaz Prezidenta Rossiyskoy Federatsii ot 20.07.2017 № 327 Ob utverzhdenii Osnov gosudarstvennoy politiki Rossiyskoy Federatsii v oblasti voyenno-morskoy deyatel'nosti na period do 2030 goda' [Decree of the President of the Russian Federation of 20 July 2017 no. 327 on approval of the fundamentals of the state policy of the Russian Federation in the field of naval activities for the period until 2030]. Official Website of Law Ministry, 20 July 2017.

33 'Utverzhdena Strategiya razvitiya sudostroitel'noy promyshlennosti do 2035 goda' [Strategy for the development of the shipbuilding industry to 2035 approved]. Government of the Russian Federation, 29 October 2019, http://government.ru/docs/38218 (accessed 8 October 2022).

34 It was reported on 2 April 2020 that Morye was to be incorporated into OSK. No further details on the timing or nature of this transfer were made available. 'Yeshche odna krymskaya verf' popolnit sostav OSK' [Another Crimean shipyard will join OSK], Flotprom.ru, 2 April 2021, https://flotprom.ru/2021/%D0%9A%D1%80%D1%8B%D0%BC/C2 (accessed 8 October 2022).

35 'SMI raskryli detali pereyezda OSK v Peterburg' [The media have revealed the details of the move of OSK to St Petersburg], Flotprom.ru, 18 May 2020, https://flotprom.ru/2020/%CE%F1%EA10 (no longer active).

36 'Glava OSK nazval sferu otvetstvennosti eks-glavkoma VMF v korporatsii' [The head of the OSK names the responsibilities of the ex-head of the navy in the corporation], RBC, 6 June 2019, www.rbc.ru/rbcfreenews/5cf8d0709a79472686589704 (accessed 14 November 2022).

37   'OSK ispytyvayet defitsit stapel'nykh mest' [OSK is experiencing a short-age of slipways], Portnews, 4 November 2020, https://portnews.ru/ news/304221 (accessed 8 October 2022).

38   'Novyy elling "Severnoy verfi" poobeshchali vvesti v stroy v 2022 godu' [Severnaya Verf's new construction hall promised to be commissioned in 2022]. Flotprom.ru, 8 February 2021, https://flotprom.ru/2021/% D0%A1%D0%B5%D0%B2%D0%B5%D1%80%D0%BD%D0%B0% D1%8F%D0%92%D0%B5%D1%80%D1%84%D1%8C1 (accessed 8 October 2022).

39   'Dve podlodki proyekta "Lada" zalozhat ne ran'she 2022 goda' [Two Lada-class submarines will be laid down no earlier than 2022], TASS, 10 July 2019, https://tass.ru/armiya-i-opk/6650513 (accessed 8 October 2022).

40   A. Frolov, 'Svoy vmesto chuzhikh: importozameshcheniye v OPK Rossii; opyt 2014–2016 godov' [Russian instead of foreign: import substitution in Russia's military–industrial complex; the experience of 2014–16]. *Russia in Global Affairs*, No. 6 (November/December 2016).

41   M. Shepovalenko, 'Predvaritel'nyye itogi GPV-2020 v chasti voyennogo korablestroyeniya' [Preliminary results from the military shipbuilding part of GPV 2020]. *Eksport Vooruzheniy*, No. 1 (January–February 2018), pp. 9–15.

42   'Prezident OSK oboznachil tri problemy v tekushchey ekonomich-eskoy situatsii' [The president of OSK has outlined three problems in the current economic situation]. Korabel.ru, 22 April 2020, www.kora bel.ru/news/comments/prezident_osk_oboznachil_tri_problemy_v_tek uschey_ekonomicheskoy_situacii.html (accessed 8 October 2022).

43   'Plan finansovogo ozdorovleniya OSK odobrilo pravitel'stvo RF' [The Russian government has approved a financial rehabilitation plan for OSK]. Flotprom.ru, 15 May 2020, https://flotprom.ru/2020/Оск9 (no longer active).

44   A. Vedyenyeva, 'Atomnyye ledokoly naydut dok v Turtsii' [Nuclear ice-breakers to find a dock in Turkey]. *Kommersant*, 14 April 2021, www.kom mersant.ru/doc/4761020 (accessed 8 October 2022).

45   S. Gorshkov, *The Sea Power of the State*. Annapolis, MD: Naval Institute Press, 1979.

6

Russia's future naval capabilities

Dmitry Gorenburg

A new goal

Through the 2010s, the Russian Navy largely gave up its aspirations either to rebuild a replica of the Soviet Navy but with more modern ships and weapons, or to build a downscale version of the early twenty-first-century US Navy. Instead, in deeds if not always in words, the Russian Navy has focused on establishing itself as a capable green-water force with a primary focus on protecting its coastline and the naval component of its nuclear strategic deterrent. In addition, it has added a powerful conventional deterrent capability through the advent of a long-range land-attack cruise missile capability. By placing such missiles on small ships in enclosed seas, the Russian Navy can protect its strike assets while becoming a more potent regional threat that carries significant firepower and presents a range of offensive options despite the small size and low numbers of its platforms. This capability gives the Russian Navy the potential of being able to threaten US allies and NATO assets, thus making it a more potent regional threat with greater firepower and a range of offensive fires capabilities despite being mostly limited to smaller platforms. In the meantime, power projection is being concentrated in the submarine fleet, at least for the near to medium term. Prospects for a serious blue-water surface fleet are put off into the indefinite long term, as the navy focuses on more limited yet achievable objectives for the foreseeable future.

Post-Soviet innovations in precision-guided munitions, specifically tactical missile systems, are at the heart of Russia's naval modernisation. Moscow regards these systems – universal vertical launching systems armed with the latest anti-ship and land-attack cruise missiles – as potent force multipliers capable of offsetting Russian shortfalls in both the numbers and quality of ships in its fleets. As shown in Table 6.1, most new Russian combat ships and submarines are being equipped with vertical launch tubes that can fire a variety of cruise missiles, depending on the specific mission of the vessel at any particular time.

Although the media often describe these cruise missiles as Kalibr missiles, there are actually several distinct missile types. Some are designed for land attack, while others primarily target other ships. The Kalibr missile itself comes in two versions, the 3M14 land-attack cruise missile and the 3M54 anti-ship cruise missile. The former has a range of 2,000–2,500 km and can pose a threat to much of Europe from the relative safety of enclosed seas such as the Black Sea or the Baltic. The latter has a range of around 600 km and differs from other anti-ship cruise missiles in that it has a terminal velocity of Mach 2.9, which greatly enhances its ability to evade short-range ship defences.[1] An anti-submarine version of the Kalibr missile is currently being completed, with initial tests under way in 2020.[2] In addition, the universal vertical launch tubes that fire these missiles can also fire the older Oniks anti-ship cruise missiles and will be able to fire the Tsirkon hypersonic cruise missile, which is currently still in testing. The Tsirkon missile has a potential range of over 500 km and can travel at speeds greater than Mach 8.[3]

The advent of cruise missiles has allowed the Russian Navy to create true multi-mission platforms, capable of providing combat-credible force across several warfare areas. This innovation allows Russia to substitute its diminishing number of large combatants

Table 6.1   The kalibrisation of the Russian Navy

Class name	Project no.	Type	Quantity ordered	Known fleet(s)	First of class entering service	Number of launchers
Yasen	885	SSGN	8	Northern and Pacific	2013	32–40
Oscar (modernised)	949AM	SSGN	2	Pacific	2022	72
Akula (modernised)	971M	SSN	4	Northern and Pacific	2022	40
Varshavyanka	636.3	SSK	13	Black Sea, Pacific, Baltic	2014	4
Lada	677	SSK	6	Northern	2010	10
Kirov (modernised)	1144	CGN	2	Northern, Pacific	~2023	72
Admiral Gorshkov	22350	FFGHM	10	Northern, Pacific, Black Sea	2016	16–24
Udaloy (modernised)	1155	DDG	4	Northern and Pacific	2021	16
Ivan Papanin	23550	FFGH	2	Northern	~2023	8
Gremyashchiy	20385	FFGHM	8	Pacific	2020	8
Merkuriy	20386	FFGHM	1	Black Sea	~2023	8
Admiral Grigorovich	11356M	FFGHM	3	Black Sea	2016	8
Vasily Bykov	22160	FFGM	6	Black Sea	2018	8
Grad Sviyazhsk (Buyan-M)	21631	FSGM	12	Caspian, Black Sea, Baltic	2014	8
Karakurt	22800	PCGM	16	Baltic, Black Sea, Pacific	2018	8

Source: Updated version of Nicholas Childs, 'Reform and Re-Equipping Russia's Naval Forces', Presentation at IISS Workshop on Russian Military Modernisation, 14 December 2016, http://bmpd.livejournal.com/2334009.html.

with smaller ships that have limited suitability for expeditionary, blue-water operations but can nonetheless support defence and deterrence goals from seas adjacent to Russia's littoral spaces. Together, the combination of thirty to forty small combat ships (frigates and corvettes) and fifteen to twenty nuclear- and diesel-powered submarines – all armed with cruise missiles – will allow the Russian Navy to maintain its ability to protect its coastline and to threaten neighbouring states. While it will not be able to project substantial combat power globally, Russia's naval capabilities will be sufficient to achieve its main maritime goals.

The future of Russian submarines

Strategic submarines

Submarines will remain the strength of Russia's naval force for the foreseeable future. The renewal of the nuclear submarine fleet has been the highest priority for the Russian Navy throughout the post-Soviet period. The leadership has largely insulated the Borei-class ballistic missile submarines from budget cuts, even when military financing was relatively scarce. A total of five are now in service, with three more under construction and to be completed by 2024. The construction of two additional submarines began in 2021 and will be completed by 2029.[4] In line with analysts' predictions of an eventual total of twelve submarines, with six located in the Northern Fleet and six in the Pacific Fleet, the Russian Navy recently announced that two more submarines of this class will be built starting in 2023.[5] All of the Borei-class submarines starting with *Knyaz Vladimir* are to be of the Project 955A subclass, with improved electronics and other updated components.[6]

In addition to the new SSBNs, the five remaining Delta IV submarines, all based in the Northern Fleet, will remain in service for the next several years, with decommissioning expected towards the end of the 2020s. The single remaining Delta III in the Pacific Fleet had its nuclear missiles removed and was reclassified as a multi-purpose submarine.[7]

The Russian Navy is also in the process of building three submarines that will carry the Poseidon (aka Status-6) autonomous, nuclear-powered unmanned underwater vehicle currently being developed by Rubin Design Bureau, which will be capable of delivering both conventional and nuclear payloads. The first of these submarines, the *Belgorod*, has already been commissioned. The other two will be completed by 2027.[8]

Multipurpose nuclear submarines

Russia's existing fleet of nuclear attack submarines is being modernised to be quieter and to carry the new cruise missiles. With new weaponry and new hydroacoustics, these Soviet-era submarines could pose a serious threat to both adversary surface combatants and critical infrastructure ashore.

Of the Russian Navy's ten Akula-class (Project 971) multipurpose nuclear powered attack submarines (SSNs), five are in the process of modernisation, which is scheduled to be completed by 2025. Modernisation of these submarines includes improvements in virtually all systems, including hydroacoustics, navigation, electronics, armaments, and propulsion.[9] As part of the modernisation, the submarines are being fitted with universal launch tubes that will enable them to fire Kalibr and Oniks cruise missiles, and also Tsirkon missiles once those enter service.[10] At the start of the process, one Russian admiral described the result as an essentially completely new submarine that can serve for an additional twelve to fifteen years.[11] The first of these submarines was completed in 2020. Of the remaining Akula-class submarines, one is expected to be leased to India, two were modernised in the recent past (though without Kalibr cruise missiles or new hydroacoustics),[12] and one is likely to be retired in the next five years.

At least two of the fleet's eight existing Oscar-class (Project 949A) cruise missile submarines (SSGNs) are currently being modernised, though this process has been moving very slowly, with initial plans for the first modernised submarine to be in service by 2017 now wildly out of date.[13] Initial announcements called for four of the submarines to be modernised, though it is not clear whether more than two will be completed.[14] Each of the modified Oscar submarines will be equipped with universal missile launchers that will allow them to launch both Oniks and Kalibr cruise missiles. Given these missiles' reduced size, each Oscar-II will now be able to carry up to seventy-two cruise missiles, which will enable them to carry out mass salvo attacks on both surface ships and land-based targets at longer range. After modernisation, these submarines are expected to remain in the fleet for another twenty years.[15] Those that are not modernised will likely be retired over the next decade.

The new Yasen-class (Project 885) series of large nuclear multipurpose attack submarines has proved to be one of the Russian Navy's most successful new projects. A total of eight Yasen-class submarines are currently in service or under construction. At the same time, their construction has been repeatedly delayed by financial constraints. Initial plans called for seven units to be in service by the end of 2020.[16] Budget cuts have resulted in delays of several years, however, so that only three are currently in service, with the others to be completed by 2028.[17]

The Yasen-class submarine is designed to be a multi-purpose attack submarine that can both provide protection for Russian SSBNs and attack enemy aircraft carriers. As such, it was designed to replace both Oscar-class SSGNs and the various existing Soviet-era classes of nuclear-powered attack submarines. The goal was to reduce the variety of submarine classes in order to save on maintenance and logistics.[18] The Yasen class has a top underwater speed of 31 knots and can submerge to a depth of 600 meters. It has ten vertical missile tubes that can launch the usual variety of cruise missiles. It also has ten 533 mm torpedo tubes and carries up to thirty Fizik torpedoes. In the future, it will be armed with Futliar heat-seeking torpedoes.[19]

This is the first Russian submarine class to be equipped with a spherical sonar, designated as Irtysh-Amfora. The sonar system consists of a spherical bow array, flank arrays, and a towed array. It is capable of detecting surface and underwater targets at a range of up to 230 km. With this equipment, the Yasen is expected to be useful for anti-submarine warfare (ASW) as part of its mission of protecting Borei-class SSBNs.[20] The Yasen class has raised concerns with Russian naval experts because of its high cost per unit. The *Severodvinsk* cost almost 50 billion roubles, double the price of each Borei SSBN. Accounting for inflation, serial production units are expected to also cost over 50 billion roubles each.[21]

For the future, the Russian Navy plans to develop a new nuclear submarine "Laika" class, with the goal of building something cheaper and smaller than the Yasen class. This would be an attack submarine with decreased missile armament but comparable hydroacoustic detection capabilities when compared to the Yasen class. The current plans call for a versatile submarine that could both protect SSBNs and capital surface ships against attack submarines and be armed with cruise missiles that could strike both ships and land-based targets. Its primary mission would be anti-submarine warfare. Such a submarine is currently being designed by the Malakhit Design Bureau in St Petersburg, with the goal of building something comparable to the American Virginia class. The first submarine of this class, if adopted by the navy, would not be ready until the end of the 2020s at best.[22]

Conventional submarines

The Russian Navy's fourth-generation diesel submarine, the Lada class (project 677), has proven largely unsuccessful, although the navy has kept it alive over the years with continued promises that it has turned the corner. The first submarine of the class was beset with problems with its propulsion, hydroacoustic sensors, and tactical data processing system. One report noted that the propulsion system could only generate half of the required power.[23] Construction was frozen for several years while these problems were resolved. For a time, the military indicated that the initial three units would become test platforms for the new air-independent propulsion systems.[24] Although the lead submarine of the class remains in sea trials ten years after it was commissioned and the second has not yet entered sea trials fifteen years after it was laid down, the navy has recommitted to the project. It has ordered three additional submarines of this class, for a total of six in construction or under contract, with the goal of all six being commissioned by 2027.[25]

Because of delays with the Lada class, the Russian Navy was forced to resume construction of third-generation Improved Kilo-class (Project 636.3) diesel submarines. These submarines have a range of 6,000 to 7,500 nautical miles and can sustain operations without resupply for forty-five days. They cannot dive as deep or stay submerged for as long as nuclear-powered submarines, but their jet propulsion system makes them very quiet and allows it to operate well in shallower coastal waters.[26] Compared to previous versions of this class, this version has a better combination of acoustic stealth and target detection range, improved navigation and automated information management systems, and more powerful torpedoes. They are also armed with eight Kalibr family anti-ship and land-attack missiles. They are designed to both defend Russia's coastline and attack enemy targets on shore or at sea with long-range cruise missiles.[27] Six of these submarines are in service in the Black Sea Fleet, with two usually on patrol in the Mediterranean Sea. Another six are being built for the Pacific Fleet and four have been contracted for the Baltic Fleet.[28] Given that Russia's shipyards can build one of these submarines quite quickly, with the most recent taking three years from the start of construction to the start of active service, these submarines are likely to continue to serve as the backbone of Russia's non-nuclear submarine patrol fleet for the next two decades.

Russia is continuing to work on air-independent propulsion systems for its diesel-electric submarines. Russian officials have said that the system will be ready for deployment by 2023, but there is little evidence of progress. Analysts have indicated that development has been slowed by the end of defence cooperation with Western states, particularly with Germany.[29] Some reports suggest that Russia plans to work with China on a new AIP-capable submarine, though little information is available, and Russia has little history of cooperation with China on submarines.[30]

The large combat ship fantasy

For many years, the Russian Navy has been discussing various options for building large combat ships to replace its aging Soviet-built cruisers and destroyers. While some of these ships have long been beset by problems, particularly with propulsion systems, age has had a negative effect even on ships that were previously considered fairly reliable. Meanwhile, projects for new destroyers continue to be postponed due to technical and financial limitations.

Aircraft carriers

Perhaps no topic in Russian military shipbuilding is as fraught as the question of whether to build a new class of aircraft carriers. The one existing carrier, the *Admiral Kuznetsov*, remains in the order of battle but is unlikely to ever sail again after almost sinking in 2018 when the floating dry dock in which it was being repaired sank. Even prior to the accident, the *Kuznetsov* was a notoriously unreliable and poorly performing ship. It had serious problems with its propulsion system, and the losses sustained by its air wing during take-offs and landings on its last deployment to the

Mediterranean resulted in the wing being redeployed to Russia's air base in Syria. If it were to be repaired, it would need new electronic and navigation systems, in addition to the replacement of the propulsion system.[31]

In the meantime, Russian leaders continue to discuss plans for a new class of aircraft carriers to be built at some point in the indefinite future. At one point, Sergei Vlasov, the head of naval shipbuilding, announced that a carrier to replace the *Kuznetsov* would be ready by 2027. Even then, though, sources in the Russian Navy dismissed such claims, arguing that construction would begin no earlier than 2025 and would take at least ten years for the first ship.[32] Official announcements have nevertheless remained quite optimistic, with the Ministry of Defence arguing that a contract could be signed in 2025 and the ship built in five years.

The prospective carrier would be a descendant of the never finished late-Soviet Ulianovsk-class aircraft carrier, with a deadweight of more than 80,000 tons and the ability to carry fifty-five to sixty aircraft. The planes would be a naval version of the Su-57 fifth-generation fighter plane, as well as some long-range airborne warning and control system (AWACS) aircraft. In addition, it would carry a variety of multi-purpose and ASW helicopters, such as the Ka-27 and Ka-31 models.[33]

The prospective carrier would have air defence and ASW capabilities, reportedly including a ship-based version of the prospective S-500 air defence system, but no strike armaments of its own. Russian designers have made clear that they have accepted the view dominant in the United States that the only job of an aircraft carrier is to carry aircraft and allow them to take off and land. All other tasks, including defending itself, are seen as making the carrier unwieldy. As a result, the prospective Russian carrier would likely have limited armament beyond an air defence system and would need a strong complement of escort ships.[34]

According to designers, a prospective carrier would most likely be nuclear powered, probably using a combined nuclear and gas turbine system that would allow for faster acceleration than a nuclear system on its own.[35] Russian designers are currently working to develop an electromagnetic catapult system, though recent designs of the future carrier show that it may also include a trampoline as an insurance policy in case the catapult breaks down.[36]

Russian experts believe that construction of such a carrier would carry substantial financial and technical risks. Some have argued that Russian shipyards could build a 60–70,000-ton carrier in four to five years but could have difficulties if the military decides to build a larger supercarrier. One problem is the lack of a suitably large drydock, as Soviet carriers were built at Nikolayev, Ukraine. A small carrier (less than 60,000 tons) could be built at Baltzavod, but the military does not want such a design. The large design currently being discussed would require construction of new facilities, most likely at Severnaya Verf' or at Sevmash, though the head of the Russian Shipbuilding Corporation has also proposed the Zvezda Shipyard in the Far East and the Zaliv Shipyard in Sevastopol as options.[37]

Cruiser modernisation programme

The modernisation of Russia's remaining heavy cruisers is now well under way, with the Kirov-class cruiser *Admiral Nakhimov* scheduled to be ready for active duty in 2023 after the replacement of its armaments and electronic components. If the target date holds, it will have taken eight years from the start of the process to the ship returning to service. As part of the modernisation, the cruiser is being equipped with new radars, electronics, internal systems, and armaments. The new armaments will include Oniks and Kalibr cruise missiles and Poliment-Redut air defence systems.[38] The *Peter the Great* cruiser is likely to be modernised once the *Nakhimov* is back in service, though the modernisation is likely to be narrower in scope and primarily focused on the propulsion system and reactor.[39] The expectation is that the project will take five years. After many years of contradictory indications on whether the *Admiral Lazarev* cruiser will be modernised in a similar manner, scrapping of the ship began in 2021.[40]

The three Slava-class cruisers (*Variag, Marshal Ustinov,* and *Moskva*) are also gradually being modernised, with the *Marshal Ustinov* completed in 2016 and, in 2020, the *Moskva* (which was subsequently sunk in April 2022).[41] As part of the modernisation, the ships received new control and communications systems and new radars. The *Moskva* also received new diesel engines.[42] Both ships were also equipped with longer-range Vulcan anti-ship missiles, with a maximum range of 1,000 km.[43] Although there have been rumours for several years that the *Varyag* is about to be sent for modernisation, for the moment it remains in active service. The expectation is that it will be modernised sometime in the next ten years, as financing and shipyard capacity permits.[44]

A new destroyer class?

Russia's existing destroyers are at present of relatively limited use. The eight Udaloy-class destroyers, which have long been the mainstay of Russian long-range naval deployments, are gradually being modernised with new electronics and armaments, including the installation of universal vertical launch systems that will allow them to launch cruise missiles. This will transform these ships from their narrow focus on ASW into multipurpose ships that can also attack targets on the sea surface and on land.[45] Meanwhile, the Russian Navy has for several years now been willing to admit that the Sovremenny-class destroyers are largely useless, due to defective propulsion systems that are considered unrealistic to replace.[46] Only three ships of this class remain in active service in late 2022, and they rarely leave the immediate vicinity of their home ports. Two of the three are currently being prepared for decommissioning.[47]

For almost a decade, the Russian Navy has been discussing the production of large 15–19,000-ton destroyers, known as the Lider class or Project 23560, ships that many analysts consider to be essentially missile cruisers in all but name. Recent announcements have indicated that these ships will have nuclear propulsion systems, officially because this will give the ships a longer range and lifespan. However, unofficial reports speculate that the decision was made in part because of uncertainty regarding the production of gas turbines domestically.[48] The ships are also expected to have a wide range of both offensive and defensive armaments, including universal vertical launch systems that can fire Kalibr and Oniks missiles and, in the future, the Tsirkon hypersonic cruise missile. The ships would also be equipped with a naval version of the S-500 long-range air defence system, as well as medium-range Poliment-Redut surface-to-air missiles and a naval version of the Pantsir-M point defence system.[49]

The start of construction of these ships has been pushed back repeatedly. Plans for the ship have been under discussion since at least 2009, with construction initially slated to start in 2012.[50] As late as 2019, there was discussion that construction could begin as early as 2022, though the absence of funding for the class in the current armament programme made this highly unlikely.[51] In 2020, it was revealed that the navy had largely given up on plans to build the destroyer in the foreseeable future, due to the project's high cost.[52] Instead, the focus will remain on the construction of smaller ships such as frigates and corvettes, with the possibility of turning back to larger ships in the 2030s.

A small ship navy?

The Russian Navy has focused on developing small ships that can launch cruise missiles to ameliorate the limitations of its lack of large combat ships. It sees such missile ships as potentially potent force multipliers capable of offsetting Russian shortfalls in both numbers and quality of ships. To this end, Russia is building a variety of frigate and corvette classes. Such multi-mission ships, once equipped with universal vertical launch systems, can support both defence and conventional deterrence goals, despite their relatively small size. The Russian Navy has in effect recognised that Russia primarily needs a fleet that can both protect its maritime approaches and hold adversary critical infrastructure at risk, as spelled out in its most recent naval doctrine.[53] In essence, the Russian Navy has determined that capabilities are more important than platforms and that a navy does not need large tonnage ships to incorporate advanced, long-range weapon systems.

Admiral Gorshkov-class (Project 22350) frigates

The navy is currently in the midst of building eight Admiral Gorshkov-class frigates, with the first two in service in the Northern Fleet and the rest scheduled to be commissioned by 2026. Two more frigates are on order, with the possibility of additional ships to be built by the end of the decade.[54] These ships have a displacement of 4,500 tons, with a length of 135 metres and a top speed of 29 knots. They are armed with the A-192 Armat 130 mm artillery gun, sixteen or twenty-four universal vertical launch tubes for cruise missiles, the Poliment-Redut air defence system, and the Palash close-in weapons system. The frigates also each carry a single Ka-27PL helicopter. The ships are expected to serve as the core of Russian naval forces in the Arctic, Atlantic, and Mediterranean.[55]

Construction of these ships was unusually slow even by the frequently glacial pace of recent Russian shipbuilding. The first ship took almost five years from the start of construction to launch and was finally commissioned twelve years after the start of construction. Serial production did not initially solve the problem, with the second ship taking even longer from start of construction to launch.

Subsequent ships are expected to take at least six years from keel-laying to commissioning, according to official schedules.[56] Despite continued promises by the United Shipbuilding Company, the goal of completing all eight ships by the initial target date of 2021 was completely unrealistic.[57] At the current rate of construction, the Russian Navy can expect to have six ships of this class by 2025, as long as there are no further delays.

Although there were initially problems with the air defence system, the main current cause of delays has been the shift in turbine production that has resulted from the end of military-industrial cooperation between Russia and Ukraine. Gas turbines for these ships were built at Zoria-Mashproekt in Ukraine, and turbines for only the first two ships had been delivered prior to the suspension of military cooperation after Russia's annexation of Crimea. Initially, Russian experts argued that two years would be sufficient to set up production of turbines in Russia, since the turbines were made with many Russian components, but in reality the delay was much longer, with serial production of the turbines being authorised only in October 2020.[58]

Russian Navy officials have long discussed the possibility of building a larger variant of the Admiral Gorshkov class of frigate. This ship design has been dubbed the Super Gorshkov, with plans calling for an 8,000-ton ship that will carry forty-eight cruise missiles and ninety-six Poliment-Redut defensive missiles. Design work on this ship is continuing at Severnoye Design Bureau, with officials claiming that the first Super Gorshkov will be completed by 2027, and as many as twelve ships of this type will be ordered altogether in the next decade.[59] The reality is that procurement of the ship has not been included in the current State Armament Programme, which means that construction is highly unlikely to begin before the mid-2020s, with completion of the first ship possible no earlier than 2030 given general timelines in Russian shipbuilding.

Admiral Grigorovich-class (Project 11356) frigates

Because of the slow pace of construction of Admiral Gorshkov-class frigates and the serious need to refurbish the Black Sea Fleet as quickly as possible, in 2010 the Russian Navy ordered six Admiral Grigorovich-class frigates. This class is an improved version of the venerable Krivak frigates, originally designed for export to India. The first three ships were built quite quickly and were all in service in the Black Sea Fleet by 2017. As with the Admiral Gorshkov-class frigates, gas turbines for these ships were built at Zoria-Mashproekt in Ukraine. Prior to the suspension of military cooperation with Ukraine, Russia had received turbines only for the first three ships of this class. Until the suspension of defence cooperation with Ukraine, the Russian Navy was considering purchasing three additional Admiral Grigorovich-class frigates for other fleets, depending on whether Severnaya Verf' was able to speed up construction of the Admiral Gorshkov-class frigates in the near future.

Once it became clear that the Ukrainian side would not provide gas turbines for the remaining ships if they joined the Russian Navy, it was determined that the two ships already under construction would be sold to India, while the sixth was cancelled.[60] Moreover, military planners eventually decided that it was not cost effective to develop a new domestically produced turbine for these ships. Consequently, there is no longer any discussion of building additional ships of this class.[61]

These ships have a displacement of over 4,000 tons and a top speed of 30 knots, powered by a two-shaft combined gas turbine system. Like the Admiral Gorshkov-class frigates, these ships are being armed with Oniks anti-ship missiles and Kalibr multipurpose missiles, which can both be fired through universal vertical launch systems, as well as Igla-1E surface-to-air missiles and Shtil-1 air defence systems.[62]

Ivan Papanin-class (Project 23550) ice-class patrol ships

As part of its effort to expand its presence in the Arctic, the Russian Navy ordered two ice-class patrol ships for the Northern Fleet, with the goal of having them in service by 2025. These 8,500-ton ships are designed to be multi-purpose and will be able to act as icebreakers, armed patrol ships, and even as tugboats for detained ships. Armaments will include two universal cruise missile launch systems for Kalibr and related missiles, as well as a 76 mm artillery system. The ships will also be equipped with two Raptor speedboats, a small hovercraft, and a helicopter. The overall goal is to have a platform that can protect sea lanes and natural resource extraction areas in the Arctic, as well as lead convoys of civilian ships along the Northern Sea Route and conduct search and rescue operations when necessary. Two similar ships, but without the cruise missiles, are being built for the border patrol.[63]

A variety of corvettes

In keeping with its tendency towards proliferation of ship classes, the Russian Navy has built a wide range of corvettes for a variety of purposes. The most numerous type is the Project 2038x range of ships, including the Project 20380 Stereguschchiy class, the Project 20385 Gremyashchiy modification, and the Project 20386 Mercury class. The Stereguschchiy-class corvette was the first major shipbuilding programme launched after the long procurement holiday of the 1990s, with the first ship commissioned in 2007. Since then, seven Project 20380 Stereguschchiy-class ships have entered the Baltic and Pacific Fleets, with an additional seven under construction for all the fleets. Another seven Project 20385 Gremyashchiy-class ships are being built for the Northern and Pacific Fleets over the next several years.[64]

This corvette programme pioneered certain features that have now become commonplace in Russian naval ship design, including modular construction and the effort to build versatile multi-mission ships to reduce the number of ship classes in the fleet. These are 1,800–2,200-ton ships with a top speed of 27 knots and a range of 4,000 nautical miles. They use Russian-built CODAD diesel engines. All of the ships carry Uran Kh-35 anti-ship missiles, which have a range of 260 km, and Paket-NK torpedoes. The ships also have a hangar for a Ka-27 helicopter. The first ship of the class is armed with the Kortik-M air defence system, though this has been replaced with the more modern and powerful Redut system in all subsequent ships. Newer ships currently under construction have replaced the Uran missiles with universal cruise missile launch systems and can therefore launch Kalibr and Oniks missiles, as can the larger Project 20385 ships.[65]

The 2,500-ton Project 20385 corvettes are designed for longer missions, and the larger size makes it easier for them to incorporate cruise missile launchers. They were designed to fix problems with the initial ship design, including inadequate defensive armament, particularly air defence and anti-missile systems, as well as unreliable propulsion systems and inadequate range.[66] They were originally designed to use German-made MTU engines for propulsion, thus rectifying one of the main problems with the original class. Because of sanctions, however, only the first two ships received the German engines, with subsequent vessels being equipped with Russian-made diesel turbines.[67]

The newest variant, the Project 20386 Mercury class, is even larger at 3,400 tons, and incorporates a more stealthy design. This modification would have newer radio-electronic equipment, including unspecified technology that would make the ship harder to detect, and would carry a helicopter and reconnaissance unmanned aerial vehicles. These innovations would allow the ship to be 'truly multi-purpose and to function in both coastal and more distant waters'.[68] It could be used for both coastal defence and power projection in nearby waters missions. Although only one ship has been ordered to date, there are reports that ten will eventually be built.[69]

Admiral Bykov-class (Project 22160) corvettes are designed to supplement the Stereguschchiy corvettes in the Black Sea. These ships have greater range and are more self-sufficient than their predecessors. They displace 1,700 tons, with a top speed of 30 knots. They can travel 6,000 miles and sixty days without refuelling, versus 3,500 miles and fifteen days for the Stereguschchiy-class corvettes.[70] Some have called these Project 22160 ships "robotic" vessels, because their weapon control systems, power plant, and onboard mechanisms are digitised and automated, making it possible to reduce significantly the size of the crew.[71] Weapons include a 57 mm A-220M gun and eight Igla surface-to-air missiles (SAM) mounted on a 3M-47 Gibka launcher. As with other recent Russian ship designs, mod-ular construction allows for a variety of weapons to be fitted on the ship, depending on mission. Hydroacoustic stations and other equipment that are housed in 40-foot shipping contain-ers installed on the ship allow for quick changes of components between missions. The vessels can be configured with two twelve-cell vertical launchers for the medium-range Shtil-1 SAM system, which uses the same missile as the SA-11 "Gadfly". They can also be armed with 3M-54 (SS-N-27 "Sizzler") or Kh-35 (SS-N-25 "Switchblade") anti-ship missiles. The ships also each carry a single Ka-27PS helicopter. Missions include protection of coastal waters, exclusive economic zone enforcement, anti-smuggling and anti-piracy operations, search and rescue, and environmen-tal monitoring.[72] Four are currently in service, with another two to be completed by 2023.[73]

The Russian Navy has modified its Buyan-class (Project 21630) small artillery ships into small missile ships designed to be used primarily in shallower enclosed seas. The Buyan-M-class ships have a displacement of 1,000 tons, a range of 2,500 miles, and can reach speeds of up to 25 knots. The ships are armed with universal 100 mm artillery, Duet 30 mm artillery, two Gibka air defence systems, and VLS systems that can launch eight Oniks or Kalibr cruise missiles with a range of 500 km. They are designed to operate in littoral zones, where they can be covered by shore-based air defence systems while threatening enemy ships or land targets with long-range cruise missiles. Using them in littoral zones ameliorates the main weaknesses of these ships, which include weak air defence, limited range, and poor seaworthiness in rough conditions. Ten of these ships are currently in service in the Caspian Flotilla and Baltic and Black Sea Fleets, with two more under construction.[74]

The Russian Navy has also chosen to develop another Kalibr-armed small missile ship class, the 800-ton Project 22800 Karakurt. Described as a 'green water multipurpose missile/artillery ship', these ships will have a larger displacement than the Bykov class, making them more suitable for high seas operations. These ships' superstructure is designed to maximise stealth.[75] Three of the sixteen Karakurts that the Russian Navy has ordered are in service in the Baltic Fleet, with the rest expected to be ready to join the navy by 2025 after some initial delays with engine production.[76]

Renewing the amphibious ship fleet

After long delays, the Russian Navy has finally started to renew its fleet of amphibious ships. The post-Soviet Russian fleet long consisted entirely of ships built in the Soviet era. The fifteen small Ropucha-class (Project 775) landing ships were built in the 1980s in Poland and can carry 450 tons of cargo or up to 340 troops. The four larger Alligator-class (Project 1171) landing ships were built in the 1960s and 1970s and can carry 1,000 tons of cargo or up to 440 troops.[77] Although troop carriers can have very long lifespans, planners have long understood that the Russian Navy needed new amphibious ships. The first ship of a successor class to the Alligator was laid down in 2004, but work on the Ivan Gren was slowed by limited financing and frequent design changes.

A plan to purchase French Mistral ships to serve as both troop carriers and as command and control vessels for overseas operations collapsed at a very late stage because of the Ukraine conflict.[78] After the start of the Syria operation in 2015, the Russian military became much more serious about building up its expeditionary capabilities. The Syrian Express operation to bring supplies and equipment to Syria showed that Russia needed more amphibious ships to bring troops and equipment to distant shores.

Construction of the Ivan Gren was accelerated, and a second ship of the class was laid down in 2014. The first ship was commissioned in 2018. The ship has a displacement of 5,000 tons and can transport up to three hundred naval infantry, thirty-six armoured vehicles, or thirteen tanks. It also carries a Ka-29 transport helicopter.[79] The second entered the navy at the very end of 2020. Both are in the Northern Fleet.[80] Two more ships of a modified version of this class were laid down in 2019 and will be commissioned into the Pacific Fleet in the mid-2020s.[81] The procurement of additional ships of this class is now under consideration.[82]

In July 2020, the Zaliv shipyard in Kerch laid down two hulls of the new Ivan Rogov-class (Project 23900) amphibious assault ship. These 25,000-ton ships are expected to serve as the domestically produced Russian answer to the never-received Mistral ships. The ships will be able to carry up to a thousand troops and seventy-five armoured vehicles and will be equipped with six landing boats. As amphibious assault ships, they will also carry sixteen helicopters, potentially including Ka-29 transport helicopters, Ka-31 ASW helicopters, and Ka-52K attack helicopters.[83] Like the Mistrals, they will be able to operate as command ships, able to control both warship strike groups and combined multi-service operations.[84] The first two ships are expected to be in service by 2030. In the long run, the Russian Navy is likely to have four such ships, one for each major fleet.

The future of the Russian Navy

Based on the plans discussed above and an assessment of the capabilities of the Russian shipbuilding industry, we can look ahead to what the Russian Navy will look like in the late 2020s. The tables below compare what the Russian Navy of the near future will look like as compared to the present day. They show that the navy will substantially renew its submarines and small ships over the next ten years but will just be starting on construction of a new generation of large surface combat ships at the start of the next decade.[85]

As shown in Table 6.2, the Russian Navy plans to have at least twelve SSBNs in active service by 2025. By this point, the core of the strategic deterrent submarine fleet will consist of eight Borei-class SSBNs. Most likely, all five Delta IV SSBNs will also still be in service in 2025. These submarines will probably be retired in 2025–30. The pace of retirement will depend on the number of Borei submarines constructed. The Russian Navy generally retires old SSBNs one year after their replacement is commissioned, so if additional contracts are signed, the RFN SSBN fleet could consist entirely of Boreis by 2030.[86]

The Russian Navy is modernising some of its Oscar-class SSGNs and Akula-class SSNs, which will extend their lifespan by twelve to fifteen years. Older classes, such as the Sierra and Victor III, might be retired before 2030, though the Sierra's titanium hull is sufficiently long-lasting that they could be modernised instead. Yasen-class construction is expected to speed up after a very slow start, though it is unclear whether any will be ordered beyond the current set. Instead, the navy is likely to focus on the new class of nuclear submarines currently being designed. Older Kilo-class diesel submarines will be gradually retired in favour of the

Table 6.2   Submarines in the Russian Navy

Class	2022	2027	2032
Borei	5	7–8	10–12
Delta IV	4	4–5	0–2
Belgorod	1	3	3–6
Delta III	1	0–1	0
Sierra II, Victor III	3	2–4	0–2
Oscar	2	6	4–6
Akula	3	6	4–6
Yasen	3	6–7	8–10
New class SS(G)N	0	0	0–4
Kilo (Project 877)	7	8–12	0–5
Imp. Kilo (Project 636.3)	9	12–14	14–20
Lada (Project 677)	0	3–6	6–8
Kalina	0	0	??

Note: Bold text denotes classes undergoing modernisation, while italic denotes classes designed in the twenty-first century.

Improved Kilo and Lada class, with long-term hopes pinned on the success of AIP development and its introduction in the next-generation Kalina class.

The Russian Navy is currently refurbishing its cruisers. As shown in Table 6.3, the programme should be complete by 2025, with two Kirov- and three Slava-class cruisers remaining in service. The three remaining Sovremenny-class destroyers are essentially inactive already and will almost certainly be decommissioned before 2025, while some Udaloy-class destroyers will be modernised to extend their lifespan through the early 2030s. Construction of Admiral Gorshkov-class frigates has been very slow, but is likely to speed up in the first half of the 2020s. New large combat ships such as the Lider-class destroyer or the Super Gorshkov frigate are unlikely to see completion this decade.

The overall number of small combat ships is expected to remain fairly steady over the next fifteen years, as shown in Table 6.4. The older classes of corvettes and missile ships will be gradually retired as new corvettes and missile ships are commissioned.

Table 6.3   Large combat ships

Class	2022	2027	2032
Kuznetsov CV	0	0–1	0–1
Kirov CGN	1	2	2
Slava CG	3	3	3
Sovremenny DDG	1	0	0
Udaloy DDG	5	5–7	4–6
Lider (new class DDG)	0	0	0–2
Krivak I & II FFG	2	0–2	0
Neustrashimyi FFG	2	2	1–2
Admiral Grigorovich FFG	3	3	3
Admiral Gorshkov FFG	2	6–8	8–12
Ivan Papanin FFG	0	2	2–6

Note: Bold text denotes classes undergoing modernisation, while italic denotes classes designed in the twenty-first century.

Table 6.4   Small combat ships

Class	2022	2027	2032
Grisha FFC	20	8–10	0
Parchim FFC	6	5–6	0–3
Stereguschchiy FFC	8	14–16	20–5
Admiral Bykov FFC	3	6–8	10–15
Gepard FFL	2	2	2
Tarantul PFG	21	20–5	10–25
Nanuchka PFG	8	6–8	4–6
Bora PFG	2	2	2
Buyan PG	3	3	3
Buyan-M PFG	9	12–15	15–25
Karakurt PFG	3	12–18	20–30

Note: Italic denotes classes designed in the twenty-first century.

The Russian Navy has finally become serious about renewing its amphibious ship fleet. As shown in Table 6.5, the overall amphibious capability of the RFN will nevertheless increase as the replacement Landing Ship (Tank) (LST)s will be larger and more capable than the ships they are replacing, while the landing

Table 6.5 Amphibious ships

Class	2022	2027	2032
Ropucha LST	15	12–15	12–15
Alligator LST	4	2–4	0–4
Ivan Gren LST	2	4–5	5–8
Ivan Rogov LHD	0	0	2–4

Note: Italic denotes classes designed in the twenty-first century.

helicopter dock (LHD) ships will add a capability that the Russian Navy has not previously possessed.

These tables clearly show that in the near to medium term, the Russian Navy will remain almost exclusively a coastal defence and deterrence force. For the foreseeable future, the strength of the Russian Navy will be in its submarines. Under any development scenario, Russian SSBNs will provide an adequate strategic deterrence capability. Meanwhile, Russian SS(G)Ns will be sufficient to protect the SSBNs and to deter enemy naval forces from attacks on Russian territory. These forces will be supported by a new generation of small and medium-sized combat ships, most of which will be equipped with anti-ship and land-attack cruise missiles. These naval forces will be fully sufficient to ensure Russian dominance in neighbouring waters. They will not, however, provide Russia with the forces to make it even a near-peer blue-water competitor for the US Navy.

Even under the most optimistic projections, the Russian Navy will not have a serious expeditionary capability for at least fifteen years. Planning for large amphibious ships and aircraft carriers is still very much in the early stages, and whether the Russian Navy should build either type of ship is still highly disputed among both the expert community and military planners. If they are built in the numbers currently being discussed and in the most likely timelines, then the United States may have to be prepared to deal with substantial expeditionary Russian forces further afield in the global ocean in the mid- to late 2030s. It is far more likely, however, that financial and industrial limitations will lead to the cancelation or significant reduction of plans to develop a naval expeditionary capability for the Russian Navy.

Furthermore, out-of-area deployment capability is likely to deteriorate in the medium term as legacy Soviet-era large combat ships age and become less reliable. This trajectory will depend to some extent on the ability of the Russia Navy successfully to modernise its existing cruisers and Udaloy-class destroyers. If these programmes are all carried out as currently planned, then the Russian Navy will be able to continue to deploy large combat ships in numbers and frequency comparable to present-day rates until the next generation of destroyers is ready in the early 2030s. If, however, these programmes are fulfilled only partially or not at all, by 2025 it will have only a few large combat ships capable of deploying regularly outside the immediate vicinity of their bases. This would make securing basing agreements (such as Sudan) all the more important.

Overall, in the 2020s the Russian Navy is going to be more than sufficient to defend the Russian coastline and ports. It will also be capable of posing a threat to its smaller neighbours and potentially to European NATO member states. The main source of the threat will be its ships' ability to launch land-attack cruise missiles from a distance of 300–2,500 km from the target, depending on the type of missile. The construction of a fairly sizeable fleet of small missile ships and corvettes equipped with land-attack cruise missiles to a large extent obviates the need to build a sizeable fleet of large combat ships.[87] Russian missile ships will be able to target most of its smaller neighbours and a large part of Europe without having to leave the relative safety of enclosed seas where Russian forces are dominant.

In summary, although the Russian Navy will continue to have problems with its platforms, its offensive capabilities will increasingly not be hull-dependent. The new generation of ships will allow the RFN to mount new generations of long-range cruise missiles in a modular fashion on a variety of platforms. As a result, while the Russian Navy will not be strong enough to challenge the US Navy directly in the open ocean (which does not appear to be the intention anyway), it will be more than sufficient to reach and potentially threaten or coerce its neighbours and even smaller NATO countries. While it will not be able to project power globally or reach the United States except in terms of strategic deterrence, it will be able to target American allies in Europe, and states it wants to influence on its borders. Since these countries are likely to be its primary targets in any case, Russia's naval capabilities will be good enough to achieve Russia's main maritime military goals in the short to medium term.

Notes

1 S. Roblin, 'Why Russia's Enemies Fear the Kalibr Cruise Missile', *National Interest*, 22 January 2017, https://nationalinterest.org/blog/the-buzz/why-russias-enemies-fear-the-kalibr-cruise-missile-19129 (accessed 8 October 2022).

2 'Antisubmarine missiles 91PE1 and 91PE2', Missilery.info, https://en.missilery.info/missile/91re (accessed 8 October 2022); 'Russian Navy Test-Fires Anti-Submarine Kalibr Missile from Admiral Kasatonov', The Eurasian Times, 1 November 2020, https://eurasiantimes.com/43091-2 (accessed 8 October 2022).

3 'Russian Navy Frigate Test-Fires Tsirkon Hypersonic Missile from White Sea', TASS, 11 December 2020, https://tass.com/defense/123402 (no longer active).

4 'Zakladka boevykh korablei Voenno-Marskovo Flota', Website of the Presidential Administration, 23 August 2021, http://kremlin.ru/events/president/news/66436 (accessed 8 October 2022).

5 'Na "Sevmashe" nachnetsya stroitelstvo dvukh roketonostsev klassa "Borei" v 2023 godu', TASS, 24 December 2021, https://tass.ru/armiya-i-opk/13298525 (accessed 8 October 2022).

6 K. Bogdanov, '"Bolshoi flot" za gorizontom', Lenta.ru, 23 January 2015, https://lenta.ru/articles/2015/01/23/bigfleet (accessed 14 November 2022).

7 Y. Rossolov, 'Garant stabilnosti v Aziatsko-Tikhookeanskom regione', *Krasnaya zvezda*, 19 March 2021, http://redstar.ru/garant-stabilnosti-v-aziatsko-tihookeanskom-regione (accessed 14 November 2022).

8 'Istochnik: tretei nositel yadernykh supertorped "Poseidon" peredadut flotu do 2027 goda', TASS, 14 January 2021, https://tass.ru/armiya-i-opk/10465325 (accessed 8 October 2022).

9 'APL Leopard posle remonta i modernizatsii vyidet na ispytaniya v 2022 godu', TASS, 8 December 2021, https://tass.ru/armiya-i-opk/13148653 (accessed 8 October 2022); 'Seriya mnogotselevykkh atomnykh podvodnykh lodok tretevo pokoleniya proekta 971 "Shchuka-B" (Akula)', Novosti VPK, https://vpk.name/library/f/971-shuka.html (accessed 8 October 2022).

10 A. Yemelianenkov, '"Leopard" poluchit "Kalibr-PL" i smozhet potyagatsya s "Yasenem", *Rossiiskaia gazeta*, 11 January 2021, https://rg.ru/2021/01/11/leopard-poluchit-kalibr-pl-i-smozhet-potiagatsia-s-iasenem.html (accessed 8 October 2022).

11 'VMF reshil provesti glubokuyu modernizatsiyu podlodok proektov 971 i 949', *Vzgliad*, 21 June 2015, https://vz.ru/news/2015/6/21/752004.html (accessed 14 November 2022).

12 'Tikhookeanskii flot do kontsa goda popolnyat dve atomnie lodki', Lenta.ru, 27 May 2015, https://lenta.ru/news/2015/05/27/upgrade (accessed 8 October 2022).

13 Communication with Ilya Kramnik, December 2016.

14 A. Shishkin, 'Chelyabinsk', Navy Korabel blog, 25 February 2020, https://navy-korabel.livejournal.com/230092.html (accessed 8 October 2022).

15 V. Karnozov, 'Kulak "Anteya": kakimi budut podlodki 949A posle modernizatsii', TV Zvezda, 13 February 2018, https://tvzvezda.ru/news/opk/content/201802131152-gphz.htm (accessed 8 October 2022); 'Kalibrovka velikanov: Zachem atomokhody "Antei" vooruzhayut novymi raketami', RIA-Novosti, 15 December 2018, https://ria.ru/2018 1215/1548001411.html (no longer active).

16 S. Safronov, '"Malakhit": budushchie submariny budut vooruzheny podvodnymi bespilotnikami', RIA-Novosti, 15 December 2014, https://ria.ru/20141215/1037925421.html (accessed 14 November 2022).

17 S. Tsygankova, 'Nositel "Poseidona": "Belgorod" peredadut flotu v 2021 godu', *Rossiiskaia gazeta*, 24 December 2020, https://rg.ru/2020/12/24/reg-szfo/nositel-posejdona-belgorod-peredadut-flotu-v-2021-godu.html (accessed 8 October 2022); V. Vasiliev, 'VMF PF v 2020 godu nedopoluchil 4 atomnie podvodnie lodki?', Regnum, 27 December 2020, https://regnum.ru/news/polit/3152134.html (accessed 8 October 2022).

18 V. Gundarov, 'Stavka na atomnie podvodnie lodki', *Nezavisimoe voennoe obozrenie*, 1 August 2014, https://nvo.ng.ru/nvo/2014-08-01/1_submarines.html (accessed 14 November 2022).

19 'Russian Navy to Receive Advanced Futlyar Torpedoes', TASS, 22 June 2016, https://tass.com/defense/883900 (accessed 8 October 2022).

20 K. Mizokami, 'The Yasen-Class vs the Virginia Class: Are Russian or American Submarines Superior?', *National Interest*, 24 January 2020, https://nationalinterest.org/blog/buzz/yasen-class-vs-virginia-class-are-russian-or-american-submarines-superior-116851 (accessed 14 November 2022).

21 M. Episkopos, 'Russia's Yasen-M Submarine Is the Deadly Gift that Keeps on Giving', *National Interest*, 13 January 2020, https://nationalin terest.org/blog/buzz/russias-yasen-m-submarine-deadly-gift-keeps-giv ing-113186 (accessed 14 November 2022).

22 'OKR "Laika" stala razitiem proekta mnogotselevoi APL pyatovo pokoleniya "Khaski", Flotprom.ru, 17 April 2019, https://flotprom. ru/2019/%D0%9E%D1%81%D0%BA13 (no longer active).

23 'VMF otkazalsya ot noveishykh podlodok proekta "Lada"', *Izvestiia*, 23 November 2011, https://iz.ru/news/507580 (accessed 14 November 2022).

24 A. Rezchikov, 'Ot "Lady" do "Kaliny"', *Vzgliad*, 19 March 2014, https:// vz.ru/society/2014/3/19/677976.html (accessed 14 November 2022).

25 'VMF Rossii poluchit dve dizelnie podlodki "Lada" po novomu gos-kontraktu', TASS, 28 June 2019, https://tass.ru/armiya-i-opk/6605634 (accessed 14 November 2022); 'Minoborony zaklyuchilo 41 kontrakt na forume "Armiya-2020"', TASS, 20 August 2020, https://tass.ru/armiya-i-opk/9285181 (accessed 14 November 2022).

26 K. Mizokami, 'The Kilo-Class Submarine: Why Russia's Enemies Fear "The Black Hole"', *National Interest*, 23 October 2016, https://nationalin terest.org/blog/the-kilo-class-submarine-why-russias-enemies-fear-the-bl ack-18140 (accessed 8 October 2022).

27 A. Latyshev and E. Komarova, '"Podvodnie raketonostsy: kak novie submariny proekta "Vashavyanka" usilit VMF Rossii"', RT, 23 October 2020, https://russian.rt.com/russia/article/795250-rossiya-podvodna ya-lodka-volhov (accessed 14 November 2022).

28 'Moshchnosti "Admiralteiskykh verfei" mogut nachat prostaivat bez kon-trakta na seriyu podlodok dlya Baltflota', Interfax-AVN, 26 August 2020, www.militarynews.ru/story.asp?rid=1&nid=536936 (accessed 8 October 2022).

29 Communication with Ilya Kramnik, 28 October 2020.

30 H. I. Sutton, 'China and Russia in Mysterious New Submarine Project', *Forbes*, 27 August 2020, www.forbes.com/sites/hisutton/2020/08/27/china-and-russia-in-mysterious-new-submarine-project/#4e96c8d01629 (accessed 8 October 2022).

31 A. Kramer, 'Russian Aircraft Carrier Is Called Back as Part of Syrian Drawdown', *New York Times*, 6 January 2017, www.nytimes.

com/2017/01/06/world/middleeast/russia-aircraft-admiral-kuznetsov-syria.html (accessed 8 October 2022).

32 A. Yudina, 'Sergei Vlasov: v Rossii uzhe hachata razpabotke elektromagnitnoi katapulty dlya avianostsev', TASS, 22 April 2014, https://tass.ru/interviews/1599621/amp (accessed 14 November 2022).

33 I. Dronina, 'Rossiya postroit krupneishii v mire avianosets', *Nezavisimoe voennoe obozrenie*, 17 January 2020, https://nvo.ng.ru/nvo/2020-01-17/1_1077_main.html (accessed 8 October 2022).

34 K. Bogdanov, '"Bolshoi flot za gorizontom", Lenta.ru, 23 January 2015, https://lenta.ru/articles/2015/01/23/bigfleet (accessed 14 November 2022).

35 H. I. Sutton, 'Russia's Next Aircraft Carrier Will Likely Be Nuclear', *Forbes*, 16 February 2020, https://www.forbes.com/sites/hisutton/2020/02/16/russias-next-aircraft-carrier-will-likely-be-nuclear/#4901ce436cc3 (accessed 8 October 2022); 'Dlya novovo rossiiskovo avianostsa vybrali kombinirovannuyu silovuyu ustanovku', Lenta.ru, 1 July 2015, https://lenta.ru/news/2015/07/01/avianosez (accessed 14 November 2022).

36 Yudina, 'Sergei Vlasov'.

37 'Po sovetskim chertezham: v Rossii sozdadut pervy avianosets', Gazeta.ru, 13 January 2020, www.gazeta.ru/army/2020/01/13/12907808.shtml (accessed 8 October 2022).

38 'Atomnyi raketny kreiser proekta 11442M posle remonta vydet na ispytaniya v 2020 godu', Interfax-AVN, 29 March 2019, www.militarynews.ru/story.asp?rid=1&nid=505043&lang=RU (accessed 8 October 2022).

39 'Modernizatsiyu "Petra Velikovo" provedut v sokrashchennom obeme', VPK, 21 February 2020, https://vpk-news.ru/news/55406 (accessed 8 October 2022).

40 V. Karnozov, 'Tikhookeanskii flot vozvrashchaet bronenostsy', *Nezavisimoe voennoe obozrenie*, 10 September 2020, https://nvo.ng.ru/nvo/2020-09-10/1_1108_fleet.html (accessed 8 October 2022); A. Shishkin, 'TARKP pr. 11442: obzor tekhnicheskovo sostoyaniya', Navy Korabel blog, 20 May 2019, https://navy-korabel.livejournal.com/203579.html (accessed 8 October 2022); 'Kreiser "Admiral Lazarev" dostavili na zavod dlya utilizatsii', Flotprom.ru, 4 May 2021, https://bit.ly/32AxfEy (accessed 8 October 2022).

41 The Ustinov was originally scheduled to be ready in 2012 but was repeatedly delayed. 'Kreiser "Marshal Ustinov" vernut flotu k kontsu 2015 goda', Lenta.ru, 1 December 2014, https://lenta.ru/news/2014/12/01/ustinov (accessed 14 November 2022).

42 'Rossiiskii kreiser poluchil modernizierovannie radary', Lenta.ru, 18 March 2015, https://lenta.ru/news/2015/03/18/ustinov; '40-letnyaya otremontirovannaya "Moskva" eshche desyati let budet zashchishchat

Krym', Lenta.ru, 7 July 2020, https://lenta.ru/news/2020/07/03/moskva (accessed 8 October 2022).

43 A. Shishkin, '"Vulkan": i vsyo-taki 1000 km', Navy Korabel blog, 10 September 2020, https://navy-korabel.livejournal.com/248867.html (accessed 8 October 2022).

44 A. Shishkin, 'O tekhnicheskom sostoyanii RKR pr. 1164', Navy Korabel blog, 5 February 2017, https://navy-korabel.livejournal.com/153675.html (accessed 8 October 2022).

45 'Modernizatsiya bolshikh protivolodochnykh korablei proekta 1155 na Dalzavode', BMPD blog, 20 September 2020, https://bmpd.livejournal.com/4145328.html (accessed 8 October 2022); L. Nersisyan, 'Na shto budut sposobny korabli postroiki SSSR posle modernizatsii?', Regnum, 25 November 2019, https://regnum.ru/news/polit/2788107.html (accessed 8 October 2022).

46 A. Shishkin, 'Esminetsy pr. 956: Chast 5; kto vinovat?', Navy Korabel blog, 14 May 2015, https://navy-korabel.livejournal.com/95871.html (accessed 8 October 2022); A. Shishkin, 'Esminetsy pr. 956: Chast 6; poslednii shans "Sarychei"', Navy Korabel blog, 14 June 2015, https://navy-korabel.livejournal.com/101314.html (accessed 8 October 2022).

47 A. Shishkin, '"Burny: schastlivchik ili donor dlya Bystrovo?', Navy Korabel blog, 17 June 2019, https://navy-korabel.livejournal.com/206465.html (accessed 8 October 2022).

48 'Perspektivnyi atomnyi esminets poluchit vozmozhnosti kreisera', Lenta.ru, 2 March 2015, https://lenta.ru/news/2015/03/02/destcruiser (accessed 14 November 2022); 'Proekt 23560: samie moshchnie eskadrennie esminitsy tipa "Lider"', Militaryarms.ru, 30 April 2019, https://militaryarms.ru/voennaya-texnika/voennye-korabli/proekt-23560 (accessed 8 October 2022).

49 J. Trevithick, 'Russia Has Abandoned Its Massive Nuclear Destroyer and Supersized Frigate Programs', The War Zone, 21 April 2020, www.thedrive.com/the-war-zone/33099/russia-has-abandoned-its-massive-nuclear-destroyer-and-supersized-frigate-programs (accessed 8 October 2022); 'Eskadrennie minonostsy proekta 23560 "Lider"', Novosti VPK, https://vpk.name/library/f/project-23560.html (accessed 8 October 2022).

50 'Perspektivny esminets rossiiskovo VMF budet mnogotselevym, osnashchen udarnym raketnym oruzhiem i pochti nevidim', Novosti VPK, 23 June 2009, https://vpk.name/news/29193_perspektivnyii_esminec_rossiiskogo_vmf_budet_mnogocelevyim_osnashen_udarnyim_raketny im_oruzhiem_i_pochti_nevidim__ekspert.html (accessed 8 October 2022).

51 'Opredeleny sroki postroiki rossiiskikh atomnykh esmintsev', Lenta.ru, 28 February 2019, https://lenta.ru/news/2019/02/28/leader (accessed 8 October 2022).

52 'Severnoe PKB priostanovilo rabotu nad perspektivnym atomnym esmintsem', Interfax, 18 April 2020, www.interfax.ru/russia/704920 (accessed 8 October 2022).

53 'Osnovy gosudarstvennoi politiki Rossiiskoi v oblasti voenno-morskoi deyatelnosti na period do 2030 goda', 20 July 2017, http://publica tion.pravo.gov.ru/Document/View/0001201707200015 (accessed 8 October 2022); D. Gorenburg, 'Russia's New and Unrealistic Naval Doctrine', War on the Rocks, 26 July 2017, https://warontherocks. com/2017/07/russias-new-and-unrealistic-naval-doctrine (accessed 8 October 2022).

54 A. Nikolskiy, 'Minfin i «Roskosmos» vstupili v publichnie prepiratelstva o sokrashenii raskhodov', *Vedomosti*, 25 August 2020, www.vedomosti. ru/politics/articles/2020/08/25/837739-minfin-roskosmos (accessed 8 October 2022).

55 A. Khrolenko, 'Antitorpeda – unikalnaya zashita rossiiskikh fregatov proekta 22350', Sputnik, 17 June 2020, https://uz.sputniknews.ru/col umnists/20200617/14352436/Antitorpeda--unikalnaya-zaschita-rossiysk ikh-fregatov-proekta-22350.html (no longer active).

56 'VMF Rossii k 2025 godu poluchit shest noveishykh fregatov proekta 22350', RIA-Novosti, 4 May 2016, https://ria.ru/20160504/1426082235. html (accessed 14 November 2022).

57 A. Shishkin, 'Severnaya verf: "sobaka, shto sidit na sene"', Navy Korabel blog, 21 June 2015, http://navy-korabel.livejournal.com/101592.html (accessed 8 October 2022).

58 Interview with Ilya Kramnik, military correspondent for Lenta.ru, April 2015; 'Pervie rossiiskie reduktornie agregaty dlya fregata proekta 22350', BMPD blog, 24 October 2020, https://bmpd.livejournal.com/4170665. html (accessed 8 October 2022).

59 'Rossiya planiruet postroit 12 modernizirovannykh fregatov proekta 22350M', TASS, 8 May 2019, https://tass.ru/armiya-i-opk/6415468 (accessed 8 October 2022).

60 'Zavod "Yantar" pristanovyl stroitelsvo fregata "Admiral Kornilov"', Lenta.ru, 20 May 2015, https://lenta.ru/news/2015/05/20/kornilov; 'Iz-za Ukrainy rossiiskie fregaty stanut indiiskimi', *Nezavisimaya gazeta*, 12 September 2017, www.ng.ru/news/593889.html (accessed 8 October 2022).

61 O. Kuleshov, 'Zachem Indii fregaty proekta 11356', Severnyi Vestnik, 10 October 2019, www.korabel.ru/news/comments/russko-indiyskie_fre gaty.html (accessed 8 October 2022).

62 'Fregat "Admiral Grigorovich" vperviye vyshel v more na ispytaniya', Lenta.ru, 24 April 2015, https://lenta.ru/news/2015/04/24/grigorovich (accessed 14 November 2022).

63 G. Kostrinskiy, 'Na patrulnie ledokoly ustanovyt "Manuly"', *Kommersant*, 8 December 2017, www.kommersant.ru/doc/3489289 (accessed 8 October 2022); A. Zakvasin and E. Komarova, 'Arktika na zamke: chem unikalen perviy krupnotonnazhnyi korabl ledovovo klassa dlya FSB "Purga"', RT, 26 July 2020, https://russian.rt.com/russia/article/767705-fsb-purga-ermak-proekt-23550-arktika (accessed 14 November 2022); R. Fakhrutdinov, '"Papanin" dlya Artktiki: v Rossii sozdan boevoi ledokol', Gazeta.ru, 25 October 2019, www.gazeta.ru/army/2019/10/25/12777104.shtml (accessed 8 October 2022).

64 A. Shishkin, 'Boevie korabli osnovnykh klassov VMF Rossii na 01.01.2022', Navy Korabel blog, 3 January 2022, https://navy-korabel.livejournal.com/257457.html (accessed 8 October 2022); A. Shishkin, 'Stroitelstvo boevykh korablei osnovnykh klassov dlya VMF Rossii na 01.01.2022', Navy Korabel blog, 3 January 2022, https://navy-korabel.livejournal.com/257030.html (accessed 8 October 2022).

65 'Korvety proekta 20380', Catalogue of Russian Arms, http://rus-guns.com/korvety-proekta-20380.html (accessed 8 October 2022); 'V Peterburge zalozhili dva korveta- "nevidimki" proekta 20380', Lenta.ru, 20 February 2015, https://lenta.ru/news/2015/02/20/skr20380 (accessed 14 November 2022).

66 Y. Apalkov, *Protivolodochnie korabli*. Moscow: Morkniga, 2010, p. 148.

67 'Project 20385 Gremyaschy Corvette to Be Powered by Russian-Made Engines', Navy Recognition, April 2016, www.navyrecognition.com/index.php/newsb/defence-news/2016/april-2016-navy-naval-forces-defense-industry-technology-maritime-security-global-news/3899-project-20385-gremyaschy-corvette-to-be-powered-by-russian-made-engines.html (accessed 8 October 2022).

68 'Korvet novovo pokoleniya so semnymi boevymi modulyami zalozhat na verfe v Peterburge', TASS, 26 February 2015, https://tass.ru/armiya-i-opk/1792507 (accessed 14 November 2022); 'Novy korvet dlya VMF Rossii osnastyat bespilotnikami', Lenta.ru, 15 October 2014, https://lenta.ru/news/2014/10/15/corvette (accessed 14 November 2022).

69 'Construction of Second Project 20386 Corvette to Start in 2018', TASS, 28 June 2017, https://tass.com/defense/953705 (accessed 8 October 2022).

70 'VMF Rossii udvoit zakaz ha modulnie korvety', Lenta.ru, 16 April 2014, https://lenta.ru/news/2014/04/16/p22160 (accessed 14 November 2022).

71 R. Kretsul and A. Ramm, 'Chas "Bykova": Korabl-robot uspeshno zavershil arkticheskii pokhod', *Izvestiia*, 27 October 2020, https://iz.ru/

1078799/roman-kretcul-aleksei-ramm/chas-bykova-korabl-robot-uspes hno-zavershil-arkticheskii-pokhod (accessed 8 October 2022).

72 K. Soper, 'Zelenodolsk Building Modular Patrol Ships for the Russian Navy', *IHS Jane's Navy International*, 3 August 2014.

73 'Zelenodolskii zavod imeni A.M. Gorkovo zalozhil shestoi patrul-niy korabl proekta 22160 dlya VMF RF', Zelenodolsk Factory, 13 January 2018, www.zdship.ru/press-center/news-events/2900 (accessed 8 October 2022).

74 'Modulny boets: Chem opasny noveishie korvety proekta 22160', RIA-Novosti, 7 July 2018, https://ria.ru/20180703/1523802694.html (accessed 14 November 2022); X. Vavasseur, 'Russia's Project 21631 Buyan-M Corvettes Fitted with Mines', Naval News, 17 March 2020, www.nav alnews.com/naval-news/2020/03/russias-project-21631-buyan-m-corve ttes-fitted-with-mines (accessed 8 October 2022).

75 'Latest Karakurt-Class Missile Corvette Laid Down for Russian Navy', TASS, 26 February 2019, http://tass.com/defense/1046432 (accessed 8 October 2022); 'V Zelenodolske nachnetsya stroitelstvo pervovo MPK proekta 22800 "Karakurt"', *Oruzhie Rossii*, 24 September 2016, https://ria.ru/20160923/1477681653.html (accessed 14 November 2022).

76 G. Kostrinskiy, '"Karakurty" razmazhut po verfyam', *Kommersant*, 30 July 2017, www.kommersant.ru/doc/3371787 (accessed 8 October 2022); 'Navy Refused to Change Engines for "Karakurt"', TopWar, 10 October 2018, https://en.topwar.ru/148177-vmf-otkazalsja-menjat-dvigateli-dlja-karakurtov.html (accessed 8 October 2022).

77 'Project 775 Large Landing Ships', Russianships.info, http://russian ships.info/eng/warships/project_775.htm (accessed 8 October 2022); 'Project 1171 Large Landing Ships', Russianships.info, http://russian ships.info/eng/warships/project_1171.htm (accessed 8 October 2022). One was sunk in March 2022 in the war against Ukraine.

78 P. Tran, 'Mistral Dispute with Russia Settled, France Eyes Exports', Defense News, 9 August 2015, www.defensenews.com/naval/2015/08/09/mis tral-dispute-with-russia-settled-france-eyes-exports (accessed 8 October 2022).

79 'V Kaliningrade zalozhili bolshoi desantny korable "Petr Morgunov"', Lenta.ru, 11 June 2015, https://lenta.ru/news/2015/06/11/morgunov (accessed 14 November 2022).

80 A. Arkadiev, 'BDK "Petr Morgunov" voshel v sostav VMF Rossii', TV Zvezda, 23 December 2020, https://tvzvezda.ru/news/forces/content/202012231630-B140I.html (accessed 8 October 2022).

81 'Novaya para BDK proekta 11711 budet otlichatsya ot "Ivana Grena" i "Petra Morgunova"', Flotprom.ru, 23 April 2019, https://flotprom.ru/2019/328108 (no longer active).

82 'VMF RF mozhet zakazat dopolnitelnie BDK modernizirovannovo proekta 11711', Korabel.ru, 24 March 2020, www.korabel.ru/news/comments/vmf_rf_mozhet_zakazat_dopolnitelnye_bdk_modernizirova nnogo_proekta_11711.html (accessed 8 October 2022).

83 X. Vavasseur, 'Russia's Project 23900 LHD to Be Able to Operate in the Arctic', Naval News, 28 August 2020, www.navalnews.com/naval-news/2020/08/russias-project-23900-lhd-to-be-able-to-operate-in-the-arctic (accessed 8 October 2022).

84 X. Vavasseur, 'Russia's Project 23900 LHD to Operate as Command Ship', Naval News, 5 August 2020, www.navalnews.com/naval-news/2020/08/russias-project-23900-lhd-to-operate-as-command-ship (accessed 8 October 2022).

85 The numbers for 2022 include ships and submarines undergoing short-term repairs, but not ones that are undergoing a long-term repair or modernisation.

86 Communication with Ilya Kramnik, July 2015.

87 D. Gorenburg, 'Is a New Russian Black Sea Fleet Coming? Or Is It Here?', War on the Rocks, 31 July 2018, https://warontherocks.com/2018/07/is-a-new-russian-black-sea-fleet-coming-or-is-it-here (accessed 8 October 2022).

Part III

The challenge: the Russian Navy in practice

7

Toward an understanding of maritime conflict with Russia

Michael B. Petersen

Russia's military modernisation since 2008 has had an impressive effect on its capabilities. Ground forces, strategic rocket forces, and aerospace defence forces in particular are vastly improved, while long-range precision strike and ground-based air defence have become special points of pride. Modernisation in the Russian Federation Navy (RFN), with its longer development timelines, greater costs, and legendary corruption and inefficiency, has been uneven but has nonetheless made significant progress. The weight of Russian effort has been on building modern nuclear-powered ballistic missile submarines (SSBNs), cruise missile submarines (SSGNs), diesel submarines, frigates, and coastal defence vessels. Moscow is now capable of putting a force to sea that is by at least one measure the third most powerful fleet in the world.[1]

Russia's recapitalisation of these forces has generated a renewed interest in its maritime warfighting capability, especially its navy, in the Euro-Atlantic community. Much of this analysis focuses on naval technologies, an important area of investigation that none-theless does not yield much insight into Russian strategy or intent. Other studies that do examine Russian intent have some rather distinct echoes with late Cold War arguments about the Soviet Navy, when debate raged over whether the Soviets intended a renewed "Battle of the Atlantic" or focused instead on "bastion defence".[2] These arguments tend to be reductive, lack analytic clarity, and frequently abjure analysis of Russian naval capabilities against its global competitors, a habit that hinders an understanding of how – and how effectively – the RFN might fight.

Other recent examinations of Russian naval warfare have focused almost exclusively on the concept of anti-access/area denial (A2/AD) in the maritime approaches to Russia.[3] These studies have effectively pointed out that Russian capabilities, while dangerous, may not be all they appear. But they only tell half the story by failing to address Russia's ability to fight at the theatre level or even across theatres of military operations (TVDs). A broader assessment that includes theatre and cross-theatre warfighting is necessary especially in light of increasing suggestions that Russia may seek to fight further from home by, for example, closing the Greenland–Iceland–United Kingdom (GIUK) Gap or even the English Channel.[4]

Indeed, the challenges of open-ocean warfare are orders of magnitude more difficult than the already significant problems associated with shore-based A2/AD. This chapter attempts to provide a more holistic picture of high-intensity naval warfare with Russia. It asks, "What is the Russian Navy for?" and uses Russian strategic and doctrinal writings to outline its broad wartime tasks. It then examines the intersection of maritime geography; combat power; and intelligence, surveillance, reconnaissance, and targeting (ISR-T) to determine how and how well the RFN might fulfil these tasks against a technologically advanced, operationally sophisticated adversary. It argues that the RFN is one component of a complex, joint offensive/defensive cost imposition and damage limitation effort. But rather than solely seeking out targets at sea for a series of navy-on-navy fights, the intersecting issues of maritime geography, order of battle, and ISR-T limitations indicate that the fleet may be more effective at operations that focus on striking "critical objects" on land rather than ship-to-ship combat at sea.

The focus of this chapter is the proverbial low-probability/high-impact event: high-end joint warfare at sea with Russia.

To borrow Russian terms, it examines regional and large-scale war, conflicts against a coalition of opponents across one or multiple theatres of war but that fall short of a global strategic nuclear exchange.[5] It bears noting at the outset that considering this possibility does not mean that war will occur or is even expected. Indeed, all potential sides agree that conflict is not in their best interest, and that such a conflict, with all its escalation risks, is to be avoided at nearly all costs. Nevertheless, scholars must confront this possibility squarely, especially given the sharp escalation in Russia's war against Ukraine in 2022.

The RFN's wartime tasks

Understanding the navy's role first requires a grasp of broader Russian wartime strategy and conflict periodisation. Recent studies demonstrate that Russian military strategy focuses on cost imposition for the purposes of escalation management. Rather than area control or denial, Russian strategists hold that the military can impose – or threaten to impose – strategic deterrence costs that restrain the adversary and outweigh the benefits of aggression, thereby undermining the adversary's political will and compelling it to end the conflict on terms acceptable to Russia. Military operations are conducted across all domains and are designed to limit damage as well as impose cost. This is part of a complex interrelationship between defence, counter-offence, and offence. In Russian thinking, carefully "dosed" cost imposition efforts and damage limitation are often two sides of the same coin. A tactical offensive, depending on the target, can be executed for the purposes of both.[6] This focus on cost imposition rather than denial or control may be borne out of the belief that at the high-end of conflict, Russia, with its smaller military capacity than the United States, must develop asymmetric strategies that have political effects beyond the military domain.[7]

Conflict periodisation is another crucial point. The two most critical elements to Russian conflict periodisation are

Table 7.1   *Russian naval tasks by conflict period, as described by the Ministry of*
         Defence

Threatening Period	Mobilisation;
	Deterrence of conflict;
	Local conflict isolation and limitation;
	Defence of navigation and economic activities;
	Standoff land attack;
	Protection of SSBN force;
Initial Period of War/ Wartime	Attack ASW capabilities and coastal installations;
	Maintain favourable operational environment;
	Provide maritime support for troops ashore;
	Coastal defence

Source: 'Navy', Ministry of Defence of the Russian Federation, n.d., https://eng.mil.
ru/en/structure/forces/navy/mission.htm.

the "Threatening Period" and the "Initial Period of War" (see Table 7.1). In the twenty-first century, the Threatening Period is generally characterised as a short, sharp crisis potentially leading to war. A common assumption among Russian thinkers is that modern combat operations occur so rapidly and decisively that wartime deployments of combat forces will be too late to affect the outcome of conflict. Russia's military doctrine, for example, points out that a characteristic feature of modern conflict is the 'reduction of the time periods required for preparing to conduct military operations'. Thus, the Threatening Period is key. This has specific implications for force readiness. The Defence Ministry notes that 'a period of threats alone will afford the time for strategic deployment of the armed forces and other troops'.[8] Military forces, therefore, must constantly be maintained at high state of readiness, and either pre-positioned for rapid combat operations or prepared for rapid deployment forward, all in order to avoid or mitigate the effects of strategic surprise.

In this Threatening Period, the Defence Ministry has assigned several tasks to the RFN. The first is rapid mobilisation and transition to wartime footing, or as Russia's official naval doctrine puts it, 'to promptly and covertly deploy forces (troops) into remote areas of the World Ocean' as part of a deterrent effort to hold adversary targets at risk.[9] Second, the navy must work to isolate local conflicts and prevent them from metastasising into a regional war. Finally, the Ministry of Defence notes that the navy's task is 'protection of navigation and industrial activities in the territorial sea and exclusive economic zone of the Russian Federation, and, if required, in the crisis areas of the World Ocean'.[10]

Thus, in the Threatening Period, the navy is responsible for a distant strategic deterrence mission as well as safeguarding the well-being of the state's maritime and coastal economic infrastructure. Russian strategists believe that destruction of these targets is an essential part of a war-winning strategy by the United States. However, given the Russian General Staff's preference for pre-emptive, or what Valeriy Gerasimov has called "preventive" action, it should be noted that protection of this infrastructure does not necessarily mean that Russia will limit itself to tactically defensive local operations.[11]

Indeed, Russia may attempt to seize the first mover advantage in the Initial Period of War. According to the Defence Ministry, this is the period in which states conduct combat operations with the forces arrayed during the Threatening Period and is considered by Russian strategists to the most crucial phase of combat.[12] It is characterised by decisive, rapid, joint, military, political, and cyber operations 'in which the warring sides will be striving to make the most of the power of its groups of forces built up in advance'.[13] Most importantly, in the Initial Period of War, even strategically defensive conflicts will include generous doses of the offensive at the tactical, operational, and even strategic level of war.

The Ministry of Defence is clear about the RFN's place in these operations. The first wartime objective enumerated in its tasks for the navy is 'to destroy enemy land-based facilities at long distances'.[14] This thinking is the result of decades of Russian thought on standoff strike, or "non-contact" warfare. Russia's official naval doctrine emphasises the RFN's importance in the Initial Period of War, noting that one of its roles is 'to attack the critically important ground-based facilities of the adversary, without violating, until a certain moment, its national sovereignty'. It further notes that '[w]ith the development of high-precision weapons, the Navy faces a qualitatively new objective: destruction of the enemy's military and economic potential by striking its vital facilities from the sea'.[15] The concept is known as "the fleet against the shore".[16]

Conceptually, these tasks are nested under the broader notion of joint "strategic operations". These are defined in the Russian military lexicon as '[a] set of coordinated and interrelated goals, tasks, place and time of strikes, operations and combat operations of the units and formations of various services of the Armed Forces, conducted simultaneously and consistently according to a single concept and plan to achieve the intended strategic goals'. They include Strategic Aerospace Operations, Strategic Operations in a Continental Theatre of Military Operations, Strategic Operations in the Oceanic Theatre of Operations, and Strategic Operations of Nuclear Forces, among other concepts. Often, these concepts serve the broader aim of Strategic Operations for the Destruction of Critically Important Targets (or "objects" in Russian), also known as SODCIT in the West.[17]

Russian navalists have consistently emphasised the value of naval forces as a key contributor to strategic operations. As early as 2001, they were arguing that '[t]he main form of employment of the Armed Forces of the Russian Federation in a sixth generation war will be a strategic defensive aerospace-sea operation' featuring integrated naval, air, and air defence forces.[18] In 2003, navy Chief of Staff Viktor Kravchenko wrote that fleet operations are

> an integral part of the strategic aerospace operation, the strategic actions of the Armed Forces in the theatre of operations ... The successful conduct of strategic aerospace operations can determine the course and outcome of a war, and when conducting non-contact

actions, its result will be the decisive, and in some cases, the only factor in achieving the final goal in the initial period of war.[19]

A dozen years later, this thinking achieved full flower.

In late 2015, ships in the Caspian Flotilla and Black Sea Fleet used the navy's new SS-N-30 Kalibr land-attack cruise missiles to destroy oil production facilities, weapons warehouses, and command centres in Syria.[20] These attacks served as proof of principle for the naval leadership, who embraced this model of long-range standoff warfare against land targets and emphasised the navy's central place in that effort. Former Black Sea Fleet Commander Admiral Alexander Vitko, for example, noted in 2017 that '[i]n the Southwest, only the Black Sea Fleet has such [Kalibr] weapons … and is capable of dealing missile strikes, using high-precision weapons, against critically important infrastructure assets belonging to the potential adversary at up to 1700 km distance'.[21] The naval leadership considers the RFN's land-attack capabilities to be decisive in the conduct of war and it currently dominates Russian strategic-operational naval thinking.

This focused effort on land attack should not obscure the fact that the naval leadership understands the necessity to engage targets at sea and in the littorals. The Defence Ministry highlights the navy's mission to 'destroy enemy antisubmarine and other forces as well as its coastal facilities', and 'maritime support of contact troops during maritime defensive and offensive operations'.[22] Just as with a land-attack mission, the Initial Period of War is critical, especially against a numerically superior adversary at sea. Soviet naval Commander Vladimir Chernavin noted decades ago that '[s]uch a specific feature as the growing role of the battle of the first salvo is becoming extremely important in modern naval combat. Pre-empting the enemy in striking a blow in battle is the main method of preventing his surprise attack, reducing losses, and inflicting the greatest damage on the enemy.'[23] Importantly, these operations focus especially on strikes against the adversary's key strategic enablers at sea. For example, an influential *Military Thought* article notes the importance of attacks against 'maritime carriers that are the global strike assets' and 'maritime components of the U.S. national [missile defence] system'.[24] This combination of strikes against critical targets ashore and afloat are at the core of the navy's offence-defence cost imposition strategy.

Geography and the challenges of naval warfighting capacity

To what extent can the RFN deliver on these ideas? The answer to this question turns on the relationship between geography, ISR-T, and order of battle. Especially against a sophisticated adversary, their interaction will tend to force Russia into concepts of operations that minimise weaknesses in large-volume open-ocean search, and to rely on less ISR-intensive theatre-level maritime efforts, such as standoff land attack against fixed targets. Alternatively, the RFN may also need to rely on operations that allow it to exploit Russia's considerable and dense land-based ISR network rather than its more problematic capabilities in the "far seas".

Basic geography often features prominently in discussions of so-called Russian A2/AD. Confined waters covered by technology "bubbles" of sensors and weapons have been a common trope of discussions on the topic. But the opposite is often ignored in discussions about Russian strategy. While geography can provide a modicum of sanctuary for Russia, as a factor in warfighting against distant targets, it also presents grave challenges. Geographers have long posited what they call a "loss of strength gradient", a unit of competitive power that is lost per some unit of distance from home shores. As such, relative military strength can change with distance.[25] In Russia's maritime domain, this loss of strength gradient is particularly relevant at the operational level of war because of capacity limitations as well as the failure to secure overseas alliances and – with the exception of Syria and Sudan – forward basing.

Russian warfighting in its littoral regions and maritime approaches is based around a densely layered and redundant network of land-based sensors, jammers, decoys, and weapons, including advanced surface-to-air missiles and tactical, fixed-wing fighter aircraft. Especially since 2009, restoring and modernising these shore-based defensive systems has been a major strategic priority for Moscow. These are not focused on defending broad areas of territory but rather on "critical objects" such as command and control nodes, nuclear weapons facilities, and economic targets.[26] That is, they play an important role in damage limitation.

Layered forward defence of this shore-based system and the strategic nuclear force afloat is the responsibility of the fleet. The navy also extends the defences around the maritime approaches and nuclear bastions. According to the US Office of Naval Intelligence, these efforts can stretch to roughly 1,000 nautical miles from a given position on the Russian coast. This force is expected to provide an initial line of defence and impose cost on expected aerospace attacks against critical Russian targets.[27]

As it moves further offshore, however, Russia's loss of strength gradient begins to take hold as the potential volume of contested geographic space increases. The Russian leadership has had success in constructing the smaller and less complex naval platforms capable of defending its near seas lines of communication in conjunction with shore-based assets. But measured against its own expectations for building a large fleet of ocean-going warships and submarines, it has struggled. This has implications for the global aspirations of its offence-defence warfighting concepts.[28]

Smaller platforms such as diesel submarines and coastal defence corvettes are armed with the Kalibr family of cruise missiles, which includes both land-attack and anti-ship variants, but they have limited range, speed, endurance, and even survivability. These combatants are generally expected to defend coastal areas and near seas under the cover of shore-based defences.[29] However, their smaller size and lack of range and survivability means that they must focus their anti-ship efforts in the local theatre of military operations only. At the same time, the Kalibr land-attack variant, with its roughly 1,000-mile range, may have a theatre role, and can even reach across different TVDs if necessary. Critically, they also carry relatively small numbers (eight to sixteen) of missiles aboard, limiting their ability to generate sustained or large salvos unless they are deployed in surface action groups of three or four vessels.

Larger platforms are less constrained and offer the Russian Navy more options. The nuclear-powered submarine force based in the Northern and Pacific Fleets is generally where most military analysts might place the Russian Navy on par with the United States. In the near term, however, this force suffers from severe order of battle constraints. According to Russian naval analyst Alexander Shishkin, the Northern Fleet may only be capable of getting five of its SSNs underway alongside its three SSGNs. The rest are undergoing extended repairs or modernisation. In the Pacific Fleet, Russia may only have one operational SSN alongside a possible three operational SSGNs.[30] If, as expected, Moscow chooses to use SSNs to defend its strategic nuclear ballistic missile submarines, then the navy's fighting strength in the Atlantic and Pacific Oceans is very limited indeed. Three to five submarines in the North Atlantic, for example (an area comprising some 6.4 million square miles), are likely to have a very difficult time locating uncooperative adversary warships in the open ocean. How might they do so?

Over-the-horizon intelligence, surveillance, reconnaissance, and targeting

Effective over-the-horizon (OTH) ISR is an essential element of long-range precision warfare. One cannot kill what one cannot find. This is especially true in blue-water, open-ocean environments, where distance and volume are orders of magnitude greater than they are in the maritime approaches to shore. Nations must have tools that not only effectively locate potential targets but also have the ability to transmit that location data to shooting platforms in a timely way. Even if they are able to accomplish this, shooting platforms must also have the ability to launch on that target data with as little time lag as possible, especially at long range, where delays as a result of distance and speed can make the difference between success and failure. A nation must therefore have enough shooting assets on hand to cover large volumes of ocean. Finally, ISR assets must also be in place to assess whether or not an attack was successful and the adversary dispatched, or if a re-attack is necessary.

While Russian fleet modernisation has resulted in a force that is in some ways as lethal as the legacy Soviet fleet, and even more flexible, those improvements have masked other ongoing shortcomings. OTH ISR-T is perhaps Russia's most critical challenge. In the great spaces of the open ocean, the navy's limited force of long-endurance platforms is dependent on large-volume search capabilities to locate targets in the open ocean. As weapon ranges have increased, the necessary search area has expanded as a square of that range. Doubling weapon range may quadruple the volume of area that requires searching.[31] Moscow has made significant strides to recapitalise its fleet of space-based, air-breathing, and ground-based ISR assets, but the Russian military may nevertheless be challenged to overcome a determined, technologically sophisticated, uncooperative peer adversary capable of exploiting gaps in Russia's large-volume OTH search capability.

Shore-based sensors can help in this regard, but they have limitations in either range or accuracy. In the open ocean, navies must rely either on space-based or air-breathing platforms, or on sensors that are organic to ships and submarines. Russia has limitations on all of these.[32] Indeed, while Russian shore-based sensors are sophisticated and capable, the further from those sensors the conflict occurs, the greater the challenges the navy faces.

Moscow has had only mixed results in renewing its space-based targeting capability. Its new family of electronic intelligence satellites is the "Liana" system, made up of Pion-NKS and Lotos-S satellites.[33] These satellites provide the RFN with a space-based targeting capability by collecting the electronic signals emitted by adversary naval vessels and providing that information to Russian anti-ship cruise missile shooters equipped with the proper satellite communications equipment.[34] But according to open sources, only one Pion-NKS satellite and three Lotos-S satellites are currently operational.[35] While the satellites' field of regard (that is, its coverage "footprint" on the earth's surface) is unknown, according to publicly available satellite tracking websites, there may be considerable coverage gaps. Furthermore, these low-earth orbit satellites have a roughly ninety-minute orbital period, meaning that they pass from view quickly and do not provide persistent coverage over a given point on the earth's surface.[36]

In the absence of constant space-based coverage, long-range air breathing maritime patrol and reconnaissance aircraft must fill gaps. In this regard, the Soviet-era Tu-142 Bear-F maritime patrol and reconnaissance aircraft is Russia's most capable asset. The Tu-142 is equipped with numerous sensors for surface and undersea search and combat and reportedly has a combat radius of over 3,000 miles.[37] Such range is impressive, but because Russia lacks forward basing, allies that could provide it, fighter aircraft with similar range, and carrier-based fighter aircraft, long-range escort missions are impossible. The massive propeller-driven aircraft, with its enormous radar cross-section, is potentially detectable on radar from hundreds of miles away and is at the mercy of modern fighter aircraft. For its own protection, it must stay within easy reach of Russian fighter patrols or land-based surface-to-air missile coverage, drastically limiting the amount of sensitive ocean it can safely cover. As a result, the Tu-142 is of limited utility in open-ocean warfare and is better used to extend Russian sensor coverage in more limited ways.[38] The Bear-F is of course not Russia's only maritime patrol and reconnaissance aircraft platform, but it is its most capable. Others are more limited with regard to either range or sensor capability or both.

Organic sensors aboard warships and submarines have critical limitations as well. Submarines rely almost entirely on sonar. They can also use an electronic support measure mast to detect ships and submarines passively, but they risk detection when doing so because the mast must come out of the water. Long-range sonar detections are possible if undersea sound convergence zones are present at certain frequencies, but even then, sonar detections of surface vessels may only be possible over a few dozen miles.[39] In the open ocean, that is unlikely to be sufficient.

Surface platforms can have much greater detection ranges but lack the survivability and endurance of nuclear-powered submarines. Ship-based ISR presents a risk to the sensor-carrying platform as it patrols further away from shore-based air defence. Most of Russia's afloat OTH detection capability is resident in its fleet of auxiliary intelligence collection ships, lumbering, lightly defended vessels. Many other warships can also serve in an ISR role and are equipped with sophisticated air defences, but those defences are nevertheless limited by shorter-range but highly accurate target engagement radars, as well as the range of the actual air-defence missile.[40] Active target engagement radar range is also limited by the curvature of the earth, allowing low-flying aircraft and missiles to avoid detection until the last moment. This detection range can, however, be extended depending on the height of surface evaporation ducts, which form as a result of vertical distribution of water vapor, air temperature, and atmospheric pressure. These ducts can refract and extend radar range. Evaporation duct height depends on seasonality and can shift in different radiofrequencies.[41]

Even ships equipped with the most modern multi-frequency active and passive radar systems are at risk, a fact that sophisticated opponents such as the United States are capable of exploiting. Passive sensors have the advantage of providing detection of enemy objects without emitting radio signals, while active sensors, such as classical radar, send out electronic signals that can provide excellent accuracy but are more range-limited and can be identified, typed, and their source often localised. Passive systems offer the benefit of "stealthier" detection and often much longer range, especially if using tropospheric scatter techniques, but they tend to be less accurate and require triangulation that either takes time and target motion analysis or multiple integrated systems simultaneously scanning a single area.[42]

Counter-ISR-T

Even the most sophisticated systems are not fool-proof, and any adversary is unlikely to cooperate with Russian efforts to locate them. Naval analyst Alexander Timokhin has observed that '[t]he idea that ships at sea are in the palm of your hand and cannot hide does not stand up to collision with reality. Satellites, radio-electronic, radio-technical and aerial reconnaissance do not provide a 100 percent guarantee that a surface ship or a group of surface ships entering an area from which a strike will be launched will be detected.'[43] With the re-emergence of global near-peer competition, the US Navy has revived its emphasis on operational counter-ISR techniques at the tactical and operational levels of war.

Some of these are redolent of the naval tactics of the Cold War, adapted to the twenty-first century. For example, radio-frequency emissions control is a technique designed to restrict or eliminate electronic emissions from combat ships so that adversaries cannot collect those emissions at long range and generate location data. Much like it was in the Cold War, the tactic is designed to frustrate modern Lotos-S and other electronic intelligence collection systems. It is receiving increased emphasis in US Navy training scenarios.[44] The US Navy is also laying heavy emphasis on alternative communications pathways and anticipating limited communications by pushing initiative to ship and submarine commanders (so-called "mission command") to further eliminate radiofrequency indiscretions and reduce electronic signatures.[45]

Operational manoeuvre, deception, and dispersal have also received enormous attention, most recently in the US Tri-Service Maritime Strategy. This strategy highlights operational concepts known as Distributed Maritime Operations, Littoral Operations in a Contested Environment, and Expeditionary Advanced Base Operations.[46] While this attention has frequently generated more heat than light, the revival of manoeuvre, deception, and dispersal is nonetheless a significant step away from static offshore deployments that characterised post-Cold War conflicts in the Balkans, Iraq, Afghanistan, Libya, and elsewhere. These tactics, designed to enhance survivability and complicate targeting, are increasingly being exercised in the US Navy.[47] Based on the evidence of US operations to strike Syrian chemical weapons facilities, they may very well be gaining traction in the force.[48] These are clear indications of a US Navy that is actively considering alternatives that are designed to frustrate ISR efforts and create difficult targeting challenges.[49]

Furthermore, Russian submarines, as dangerous as they are, face the extraordinarily difficult challenge of large numbers of adversaries with sophisticated technology and advanced tactics. For example, historical fixed sonar arrays on the ocean floor have recently been upgraded, and may have the effect of constraining the geographical area in which Russian submarines can deploy undetected.[50] The United States and NATO may also be prepared to degrade extraordinarily complex OTH sensor and communications networks through kinetic, electronic, or cyber-attacks, forcing submarines to rely on limited organic sensors.[51] Thus, the Russian Navy may face an adversary that will use these tactics to exploit the combination of geographic distance, order of battle challenges, and ISR-T shortcomings.

Russian analysts themselves acknowledge these issues. In typically dry fashion, they note that the

lack of sufficient amounts and standards of available Navy reconnaissance forces and assets (removal from combat duty of the space
reconnaissance and target designation system; inadequate numbers
of reconnaissance aircraft, reconnaissance ships, and also surface
ships and submarines, that can conduct reconnaissance along with
their major tasks; location of ground centers of radio and radio
technical reconnaissance exclusively on RF territory) ... do not
make for radically improving the efficiency of naval EIC [electronic
intelligence collection] to disclose in time the intent of the potential
adversary and diminish the surprise effect of its actions.[52]

In the contest to exploit asymmetric advantages and minimise
disadvantages, these dynamics tend to have a shaping effect on
Russia's defence-offence cost imposition measures. They mean
that Russian tactical ship-to-ship actions, while possible, may be
higher-risk and yield less success, especially against an uncooperative target hundreds of miles from Russian shores. Further, even
when the RFN is able to execute complex strikes at sea, given
the limited number of missiles available on Russian warships, the
margin for error is razor thin. The Russian Navy simply cannot
afford to miss, or it has shot itself out of business.

Of course, these tactics provide few guarantees against a high
attrition rate at sea or on land. The Russian military is a thinking,
learning organisation and actively seeks asymmetries in its favour,
either via technology development or inventive concepts of operations or both. Adversary ships at sea remain at risk, and the navy
and air force have the capability to wickedly punish naval vessels
that fall into their crosshairs. Russia's adversaries may suffer high
casualties and struggle to achieve victory at sea. Given the cognitive and political costs this can have against their adversaries, the
RFN would gladly trade its frigates or a substantial portion of its
strike capability for a US aircraft carrier. Nevertheless, the RFN
still has other, less expensive cost imposition options at its disposal.

Their thinkers have identified long-range naval strikes against
fixed landward targets – the ship against the shore – as one such

opportunity for Russia to realise its preferred way of war. The navy may be challenged to defeat highly manoeuvrable combat units at sea, but it is likely to excel at the comparatively easier task of destroying non-manoeuvring, fixed landward targets. Nevertheless, the risk to ships remains significant, and the RFN will attempt strikes at sea, particularly against high-value targets such as aircraft carriers. Russian anti-ship missile capabilities have far outstripped those of the United States and its allies, and with the coming of the Tsirkon hypersonic anti-ship cruise missile, Moscow stands likely to maintain that advantage.[53]

Waging a maritime conflict

How might these dynamics manifest themselves in a theoretical, high-intensity, regional, or large-scale war in the near term (one to five years)? It is possible to gain a sense of the broad contours of such a conflict by combining these relative military concepts at the operational and strategic level of war as well as Russian strengths and limitations and pitting them against a sophisticated adversary such as the United States and NATO with its own strengths and limitations.

At the outset, as the Russian leadership senses that it has entered the Threatening Period, it is likely to begin dispersing naval forces out of their bases. SSBNs will move into seaborne bastions protected by surface combatants and SSNs. Smaller diesel submarines and surface combatants will also put to sea, as will large surface combatants and SSGNs.[54] The navy would deploy with a crisis deterrence mission, threatening damage infliction if an adversary does not take off-ramps to conflict. The Fundamentals of Russia's State Naval Policy calls out these tasks explicitly, noting that '[t]he Navy is one of the most effective instruments of strategic (nuclear and nonnuclear) deterrence', due in part to its ability 'to deploy naval expeditionary groups in a short period of time into the areas of conflict and remain in these areas for an extended period of time'.[55] Ashore, theatre-level Aerospace Defence Forces and ground force air defence forces deployed along maritime frontiers will be brought up to higher states of readiness and possibly deployed from garrisons. The goal of these forces would be to threaten "deterrent" or unacceptable damage to the potential adversary.[56]

Cruise missile shooting submarines are especially crucial in this regard, as they are likely to be called upon 'to perform a number of tasks in coastal areas', including 'the destruction of military-industrial facilities, command centres, disruption of enemy communications'.[57] Indeed, during the Threatening Period, it is even possible that Russia would attempt to deploy the Yasen-class SSGN *Severodvinsk* off the coast of the United States as part of a strategic deterrence mission and to be prepared to carry out strikes on critically important objects, should that become necessary.[58] It is important to note, however, that with only two potential submarines in this class available in the near term, order of battle shortfalls place limitations on Russia's ability to execute this mission.

During the Threatening Period, Russia may also make every effort to locate and hold at risk high-value naval units before combat operations make strict counter-ISR measures necessary.[59] Vice Admiral Andrew Lewis, the commander of the US Second Fleet, noted in early 2020 that '[o]ur ships can no longer expect to operate in a safe haven on the East Coast or merely cross the Atlantic unhindered to operate in another location'.[60] Indeed, the US and European military leadership must balance the deterrence value offered by naval presence in a crisis against blue-force survivability and increased instability when highly mobile strike platforms like warships "disappear" in the Threatening Period.[61]

For the US Navy, there is a clear tension between open declarations of presence during crisis deterrence operations on the one hand, and more covert deployments and preparation for war on the other, especially if it is intent on taking advantage of Russian open-ocean ISR challenges. In any case, while US naval forces will need to make clear shows of partner support and commitment, they are unlikely to do so in ways that make Russia's targeting challenges simple. Given the sheer volume of ocean and Russian naval and OTH ISR limitations noted above, it is likely that the greatest risk from Russian submarines is at the ends of sea lines of communication, where ships are more easily located and tracked departing or arriving in port.

If Moscow believes that deterrence is failing, it may initiate hostilities and shift into the Initial Period of War. Given the General Staff's traditional sensitivities to correlations of forces over time, and its emphasis on pre-emptive warfare, Moscow may believe that it needs to seize the initiative from its adversaries in this period.[62] Rapid, decisive strategic aerospace operations, or strategic operations for the destruction of critically important targets are key elements of potential Russian campaigns. The scope and intensity of these campaigns can vary depending on the level of conflict and the type of damage that Russia wishes to inflict, but in any case, such campaigns feature prominently in the Initial Period.

The navy will likely comprise one component of a larger effort to achieve local superiority during this period, especially to enable follow-on operations. For example, in a hypothetical conflict in which Norway is involved, there are several critical tasks that the General Staff may wish to carry out in the Initial Period. To deepen its northern bastion, blind adversary sensors, and ensure air superiority, Russian aircraft and ships may attempt to roll back neighbouring air and surface surveillance sites as well as restrict the use of military airfields in northern Norway.[63] Indeed, in March 2017, nine Su-24 fighters conducted a mock attack against the Globus radar in Vardø, across Varanger Fjord from Russia. That same year, in May, a similar mock attack took place at military installations around Bodø, as did a mock attack against naval assets around Tromsø and Bodø.[64] In 2018, eleven Russian Su-24 fighters once again conducted a mock attack against Vardø.[65]

In some cases, air attack may not even be necessary, as Russian surface ships can merely shell certain coastal surveillance sites.[66] This campaign could be part of a larger effort to eject Norwegian and allied air and air defence assets from sites north of Vestfjord. A combined offensive operation, with precision-strike land-attack cruise missiles, SS-26 Iskander-M ballistic missiles, and even unguided "dumb" bombs, especially at the outset of a conflict, may be capable of destroying NATO's integrated air defence radar network north of Vestifjord in Norway, and of effectively closing airfields that tactical fighters might otherwise utilise.[67] This campaign may be especially critical for removing or pushing back Norway's fleet of F-35 stealth fighters, which likely provide that country with a key asymmetric military advantage over Russia.

This strategic aerospace operation in the Initial Period can open the door to follow-on attacks with long-range theatre strike munitions. In the NATO northern flank scenario, with northern Norway cleared, Russian Tu-95 bombers carrying Kh-101 air-launched cruise missiles as well as Kalibr-carrying warships could initiate a campaign (the execution of strikes against different targets at different times) against critical military and civilian targets as far away as the United Kingdom and Iceland. These targets can include military bases housing important enabling capabilities such as command and control facilities, P-8 reconnaissance aircraft, air refuelling tankers, and even strategic strike aircraft, among many other potential targets.[68] Each bomber can carry up to eight missiles (the same as a Kalibr-capable corvette or Grigorovich frigate), so salvo sizes may be much larger, and their ability to conduct multiple sorties raises the prospect of repeated salvo attacks.[69]

Indeed, a crucial and overlooked point regarding war with Russia is that Russian Long-Range Aviation (LRA) bombers firing long-range precision-guided munitions from sanctuary may be far more dangerous than the navy's limited number of cruise-missile shooting submarines and their relatively small potential salvo size.

One Russian analysis notes that in wartime, '[t]he importance of strike aircraft is growing sharply, while the role of ships as a strike weapon is decreasing, but not disappearing'.[70] Thus, LRA assets launching theatre-level weapons from an air bastion will be an equally serious challenge as surface ships launching Kalibr cruise missiles from a naval bastion.

Nevertheless, modern Kalibr-capable vessels should not be dismissed. The RFN has gained valuable experience in Syria, where Kalibr missiles demonstrated impressive capability at long ranges. Even if "bottled up" in their home waters in the Barents, Baltic, or Black Seas, frigates, smaller corvettes, and diesel submarines can strike most of Northern, Central, and Eastern Europe. The former Commander of US Naval Forces Europe, Admiral James Foggo, noted that '[t]hey have shown the capability to be able to reach pretty much all the capitals in Europe from any of the bodies of water that surround Europe'.[71] While they might individually lack the large salvo capability resident in the LRA force of strategic and theatre bombers, Yasen and Yasen-M submarines also carry at least thirty-two land-attack and anti-ship cruise missiles and can pose a substantial threat, especially to European critical infrastructure and high-value naval units. These can have a decisive political effect on the course of a conflict.

Older, non-kalibrised platforms will also present a risk to US and NATO vessels. Oscar II SSGNs in the Northern and Pacific Fleets, dispersed in the Threatening Period, may attempt to overcome open-ocean ISR-T shortcomings by lying in wait in maritime choke points where Moscow anticipates high-value units may transit. Though limited in number, they will play a crucial role in both offensive cost imposition and defensive damage limitation by seeking out these vessels far from Russian shores, 'before these can move into the line of weapon employment'.[72]

Standoff strikes against landward targets will present a difficult problem to the United States and its allies. While NATO states and other partners could provide enviable basing resources,

Russia is likely to use its land-attack capabilities to reduce or deny NATO or US access to bases that are closer to its sensitive facilities, pushing tactical strike aircraft out of unrefuelled range. This is especially true in Europe. Put another way, Russia may attempt to "expand" its adversary's relative geography by pushing its opponents out of bases closer to Russian soil and forcing a more costly application of resources, while a nation like the United States may attempt to "shrink" its own by using standoff strike in order to bring follow-on military power forward.

But the use of impressive Western long-range precision strike against land targets should not be assumed. Moscow's declared nuclear use policy is that Russia reserves the right to use nuclear weapons in part '[i]n the event of aggression with conventional weapons when the very existence of the state is in jeopardy'. A second potential nuclear use scenario offered by Moscow is an 'attack by [an] adversary against critical governmental or military sites of the Russian Federation, disruption of which would undermine nuclear forces response actions'.[73] Conventional strikes near nuclear weapons storage and handling facilities like those on the Kola or Kamchatka Peninsulas would likely meet such a standard, as might strikes on Russian economic infrastructure in the Arctic.[74] To avoid potential nuclear escalation, it is conceivable – though not guaranteed – that US national leadership would forbid conventional strikes against Russian territory, especially where conventional and nuclear forces are co-located. If destruction of airfields and ports that provide force generation for these attacks is forbidden, long-range strike platforms will have to be destroyed in the air and at sea.

This is where the geographic loss of power gradient may affect Russia's adversaries, especially on the so-called "northern flank". If Russia is successful in stretching the geography by eliminating the use of forward air basing, the United States and its partners must invest greater resources to move large amounts of combat strength northward. The flight from air bases in the central United

Kingdom and southern Norway is between 1,200 and 1,700 miles, well beyond the unrefuelled combat radius of any tactical aircraft in the US or allied inventory. The United States will be forced to use either carrier strike groups or increasingly larger numbers of finite in-flight refuelling tankers from the US Air Force. The longer flight time will likewise limit the number of sorties that aircraft can fly in a given time.

Absent long-range land attack, and possibly lacking in tankers, the US Navy may need to manoeuvre to within range of its tactical naval strike capabilities, where it could be exposed to attacks from strike aircraft, surface ships, and any submarines that may be lying in wait, unlocated by undersea warfare forces.[75] Here, deceptive operations, manoeuvre, creative exploitation of the electromagnetic spectrum, and kinetic counter-ISR will be critical to survivability. If the navy must come forward, the searchable volume of ocean may shrink. Counter-ISR-T techniques are likely to be the difference between life and death in the face of a determined effort to extract as much cost against naval assets as possible.[76]

While US carrier strike groups will pack the majority of the firepower, it may require supplemental fifth-generation aircraft, possibly embarked aboard the British carrier *Queen Elizabeth* or as part of the complement on a US Marine expeditionary strike group, to enhance aircraft survivability in an air defence environment that will become more dense and complex the further north the navy proceeds. The combination of logistics needs, geography, and potential poor weather may also impact operations as resupply ships may struggle to cover longer geographic distances in short windows of clear weather.[77] Given these conditions, it is possible that the relative power gradient may shift to favour Russian strengths if a carrier strike group comes forward. Thus, a crucial question is whether or not long-range precision land attack would be authorised by US and NATO national leadership.

This stage of warfare may be more akin to what might be called A2/AD. But again, the bulk of Russian military and naval warfighting theory points not to sea denial, but to punishment and cost imposition. Russian surface combatants, including frigates, destroyers, and cruisers, will provide air defence and surface strike. Smaller corvettes, many equipped with Kalibr anti-ship cruise missiles, will support their larger cousins. But given limitations in numbers of missiles on board and the absence of at-sea reloads, an equal contribution in the effort to dole out punishment on any naval forces that come forward will be made by land-based strike aircraft such as Tu-22M3 bombers and Su-34 fighter-bombers, supported by tactical fighters and shore-based missile systems.

Strategic dilemmas

In high-end regional and global conflicts, the combination of doctrine and geography present Russia with a strategic dilemma. A critical aspect of Russian warfighting is careful escalation management, but for Moscow, operational realities may clash with strategic desires. To conduct dosed strikes against critical objects against an adversary like the United States, Moscow must risk horizontal escalation and expansion of the conflict. For example, one can imagine a scenario, however remote, in which Russia paralyses leadership and decision-making institutions in NATO countries to the extent that the latter refused to make military contributions during wartime. Consequently, there is a possibility that only a small coalition of nations, perhaps led by the United States, would participate in efforts to defeat Russia. Russia's list of critical targets would be drastically narrowed in such a scenario.

But the doctrinal instinct and operational imperative to strike critical US targets in Europe would clash with Moscow's greater strategic effort to keep the war from widening into a general conflict with NATO. Aviano Air Force Base, for example, is a major US combat, maintenance, and logistics hub. At least two F-16 squadrons are based there, and it is a suitable basing area for fifth-generation aircraft such as F-35s.[78] As such, it would likely play a critical role in any war in Europe. Russian efforts to strike the US base in Aviano with long-range precision guided munitions (PGMs) would necessarily involve shaping operations that allow Russian weapons to reach the target and non-permissive overflight of NATO countries by long-range PGMs. A Russian strike sourced from the Black Sea, for example, would likely involve first destroying US forces in Romania. An attack there would place pressure on Bucharest to respond militarily. A similar situation would exist for many potential fixed Russian targets, such as Souda Bay in Greece, İncirlik in Turkey, and Andøya in Norway, among many others. Thus, potential Russian efforts to de-escalate a conflict by imposing cost on critical US targets in Europe actually create horizontal escalation pressures and unwittingly draw more nations into the conflict.

In addition, even conventional strikes such as those postulated here against a nuclear-armed opponent like the United Kingdom are likely to put significant escalation pressure on the UK government. London may feel pressured, or may pressure the United States, to respond in kind with combined US/UK attacks on Russian soil. Thus, Russian conventional precision strikes in the UK may inadvertently provide the United States with enough justification to use its overwhelming long-range precision land-attack capabilities to target fixed installations in Russia, driving up escalation pressures dramatically. In addition, London describes its nuclear use policy as 'purposefully ambiguous', a factor that complicates Russian decision-making about the necessary "dosage" of strikes that would force the UK from the conflict.[79] 'We would consider using our nuclear weapons,' states an official explanation of the United Kingdom's nuclear strategy, 'only in extreme circumstances of self-defence, including the defence of our NATO Allies.'[80] What exactly those "extreme circumstances" may be remains unclear.

Implications for analysis and planning

This analysis has several implications. First, Russia-watchers must be cautious about making statements regarding threats to trans-Atlantic sea lines of communication. These arguments require much greater analytic clarity because they run the risk of warping strategic realities. Given Russian capacity and OTH ISR challenges, it seems likely that points of embarkation and debarkation – the *ends* of the Sea Lines of Communication (SLOCs), not the vast middle of them – are at risk, primarily because it is comparatively easier to destroy a ship in port than it is to do so at sea. Moscow has the intent and the capability to threaten landward targets on both sides of the Atlantic, though their ability to do so in the Western Atlantic is somewhat reduced. The circumstances of geography and the state of their own military modernisation would likely drive them in this direction.

Their weight of effort, as Michael Kofman and others have explored elsewhere, is dedicated to inflicting carefully dosed conventional damage effects in an effort to disorganise responses, interrupt logistics flows at fixed points, and generally impose "deterrent" or "unacceptable" damage that coerces an adversary to sue for peace on terms favourable to Russia.[81] Thus, the bulk of offensive activity is likely to be on landward, fixed targets as part of a joint campaign aimed at cost imposition. Long-range precision-guided munitions may be used either from the sanctuary of distant bastions or from the far seas. Russian joint assets, with some exceptions, will less commonly go on long and frustrating hunting missions for moving targets in a very large ocean. Such attacks, while possible, are far more ISR-intensive and tactically complex. But long-range strikes from sanctuary mean that NATO forces must be prepared to defend against such strikes while accepting risk and bearing what may be a high cost in order to defeat them where they are generated.

Similarly, in light of the interaction of geography with warship and ISR capacity, the concerns about Russia's purported ability to threaten targets south of the GIUK Gap appears to be inflated. While Russia may *technically* be able to close the GIUK Gap or even the English Channel, the likelihood of such an attempt is low, as the risk is high and the probability of success suboptimal. Rather, Russian warfighting strategy is partially shaped by its need to minimise its asymmetric disadvantages in warship capacity and ISR. Effectively challenging forces in the "far seas" of the GIUK Gap or south requires more high-volume, survivable, OTH search capability as well as greater numbers of survivable combat platforms than are currently available to Russia. In short, Russia still lacks the open-ocean capacity necessary to meaningfully overcome the geographic loss of strength gradient and successfully conduct ship-to-ship fighting in the central Atlantic at a scale to defeat the United States and NATO.

Even so, this analysis also suggests that the United States and NATO should not ignore investments in key future capabilities. Continued development of ISR and counter-ISR capabilities will remain essential. But counter-ISR will be no guarantee against attack. As Russia fields more advanced sensors to feed more combat platforms equipped with increasingly sophisticated hypersonic anti-ship missiles, avoiding that ISR and shooting down those missiles in flight will become ever more difficult, necessitating greater investment in so-called "soft-kill" technologies that seduce missiles to strike false targets.[82] In addition, if Russia is able to successfully expand the maritime geography, US and NATO partners are likely to require greater investments in aerial refuelling to ensure that tactical combat aircraft are able to transit and fight at long distance.

Finally, it is worth remembering that any wartime adversary of Russia gets a vote. Too much of what passes for analysis of the Russian military, particularly its maritime warfighting capabilities, is carried out in the absence of what a sophisticated adversary may do with its own capabilities and capacities. Russia is a dangerous opponent in the maritime domain and, despite its problems, is developing the strategy, operational concepts, and capabilities to impose substantial cost on potential adversaries. But war is a dynamic interaction. Moscow's potential opponents have effective and powerful militaries of their own and are developing sophisticated concepts to deter or defeat Russia. Any clear-headed assessment of Russian maritime warfighting must take both perspectives into account.

Notes

The views expressed here are the author's only, and do not reflect the opinion of the US Navy, Department of Defense, or any other segment of the US government.

1   K. Patton, 'Battle Force Missiles: The Measure of a Fleet', CIMSEC, 24 April 2019, https://cimsec.org/battle-force-missiles-the-measure-of-a-fleet (accessed 8 October 2022).

2   A good critique of these discussions is offered by S. Wills, '"These Aren't the SLOCs You're Looking For": Mirror-Imaging Battles of the Atlantic Won't Solve Current Atlantic Security Needs', *Defense & Security Analysis*, Vol. 36, No. 1 (2020), pp. 30–41. One of the more influential books supporting a new "Battle of the Atlantic" theory is M. Nordenman, *The New Battle for the Atlantic: Emerging Naval Competition with Russia in the Far North*. Annapolis, MD: US Naval Institute Press, 2019.

3   The Swedish Defence Research Institute has been on the cutting edge of this valuable work. See, for example, R. Dalsjö, C. Berglund, and M. Jonsson, *Bursting the Bubble, Russian A2/AD in the Baltic Sea Region: Capabilities, Countermeasures, and Implications*. Stockholm: FOI, 2019.

4   M. Melino and H. A. Conley, 'The Ice Curtain: Russia's Arctic Military Presence'. Washington, DC: Center for Strategic and International Studies, 2019, www.csis.org/features/ice-curtain-russias-arctic-military-presence (accessed 8 October 2022); M. Boulégue, 'Mitigating Russia's Military Posture in the European Arctic: Towards a High North Hard Security Architecture', in D. Depledge and P. Whitney Lackenbauer (eds), *On Thin Ice? Perspectives on Arctic Security*. Peterborough, Ontario: North American and Arctic Defence and Security Network, 2021, pp. 71–7.

5   Russian conflict definitions are embedded in its official military doctrine. See 'Voyennaya doktrina Rossiyskoy Federatsii', *Rossiiskaia gazeta*,

30 December 2014, https://rg.ru/2014/12/30/doktrina-dok.html (accessed 8 October 2022).

6 Michael Kofman, Anya Fink, and Jeffrey Edmonds explore these ideas in greater depth in *Russian Strategy for Escalation Management: Evolution of Key Concepts*. Arlington, VA: Center for Naval Analyses, 2020. They also point out an important distinction between strategic deterrence roles and general purpose warfighting roles played by conventional Russian forces.

7 T. L. Thomas, *Russian Military Thought: Concepts and Elements*. McLean, VA: Mitre Corporation, 2019, pp. 5–9, 5–10.

8 'Ugrozhayemyy period', in Russian Ministry of Defence, *Russian Military Encyclopaedic Dictionary*, https://encyclopedia.mil.ru/encyclopedia/dictio nary/details_rvsn.htm?id=10643@morfDictionary (accessed 8 October 2022). V. N. Gorbunov and S. A. Bogdanov, 'Armed Confrontation in the 21st Century', *Military Thought*, Vol. 18, No. 1 (2019), p. 27.

9 A. Davis (trans.), 'Fundamentals of the State Policy of the Russian Federation in the Field of Naval Operations for the Period until 2030', Russia Maritime Studies Institute, United States Naval War College, 2017, https://dnnlgwick.blob.core.windows.net/portals/0/NWCDepar tments/Russia%20Maritime%20Studies%20Institute/RMSI_RusNavy FundamentalsENG_FINAL%20(1).pdf?sr=b&si=DNNFileManagerPoli cy&sig=fjFDEgWhpd1ING%2FnmGQXqaH5%2FDEujDU76EnksAB %2B1A0%3D (accessed 8 October 2022).

10 'Navy Missions', Website of the Ministry of Defence of the Russian Federation, https://eng.mil.ru/en/structure/forces/navy/mission.htm (accessed 8 October 2022).

11 V. Gerasimov, 'Vektory razvitiya voennoi strategii', *Krasnaya Zvezda*, 4 March 2019.

12 'Nachal'nyy period voiny', in Russian Ministry of Defence, *Russian Military Encyclopedic Dictionary*, http://encyclopedia.mil.ru/encyclopedia/ dictionary/details.htm?id=6941@morfDictionary (accessed 8 October 2022).

13 S. G. Chekhinov and S. A. Bogdanov, 'Strategic Deterrence and Russia's National Security Today', *Military Thought*, Vol. 21, No. 1 (2012), pp. 29–30.

14 'Navy Missions'.

15 Davis, 'Fundamentals of the State Policy'.

16 A. Tsyganok, 'Voina na more v XXI veke', *Nezavisimoye Voyennoye Obozhreniye*, 5 April 2019, https://nvo.ng.ru/nvo/2019-04-05/1_1040_ war.html (accessed 8 October 2022).

17 See D. Johnson, *Russia's Conventional Precision Strike Capabilities, Regional Crises, and Nuclear Thresholds*. Livermore, CA: Lawrence Livermore Institute, 2018, p. 32, https://cgsr.llnl.gov/content/assets/docs/Prec

ision-Strike-Capabilities-report-v3-7.pdf for a good discussion of these concepts.

18 I. Kapitanets, *Voina na more: aktual'nyye problemy razvitiya voyenno-morskoy nauki*. Moscow: Vagrius, 2001.

19 V. Kravchenko, 'Flot v sovremennoy voine', *Krasnaya Zvezda*, 45, 14 March 2003, p. 1.

20 S. LaGrone, 'Kurdish Video Lends Credibility to Russian Navy Caspian Sea Strike Mission Claims', USNI News, 7 October 2015, https://news. usni.org/2015/10/07/kurdish-video-lends-credibility-to-russian-navy-ca spian-sea-strike-mission-claims (accessed 8 October 2022); 'Russian Navy Caspian Flotilla Vessels Launched 2nd Cruise Missile Strike against IS Targets in Syria', Navy Recognition, 22 November 2015, https://www. navyrecognition.com/index.php/news/defence-news/year-2015-news/ november-2015-navy-naval-forces-defense-industry-technology-maritime- security-global-news/3255-russian-navy-caspian-flotilla-vessels-launched- 2nd-cruise-missile-strike-against-is-targets-in-syria.html (accessed 8 October 2022); A. Mathew, 'Russian Navy Submarines Fire Kalibr Cruise Missiles at Targets in Syria', DefPost, 5 October 2017, https://defpost.com/rus- sian-navy-submarines-fire-kalibr-cruise-missiles-targets-syria (accessed 8 October 2022); 'Russia Hits Targets in Syria from Mediterranean Submarine', BBC News, 8 December 2015, https://www.bbc.com/ news/world-middle-east-35041656 (accessed 8 October 2022).

21 A. V. Vitko, 'The Black Sea Fleet: A Factor for Expanding Combat Capabilities in the Responsibility Zone', *Military Thought*, Vol. 26, No. 3 (2017), p. 40.

22 'Navy Missions'. Emphasis added. The latter task is one that has been long-held by the navy.

23 A. Timokhin, 'Morskaya voina dlya nachinayushchikh: vzaimodeyst- viye nadvodnykh korabley i udarnoy aviatsii', *Voyennoye Obozreniye*, 20 December 2020, https://topwar.ru/177552-morskaja-vojna-dlja-nachi najuschih-vzaimodejstvie-nadvodnyh-korablej-i-udarnoj-aviacii.html (accessed 8 October 2022).

24 O. V. Alyoshin, A. N. Popov, and V. V. Puchnin, 'The Naval Might of Russia in Today's Geopolitical Situation', *Military Thought*, Vol. 25, No. 3 (2016), p. 17.

25 See, for example, H. Starr, 'Territory, Proximity, and Spatiality: The Geography of International Conflict', *International Studies Review*, Vol. 7, No. 3 (September 2005), pp. 387–406.

26 See M. Kofman, 'It's Time to Talk About A2/AD: Rethinking the Russian Military Challenge', War on the Rocks, 5 September 2019, https://warontherocks.com/2019/09/its-time-to-talk-about-a2-ad-reth inking-the-russian-military-challenge (accessed 8 October 2022).

27 'The Russian Navy: A Historic Transition', Suitland, MD: Office of Naval Intelligence, 2015, www.oni.navy.mil/ONI-Reports/Foreign-Naval-Capabilities/Russia (accessed 14 November 2022).

28 See M. B. Petersen, 'Strategic Deterrence, Critical Infrastructure, and the Aspiration–Modernization Gap in the Russian Navy', in J. Mankoff (ed.), *Improvisation and Adaptation in the Russian Military*. Washington, DC: Center for Strategic and International Studies, 2020, pp. 30–7.

29 I. Dygalo and A. Gavrilenko interview with Vladimir Korolev, 'Podvodnyye lodki – glavnaya udarnaya sila flota', *Krasnaya zvezda*, No. 28, 19 March 2018, p. 1.

30 A. Shishkin, 'Korabel'nyy sostav VMF Rossii (boyevyye korabli osnovnykh klassov) na 01.01.2021', Navy-Korabel, https://navy-korabel.livejournal.com/256211.html (accessed 8 October 2022).

31 W. P. Hughes, *Fleet Tactics: Theory and Practice*. Annapolis, MD: Naval Institute Press, 1986, pp. 166–7.

32 Russia's longest-range land-based radar is the Konteyner OTH radar. According to an image presented on Russia's TV Zvezda, the system, based in western Russia, tracks aircraft and currently provides maritime coverage over parts of the North Sea, the Eastern Mediterranean, and the Caspian Sea, hardly what Russia considers the "World Ocean". I. Levin and D. Shurygin, '"Nebesnyy nablyudatel": v RF sozdadut sploshnoye radiolokatsionnoye pole dlya obnaruzheniya vrazheskoy aviatsii', TV Zvezda, 2 December 2019, https://tvzvezda.ru/news/2019122121-lHScW.html (accessed 8 October 2022).

33 '"Soyuz" vozvrashchayetsya k polotam, zapustiv sputnik-razvedchik "Lotos-S1" iz Plesetska', 5 May 2020, https://avianews.info/soyuz-voz vrashhaetsya-k-polyotam-s-zapuskom-razvedyvatelnogo-sputnika-lotos-s1-iz-plesetska (accessed 8 October 2022).

34 P. Rumyantsev, '"All-Seeing" Space-Based Reconnaissance and Targeting System', New Defence Order Strategy, No. 5 (2018), https://dfnc.ru/en/kosmos/all-seeing-space-based-reconnaissance-and-target ing-system (accessed 8 October 2022).

35 The newest Lotos-S was launched on 2 February 2021. See 'Lotos-S Spacecraft for the Liana System', Russian Space Web, n.d., www.russi anspaceweb.com/liana.html (accessed 8 October 2022). Pion-NKS was launched on 25 June 2021. See W. Graham, 'Russia's Soyuz Launches Pion-NKS Naval Intelligence Satellite', 25 June 2021, www.nasaspaceflight.com/2021/06/soyuz-launches-pion-nks (accessed 14 November 2022).

36 Satellite orbits and periodicity for Cosmos 2524, 2528, and 2549, the designators for Russia's ELINT satellites, can be found at www.celestrak.com. See also www.n2yo.com/?s=47546&live=1 (accessed 8 October 2022).

37 'Tupolev Tu-142', Military Today, n.d., www.military-today.com/air craft/tu_142.htm (accessed 8 October 2022).

38 A 1983 incident near the Kuril Islands in the Pacific also illustrates the extraordinary challenges of open-ocean searches using maritime patrol and reconnaissance aircraft. See V. Mikhailov, 'Russkiy Perl-Kharbor', VKS Zhurnal, 27 March 2019, www.vesvks.ru/vks/article/russkiy-perl-harbor-16399 (accessed 8 October 2022).

39 For a description of how convergence zones function, see 'Sound Channel Convergence Zones', Naval Postgraduate School, n.d., www.oc.nps. edu/~bird/oc2930/acoustics/soundchannel.html (no longer active).

40 A ship's embarked helicopter may extend its sensor coverage but only at limited ranges. For an excellent introduction to radar performance in various bandwidths, see Massachusetts Institute of Technology Open Courseware, 'Introduction to Radar Systems', https://ocw.mit.edu/ resources/res-ll-001-introduction-to-radar-systems-spring-2007 (accessed 8 October 2022).

41 See P. Østenstad and M. M. Meltzer, 'Evaporation Duct Height Climatology for Norwegian Waters Using Hindcast Data', NATO paper, n.d., www.sto.nato.int/publications/STO%20Meeting%20Proc eedings/STO-MP-SET-244/MP-SET-244-10A.pdf (accessed 8 October 2022).

42 See Z. Liu and X. Chen, 'Prediction on Operating Range of Passive Troposcatter Detection System', *International Journal of Microwave and Wireless Technologies*, Vol. 11, No. 1 (February 2019), pp. 22–6. A helpful introduction to the topic is H. D. Griffiths and C. J. Baker, *An Introduction to Passive Radar*. Boston: Artech House, 2017.

43 A. Timokhin, 'Morskaya voina dlya nachinayushchikh: vyvodim avia-nosets "na udar"', *Voyennoye Obozreniye*, 16 October 2020, https://topwar. ru/176082-morskaja-vojna-dlja-nachinajuschih-vyvodim-avianosec-na-u dar.html (accessed 8 October 2022).

44 Z. Hoyt, 'Get Used to EMCON', *U.S. Naval Institute Proceedings*, Vol. 143, No. 7 (July 2017), pp. 75–6, www.usni.org/magazines/proceedings/2017/ july/professional-notes-get-used-emcon (accessed 14 November 2022). EMCON does impart risk, as a ship with its self-defence radars turned off is entirely reliant on passive detection to provide attack warning. But given the periodicity of Russian ELINT satellites, self-defence radars do not need to be turned off full-time.

45 P. Kime, 'Navy to Embrace "Mission Command" Concepts to Match Adversaries', Military.com, 15 January 2019, www.military.com/daily-news/2019/01/15/navy-embrace-mission-command-concepts-match-ad versaries.html#:~:text=Richard%20Brown%20calls%20%22Great%20 Power,actions%20support%20the%20commander's%20intent (accessed

8 October 2022). For specific examples of potential alternative communications pathways, see D. P. Brutzman, 'Low Probability of Intercept (LPI) Optical Signaling in Anti-Access Environments', Naval Postgraduate School Cyber Academic Group study, 17 April 2018, https://nps.edu/web/cag/-/low-probability-of-intercept-lpi-optical-signaling-in-anti-acc ess-environments (accessed 8 October 2022).

46 United States Navy, 'Advantage at Sea: Prevailing with Integrated All-Domain Naval Power', December 2020, https://media.defense.gov/2020/Dec/16/2002553074/-1/-1/0/TRISERVICESTRATEGY.PDF (accessed 8 October 2022).

47 M. Eckstein, 'Massive 2021 U.S. Naval Drills Will Include Multiple Carriers and Amphibious Ready Groups', USNI News, 3 December 2020, https://news.usni.org/2020/12/03/massive-2021-u-s-naval-drills-will-include-multiple-carriers-and-amphibious-ready-groups (accessed 8 October 2022).

48 T. Olorunnipa, J. Jacobs, A. Capaccio, and M. Talev, 'Warship Ruse and New Stealth Missiles: How the U.S. and Allies Attacked Syria', Bloomberg, 14 April 2018, www.bloomberg.com/news/articles/2018-04-14/warship-ruse-and-new-stealth-missiles-how-they-attacked-syria (accessed 8 October 2022).

49 See also J. F. Solomon, 'Maritime Deception and Concealment: Concepts for Defeating Wide-Area Oceanic Surveillance Reconnaissance-Strike Networks', *Naval War College Review*, Vol. 66, No. 4 (2013), https://digital-commons.usnwc.edu/nwc-review/vol66/iss4/7 (accessed 14 November 2022).

50 S. Stashwick, 'US Navy Upgrading Undersea Sub-Detecting Sensor Network', The Diplomat, 4 November 2016, https://thediplomat.com/2016/11/us-navy-upgrading-undersea-sub-detecting-sensor-network (accessed 8 October 2022).

51 M. Glynn, 'Deception Operations in Full-Spectrum ASW', *U.S. Naval Institute Proceedings*, Vol. 143, No. 7 (July 2017), pp. 73–5.

52 V. V. Schell and R. V. Yurov, 'The Role and Place of Electronic Intelligence Collection in Navy Combat Support', *Military Thought*, Vol. 28, No. 3 (2019), pp. 175–6.

53 'The Frigate Admiral Gorshkov Performed Another Test Firing with a Hypersonic Missile Zircon in the White Sea', Russian Ministry of Defence Press Report, 11 December 2020, http://eng.mil.ru/en/news_page/country/more.htm?id=12329718@egNews (no longer active).

54 T. Nilsen, 'Russian Subs Honing Stealth Skills in Major North Atlantic Drill, Says Norwegian Intel', The Barents Observer, 29 October 2019, https://thebarentsobserver.com/en/security/2019/10/russian-northern-fleet-massive-submarine-show (accessed 8 October 2022).

55 Davis, 'Fundamentals of the State Policy'.

56 See especially Kofman, Fink, and Edmonds, *Russian Strategy for Escalation Management*, pp. 12–16.

57 'Napravleniya razvitiya i ispol'zovaniya podvodnykh flotov v sovremennykh usloviyakh', *Morskoi sbornik*, No. 9 (September 2018), p. 65.

58 V. Puchnin, 'Rossii nuzhen sbalansirovannyy okeanskiy flot', *Nezavisimoye Voyennoye Obozreniye*, 25 February 2020, https://nvo.ng.ru/nvoexpert/2020-02-25/100_fleet250220.html (accessed 8 October 2022). Many of Puchnin's earlier ideas were adopted by Russia's state naval policy.

59 Schell and Yurov, 'The Role and Place of Electronic Intelligence Collection in the Navy', p. 178.

60 J. Trevithick, 'Admiral Warns America's East Coast Is No Longer a "Safe Haven" Thanks to Russian Subs', The Drive, 4 February 2020, www.thedrive.com/the-war-zone/32087/admiral-warns-americas-east-coast-is-no-longer-a-safe-haven-thanks-to-russian-subs (accessed 8 October 2022).

61 E. Gartzke and J. R. Lindsay, 'The Influence of Sea Power on Politics: Domain- and Platform-Specific Attributes of Material Capabilities', *Security Studies*, Vol. 29, No. 4 (2020), pp. 601–36.

62 Gerasimov, 'Vektory razvitiya voennoi strategii'.

63 A 2020 RAND study identified 'limited defensive depth' and 'resilience of air bases and other critical infrastructure' as critical vulnerabilities in northern Norway. J. Black et al., 'Enhancing Deterrence and Defence on NATO's Northern Flank: Allied Perspectives on Strategic Options for Norway', Santa Monica, CA: RAND Corporation, 2020, p. 18, www.rand.org/content/dam/rand/pubs/research_reports/RR4300/RR4381/RAND_RR4381.pdf (accessed 14 November 2022). See also T. O'Connor, 'Russia Will "Take Measures" against U.S. Radar Near Its Border, Thought to Be Part of Missile Defense', *Newsweek*, 23 May 2019, www.newsweek.com/russia-us-radar-norway-defense-1434756 (accessed 8 October 2022).

64 T. Nilsen, 'Norway Says Russia's Mock Attack on Vardø Radar Troubles Stability in the North', The Barents Observer, 13 March 2018, https://thebarentsobserver.com/en/security/2018/03/oslo-such-behavior-does-not-promote-good-neighborly-relations (accessed 8 October 2022).

65 T. Nilsen, '11 Russian Fighter Jets Made Mock Attack on Norwegian Arctic Radar', The Barents Observer, 12 February 2019, https://thebarentsobserver.com/en/security/2019/02/11-russian-fighter-jets-made-mock-attack-norwegian-arctic-radar (accessed 8 October 2022). Such attacks are also possible in other regions. In 2013, Russian aircraft conducted a mock attack against Sweden that was eventually revealed to be a mock attack with nuclear weapons. See 'Russia Carried Out

Practice Nuclear Strike against Sweden', TheLocal.Se, www.thelocal.se/20160203/russia-did-practice-a-nuclear-strike-against-sweden (accessed 8 October 2022).

66 T. Nilsen, 'Large Russian Missile Cruiser Sails Varanger Fjord Close to Norway's Border', The Barents Observer, 22 February 2021, https://thebarentsobserver.com/en/security/2021/02/large-russian-missile-cruiser-sails-varanger-fjord (accessed 8 October 2022).

67 Russia has gained much experience in joint bombardment using SS-26 Iskander-M SRBMs and air force bombers in Syria. See R. E. Hamilton, C. Miller, and A. Stein, *Russia's War in Syria: Assessing Russian Military Capabilities and Lessons Learned.* Philadelphia, PA: Foreign Policy Research Institute, 2020.

68 See 'SODCIT Target Categories', in Johnson, *Russia's Conventional Precision Strike Capabilities*, p. 54.

69 P. Butowski, *Russia's Air-Launched Weapons: Russian-Made Aircraft Ordnance Today.* Houston, TX: Harpia Publishing, 2017, pp. 16–17; 'Kh-101/102', Missile Threat, n.d., https://missilethreat.csis.org/missile/kh-101-kh-102 (accessed 8 October 2022).

70 A. Timokhin, 'Morskaya voina dlya nachinayushchikh', *Voyennoye obozreniye*, 2 December 2020, https://topwar.ru/177552-morskaja-vojna-dlja-nachinajuschih-vzaimodejstvie-nadvodnyh-korablej-i-udarnoj-aviacii.html (accessed 8 October 2022).

71 C. Woody, 'Russia's Submarines Are Showing They Can Strike Deep Inside Europe, and They've Got the U.S. Navy on Edge', Business Insider, 5 October 2018, www.businessinsider.com/russian-submarine-ability-to-hit-targets-in-europe-us-with-missiles-2018-10 (accessed 8 October 2022).

72 Alyoshin, Popov, and Puchnin, 'The Naval Might of Russia', p. 17.

73 'Basic Principles of State Policy of the Russian Federation on Nuclear Deterrence', Website of the Presidential Administration, 2 June 2020, http://kremlin.ru/acts/bank/45562 (accessed 8 October 2022).

74 'Rossiya budet narashchivat' gruppirovku strategicheskogo yadernogo i neyadernogo sderzhivaniya v Arktike', *Morskiye vesti Rossii*, 21 March 2014, http://www.morvesti.ru/news/1679/40312 (no longer active).

75 M. Eckstein, 'Truman Carrier Strike Group Operating North of Arctic Circle; First Time for US Navy since 1991', USNI News, 19 October 2018, https://news.usni.org/2018/10/19/truman-carrier-strike-group-operating-north-arctic-circle-first-time-us-navy-since-1991 (accessed 8 October 2022). A carrier strike group's primary anti-surface capability resides in the carrier air wing's fleet of F/A-18-E/F Super Hornet strike fighters. The US Navy states that their combat range (vice combat radius) is 1,275 miles when loaded with two AIM-9 air-to-air missiles. 'F/A-18A-D Hornet and F/A-18E/F Super Hornet Strike Fighter', United

States Navy, 4 February 2021, www.navy.mil/Resources/Fact-Files/ Display-FactFiles/Article/2383479/fa-18a-d-hornet-and-fa-18ef-super-hornet-strike-fighter (accessed 14 November 2022). This is an inadequate combat loadout, especially for anti-ship missions, which must include heavier Harpoon anti-ship missiles. Combat range is the maximum range an aircraft can fly when carrying specified ordnance. Combat radius is based on the maximum distance a warplane can fly with ordnance from its base, accomplish its mission, and return to its original base. As such, it is roughly half (likely less) of combat range.

76 Russian aircraft commonly simulate attacks against US surface ships. See, for example, D. Malyasov, 'Russian SU-24 Jets Practiced Attack on a U.S. Navy Destroyer in the Black Sea', Defence Blog, 24 December 2019, https://defence-blog.com/russian-su-24-jets-practiced-attack-on-a-u-s-navy-destroyer-in-the-black-sea (accessed 14 November 2022), and D. Cenciotti, 'Report: Russia Is Practicing Attack Runs against NATO Warships in the Black Sea', Business Insider, 4 March 2015, www.businessinsider.com/david-cenciotti-russia-practiced-attack-runs-against-nato-warships-2015-3 (accessed 8 October 2022). Several incidents of such mock attacks have taken place since 2015.

77 M. Eckstein, 'Truman CSG: Arctic Strike Group Operations Required Focus on Logistics, Safety', USNI News, 6 November 2018, https://news.usni.org/2018/11/06/truman-strike-group-operating-in-arctic-circle-required-more-consideration-of-logistics-safety (accessed 8 October 2022). According to Rear Admiral Eugene Black, during the Trident Juncture exercise, the Harry S. Truman carrier strike group had to carry its own extra supplies north into the Norwegian Sea because weather conditions made resupply via logistics ships uncertain.

78 R. G. McGarvey et al., 'Assessment of Beddown Alternatives for the F-35', Washington, DC: RAND Corporation, 2013, pp. 80–4, www.rand.org/content/dam/rand/pubs/research_reports/RR100/RR124/RAND_RR124.sum.pdf (accessed 14 November 2022).

79 United Kingdom Defence Nuclear Organisation and Ministry of Defence, 'Integrated Review of Security, Defence, Development and Foreign Policy 2021: Nuclear Deterrent', 17 March 2021, www.gov.uk/guidance/integrated-review-of-security-defence-development-and-foreign-policy-2021-nuclear-deterrent (accessed 8 October 2022).

80 United Kingdom Defence Nuclear Organisation and Ministry of Defence Fact Sheet, 'The UK's Nuclear Deterrent: What You Need to Know', 17 February 2022, www.gov.uk/government/publications/uk-nuclear-deterrence-factsheet/uk-nuclear-deterrence-what-you-need-to-know (accessed 8 October 2022).

81 Kofman, Fink, and Edmonds, *Russian Strategy for Escalation Management.*

82 The Tsirkon hypersonic ASCM reportedly flies at Mach 8, over 6,100 miles per hour. Assuming the radar horizon is thirteen miles away at the surface, a sea-skimming Tsirkon will cross that distance in eight seconds. Kinetic engagements at such speed is virtually impossible. The presence of atmospheric ducts noted above may lengthen the radar horizon, but not to tactically relevant distances. 'Russia Test-Fires "Tsirkon" Hypersonic Missile', *Moscow Times*, 27 November 2020, www.themos cowtimes.com/2020/11/26/russia-test-fires-tsirkon-hypersonic-missile-a72158 (accessed 8 October 2022). Examples of current soft kill naval technologies include the US Mk53 "Nulka" decoy and the Mk59 floating decoy.

Index

Literary works can be found under authors' names. Note: 'n.' after a page reference indicates the number of a note on that page. Page numbers in *italic* refer to figures or tables.

242

Index

Index

Index

Index

Index

Index

Index